D0322491

Observing Children with Attachment Difficulties in School
A Tool for Identifying and Supporting Emotional and Social Difficulties in Children Aged 5–11
Kim S. Golding, Jane Fain, Ann Frost, Cathy Mills, Helen Worrall, Netty Roberts, Eleanor Durrant and Sian Templeton
Foreword by Louise Bombèr
ISBN 978 1 84905 336 5
eISBN 978 0 85700 675 2

Observing Children with Attachment Difficulties in Preschool Settings
A Tool for Identifying and Supporting Emotional and Social Difficulties
Kim S. Golding, Jane Fain, Ann Frost, Sian Templeton and Eleanor Durrant
Foreword by Louise Bombèr
ISBN 978 1 84905 337 2
eISBN 978 0 85700 676 9

Using Stories to Build Bridges with Traumatized Children
Creative Ideas for Therapy, Life Story Work, Direct Work and Parenting
Kim S. Golding
ISBN 978 1 84905 540 6
eISBN 978 0 85700 961 6

Nurturing Attachments Training Resource
Running Parenting Groups for Adoptive Parents and Foster or Kinship Carers
Kim S. Golding
ISBN 978 1 84905 328 0
eISBN 978 0 85700 665 3

Creating Loving Attachments
Parenting with PACE to Nurture Confidence and Security in the Troubled Child
Kim S. Golding and Daniel A. Hughes
ISBN 978 1 84905 227 6
eISBN 978 0 85700 470 3

Nurturing Attachments
Supporting Children who are Fostered or Adopted
Kim S. Golding
ISBN 978 1 84310 614 2
eISBN 978 1 84642 750 3

The Teacher's Introduction to Attachment
Practical Essentials for Teachers, Carers and School Support Staff
Nicola Marshall
Foreword by Phil Thomas
ISBN 978 1 84905 550 5
eISBN 978 0 85700 973 9

Learning Through Child Observation
Second Edition
Mary Fawcett
ISBN 978 1 84310 676 0
eISBN 978 1 84642 964 4

Educating Children and Young People in Care
Learning Placements and Caring Schools
Claire Cameron, Graham Connelly and Sonia Jackson
ISBN 978 1 84905 365 5
eISBN 978 0 85700 719 3

Observing Adolescents with Attachment Difficulties in Educational Settings

A Tool for Identifying and Supporting Emotional and Social Difficulties in Young People Aged 11–16

Kim S. Golding, Mary T. Turner, Helen Worrall, Jennifer Roberts and Ann E. Cadman

Foreword by Louise Michelle Bombèr

Jessica Kingsley *Publishers*
London and Philadelphia

First published in 2016
by Jessica Kingsley Publishers
73 Collier Street
London N1 9BE, UK
and
400 Market Street, Suite 400
Philadelphia, PA 19106, USA

www.jkp.com

Library of Congress Cataloging in Publication Data
Golding, Kim S.
  Observing adolescents with attachment difficulties in educational settings : a tool for identifying and supporting emotional and social difficulties in young people aged 11-16 / Kim S. Golding, Mary T. Turner, Helen Worrall, Jennifer Roberts and Ann E. Cadman.
    pages cm
  Includes bibliographical references.
  ISBN 978-1-84905-617-5 (alk. paper)
  1. Middle school students--Psychology. 2. High school students--Psychology. 3. Emotional problems of children. 4. Attachment behavior in children. 5. Behavioral assessment of children. 6. Educational psychology. I. Title.
  LB1623.G58 2015
  371.94--dc23
                    2015012008

British Library Cataloguing in Publication Data
A CIP catalogue record for this book is available from the British Library

ISBN 978 1 84905 617 5
eISBN 978 1 78450 174 7

Printed and bound in Great Britain

We dedicate the observation checklist
books to the memory of Annie Wise,
a much-missed colleague and friend.

Contents

Foreword

For many pupils around the UK current traditional behaviourist strategies are clearly not working. Why is it that I still visit schools to discover that a vulnerable pupil is now on their twelfth exclusion with no appropriate, developmentally matched support plan or key adult attached to them? Why continue 'doing school' the same when it isn't working? Forgive my presumption, but who has the learning difficulty? This is a long-awaited book and I am so glad that Kim and her team have invested their time, energy and wisdom into producing it. It was well worth the wait…

It is crystal clear that now is the time for secondary schools to update their whole-school policies and practices to include fully the pupils focused on within these pages. That now is the time to say a loud and resounding 'no' to any more screaming, shouting, shaming, threats, time out, seclusion and exclusion, and 'no' to staff misusing their power, authority and control to attempt to get those who are hurting to conform and behave. These pupils need our sensitive, attuned care, and this will mean maximizing our flexibility and enhancing our creativity within the school context, not only by discrete provisions such as special needs rooms/units/services but also by support integrated into the wider school system.

Our pastoral colleagues know what these pupils need and what works for them, but have often not had their voices heard. Many of our schools have become vast, complex systems that are often run more like businesses than relational communities. This important book gives the structures necessary for beleaguered headteachers, deputies, heads of year, form tutors and subject specialists to adapt current practice. We can no longer ignore the findings of child development, attachment and neuroscience.

Let's get relationship back on the map in secondary schools. *Relationship security is at the heart of what is needed to engage our exploratory systems, that is, our capacity to learn.* We would be wise to start investing in relationships between staff and pupils if we want to see academic success; to invest our limited resources into allocating key adults to build relationships with vulnerable pupils; to allow permanency for these key relationships, not chopping and changing, but remaining over time; and to create small, consistent teams around pupils to build safety, security and stability. So let's be brave enough to do secondary school differently. Others will follow!

For such a time as this…

Louise Michelle Bombèr
www.theyellowkite.co.uk
www.attachmentleadnetwork.net

Acknowledgements

This secondary school version of the observation checklist would not have been produced if it wasn't for the persistence of Louise Michelle Bombèr who told us that we should develop it, and suggested this to Steve Jones at Jessica Kingsley Publishers. Between the two of them we finally succumbed! Thank you, Louise, for giving us the confidence to believe in this project.

As with our previous two observation checklist books we also wish to acknowledge and remember Annie Wise who had the initial idea for developing this tool for education staff.

Thanks to members of the Virtual School (formerly ISL education support) past and present for their advice and guidance during the development of this version. Special thanks to those who attended our workshop which explored issues and support needs for adolescent students.

Thanks to the school practitioners and the young people who we have worked with over the years who have taught us so much.

Again thanks are due to managers who have given us the time to work on this development, a challenge which gets harder and harder as resources get tighter. For this version we thank Ellie Ballard, Anne Griffin, Stuart Watkins and Philippa Coleman for allowing us to take some time from the day-to-day tasks to focus on this development.

Inevitably we all had to put our own time into producing this as well, so thanks are also due to our families for putting up with our distraction from family time.

Finally, thanks to the staff at Jessica Kingsley Publishers for taking good care of these observation checklist books.

Introduction

ABOUT THIS RESOURCE

This resource has been designed to assist those working in educational settings to recognize the emotional needs of adolescent students and the difficulties they may have in benefiting from the support on offer.

It is intended to be used as a tool to reflect on the student's behaviour and, using attachment theory as a guide, consider what this may be communicating and how this can be supported. The observation checklist which forms the heart of the resource is designed to help structure observations of the young people in their educational settings. It will help to identify their support needs, being especially helpful in understanding the young person with attachment insecurities or difficulties.

With the information acquired through structured observations, staff will be better equipped to find creative ways of meeting the relationship needs of their students, building emotional health where there is emotional difficulty and equipping the young people for a continuing journey through education within which they will be able to benefit relationally, emotionally, socially and then educationally.

We will first provide readers with accessible summaries of the information and background theory they need in order to understand the developmental challenges and difficulties that these young people face, before providing more information about the checklist and how it can be used in Chapters 4 to 8.

We then provide guidance on how to help support the students within the educational setting. Before reading on, you may prefer to take a quick look at the checklist itself in Appendix 1 to get a sense of what it looks like and the form it takes. The appendices contain further, more detailed information for those interested in reading in more depth.

This book focuses on observing adolescents with attachment difficulties in educational settings. It follows on from the two previous books which focus on observing children in preschool and school settings. In this book we have been mindful of the developmental stage of adolescence, and the range of settings that young people might be attending, including middle and high schools in the UK as well as a range of short break schools or special schools. We have developed a new observation checklist for this developmental stage. This follows the format of the previous ones but includes a greater range of adolescent behaviours related to social and emotional functioning. We have additionally updated the examples based on fictional and composite children from the original books. Within this book these children are growing up and developing into young people dealing with the challenges of adolescence and the move to secondary education. In addition we introduce some new adolescents, based upon young people we have known, to illustrate the additional information that we provide within the appendices. This includes two completely new sections (Appendices 2 and 4) written specifically for this book. These provide further information about the developmental stage of adolescence and consider what support young people might need as they make their way through their secondary education.

The material in this checklist is universal, and applicable for professionals working with students in any country, even though terminology (such as Key Stages 3, 4 and 5; middle school; secondary school; and further education) differs. As this observation checklist was developed and piloted in Worcestershire, England, we use UK terminology throughout, but include a short glossary in Appendix 6 which explains specific UK terminology.

Many chapters contain useful summaries; these are marked with ⌒🖱 and readers have permission to download them for their personal use from www.jkp.com/catalogue/book/9781849056175/resources.

1
Child Development in the Early Years and Beyond

The human infant, beyond any other species, is born immature and dependent. This is partly a consequence of our evolutionary development. As our species developed, our brain size increased and therefore our heads became larger compared to other mammals. If we were born with fully mature brains babies would need larger heads, making it impossible for them to pass through the birth canal. For this reason babies are born with immature brains and relatively small heads. This means that much of brain development needs to occur postnatally. This result of human development works very well for us as a social species, pushing brain development as it does into the social world. We are a product of how we are cared for (for an accessible text exploring this, see Gerhardt 2014).

Here are a few facts to support the importance of early experience and how it impacts on children coming into education and how they relate to others (see Gerhardt 2014; Nash 1997):

- A human infant's brain almost doubles in size during the first year.
- At birth the baby has all the brain cells (neurons) it needs in place, but these cells are immature. At birth the neurons are mostly unconnected, but by three years of age there is a dense network of connections.
- Genes begin the process of brain development, but it is experience that triggers the electrical activity which will determine how the neurons connect and grow.
- The development of the brain is therefore experience-dependent. It develops as a consequence of experience and through interactions with others.
- Between birth and the age of two, there is a critical period for emotional growth that supports cognitive development, thinking and growth.
- If the child lives in fear, the brain chemistry changes. This means that children come into settings with an altered or distorted way of thinking and processing information.

Human babies are well equipped for development within a social world, being attracted to other people and equipped to seek nurture and care from those around them.

They instinctively elicit from others what they need to nourish the brain. This also gives them their greatest vulnerability. If the social world is not able to give the babies what they need, brain development will suffer. When children's early dependency needs are not met, this can have a lifelong impact, not only on emotional and social development but also on learning. A critical factor in whether children recover from this earliest of traumas is the quality of the later relationships they encounter throughout their childhood and adolescence. Many of these relationships will be in educational settings.

An early sign of emotional difficulty is displayed through the development of first attachment relationships. Children who are not able to receive sensitive, responsive, nurturing care for a variety of reasons will develop attachment relationships adapted to this lack. Described as attachment insecurities or, for the most severely affected, attachment difficulties, these are adaptations to a world which is not meeting the most fundamental of emotional needs: to be kept safe and secure. This can impact on the child's journey into the wider world outside of the home.

Children may not get their attachment needs met for a variety of reasons. Illness and/or hospitalization in child or parent, neurodevelopmental difficulty in child or parent or experience of separation, loss, abuse and neglect for the child can all be factors in the development of attachment difficulties. This leaves these children disadvantaged at the very beginning of their life. The secure base of home is missing and they adapt to a world without it. The cost is a slowed or disordered emotional development, and an emotional immaturity which will have later impact on the rest of development. This leaves the child at risk for a range of emotional, social and cognitive difficulties. Most importantly the ability to form and benefit from relationships is compromised. In adapting to the lack of relationship in their early life, the children are affected in the area that could also provide them with greatest healing. Parents and other significant adults who want to help these children are ready to offer relationships to the children. The children, however, have not learnt how to use and benefit from such relationships because of the lack of experience in their earliest months or years. To help these children, we cannot just offer them relationships; we also need to help them to use and benefit from these relationships.

As the children continue along their life's journey, their horizons will widen to also include the world of education. Children enter school according to their chronological age and not dependent upon the stage of development that they are at. Some are ready for this step into the wider world, while others are not. School staff are prepared for these differences and will provide individualized support. The biggest challenge facing them, however, is how to meet the needs of the children who have not had their earliest dependency needs met and are therefore least ready for the relative independence of school. Louise Michelle Bombèr tells us:

> We cannot fast-track children who have experienced trauma and loss into emotional and sensory literacy, without first giving them the opportunity to fully negotiate the developmental stage of dependency. Self and other awareness grows in the context of a positive, sensitive and caring relationship, in which the child is initially dependent on an adult: this relationship is what we must provide in schools. (Bombèr 2007, p.10)

Recognizing the dependency needs of small children in school is relatively straightforward. School staff will be familiar with the range of maturities that children come into school with and be able to adapt their approach tailored to the child's need. As the children progress through their early years in school they will also be maturing and with support will become more independent and more able to cope with a growing range of relationships, including managing the strain and conflicts inherent in forming friendship groups.

Children with attachment difficulties can struggle with these developmental challenges and often need more support to navigate successfully through the middle childhood years. Typically these children are more immature emotionally compared to their peers. Additionally their early experience has not equipped them well for handling reciprocal relationships; the give and take of peer relationships can be a challenge for them. Children with the most severe attachment difficulties tend to be the most controlling within their relationships. This can put an added strain on the child, teachers and peers. These children are helped by consistent, understanding school staff and the tolerance of the other children. They survive these school years, and with excellent support can thrive and grow emotionally.

The move into adolescence brings another set of challenges, coinciding with the move to high school, or the equivalent educational setting, and all the extra demands and challenges that this brings. Friendships become even more important and the young person revisits their sense of identity – what sort of person am I? This coupled with the biological changes, both hormonally and within the developing brain, is a heady mix. Children with attachment difficulties have to cope with all these changes, although emotionally and socially they are not ready for them.

School staff will notice young people taking a jump in their maturity to sustain them with the new expectations upon them. The maturity in the ability to think, problem solve and manage relationships, and increased organizational abilities, all help the young person to make the move to secondary education.

These staff will also notice how young people with attachment difficulties struggle to make this maturational leap. The gap between them and their peers becomes wider, and their slowly maturing cognitive and emotional abilities means that they struggle to meet the expectations of the new educational environment. This in turn undermines their confidence, and their search for an adolescent identity becomes coloured by fears of not being good enough.

Young people vary in their ways of coping with this. Some students try their hardest to fit in academically and socially, but the pressure of this is revealed at home where stress is released often through aggression and sullenness or by withdrawing. Other students find a range of ways to try to manage peer relationships. This can include bullying, becoming a victim of bullying, falling in with the 'wrong crowd', becoming clingy and demanding of friends, becoming withdrawn or focusing on school work at the expense of friendships. Academic progress can suffer as the students try to deal with the extra social and emotional demands upon them. A range of behaviours can alert staff that a student is encountering these struggles. Lying, stealing, self-harm behaviours, increased neediness of adult attention, increases in self-reliant behaviour and a range of peer-related difficulties can all be indicators of emotional and social struggles during adolescence. Attention to academic performance will need to be secondary for these students who are in need of social and emotional support. Once this support is in place then academic performance is likely to improve again or the student will be receptive to increased academic support.

If young people are to be successful social beings, if they are to be successful learners and if they are to be emotionally healthy enough to have relationship success, it is imperative that those working in educational settings are equipped to recognize and meet the emotional needs of the students in their care. For young people with attachment difficulties, these needs can be presented in a range of ways, not all of which are obvious, and the young people can have a range of challenges in being able to use the support and nurture being offered.

2 Recognizing the Emotional Needs of Students in Educational Settings

This chapter features scenarios to illustrate the different emotional needs of a number of different students.

It is the beginning of the week and Amanda, John and Niko all have to get up and ready so that they can catch the school bus.

Mum has called upstairs to Amanda to let her know that she has ten minutes. Amanda is almost ready. She runs downstairs and picks up her bag which she got ready the evening before. Mum hands her a drink and a slice of toast, checking that these are not neglected in her haste to get on with her day. Amanda groans but stops long enough to please her mother and then with a quick wave she leaves the house in good time. She meets her friends on the bus and they chat happily about their respective weekends. They all wait together for the bell, and then with arms linked they go into school ready to start another week.

John is less confident. Dad wakes him up with lots of time to spare, knowing that he will need the extra time to get up and ready. With ten minutes to go John has reluctantly got up and eaten breakfast and is ready to leave the house. He waves goodbye and walks down the driveway, but then returns worried that he hasn't got his PE kit. Dad reassures him that it is in his bag and watches him as he walks in the direction of the bus stop. John remains anxious until he is on the bus and with his friends. He is then able to relax a little as they get into the usual banter. He follows them off the bus and into school. Like Amanda, John and his friends wait together for the bell to go and then John follows them into school.

Niko is the most reluctant of these three young people to attend school. He oversleeps and as usual on a Monday morning is difficult to rouse. Mum encourages him into the shower whilst she makes him his breakfast. Niko eats slowly but is finally ready. Mum helps him check that he has everything in his school bag and finds his tie, which had fallen behind the chair. They are just about to leave the house when she notices he has his trainers on instead of his school shoes. Finally ready, Niko and his mum walk to the bus stop together. Niko is worried that his friends won't be there and checks that Mum will take him to school if his fears are realized. The bus arrives and Mum points out Charlie and Nick, sitting in their usual place at the back of the bus. Niko hangs back a little, but then gets on the bus. He is the last to get off the bus when it arrives at school but, remembering to pick up his bag at the last minute, he follows Charlie and Nick and they go into school together.

These students will be familiar to anyone working in secondary school. They represent the range of individual differences that students can display. Some students are sociable, confident and bubbly; others are more reserved, while others are shy and uncomfortable. Young people of the same age vary in maturity and the degree to which they demonstrate temperamental traits, such as sociability and shyness. Some young people take everything in their stride, thriving on the unexpected, while others are slower to warm up, preferring predictability and consistency. This represents the individual differences within the emotional and social development of young people. The sensitive school staff adapt their approach to each of the students depending upon their needs, and each student is able to grow in confidence and security as the school year progresses. They remain different from each other, but each student is able to benefit from the experience of school. Students have individual differences but with appropriate support will make progress in their social and emotional development. This in turn allows them to benefit from everything the school has to offer and thus to progress in their learning.

What makes these young people different from those we would describe as having an emotional difficulty? These are young people who will require more specialized help from the teachers and assistants in the school. In many ways recognizing young people with emotional difficulties can be difficult precisely because young people show a range of individual differences.

Amanda is sociable and confident. How can we distinguish her from Karen, who also comes in confidently in the morning? Karen, however, is a little overly boisterous. Other young people warm to Amanda but appear more wary of Karen, who can be controlling and domineering. When it is time for assembly, Amanda and Karen are keen to go in. Amanda walks into the hall, seeking out her friends to sit with, while being aware of where her teacher is. Karen rushes into the hall, pushing herself among the other young people. She takes no notice of the teacher as she demands that the person next to her move up a little.

John is quieter and more reserved. Jack also appears quiet and reserved, but when the boys are observed together, there is a confidence in John that is not apparent in Jack. John will get on with the task in front of him, but as the adult approaches he is able to accept support and to go further in what he is doing as a result. He tends to gravitate to one or two of the other young people, but is not overly concerned when paired up with a different peer. Jack is less easy to support, and progresses less well under the adult's careful gaze. He finds it harder to adjust to young people outside of his small group. When it is time for assembly, both boys will respond to the teacher's instruction and move on into the hall. Jack, however, will appear more on edge during the assembly. He complies, with the teacher's encouragement, but is less comfortable doing so.

Niko is shy and quiet. He needs extra support to cope with daily routines and to cope with change and transition. George also appears shy, but is much more clingy and needy of support. Neither Niko nor George cope well with assembly. Niko can cope as long as he is supported by a familiar adult, whereas George is more likely to go to pieces. He tries to avoid assembly and will even become verbally aggressive, drawing the adult into an argument in the hope that assembly is over before it is resolved.

Throughout the year it is Amanda, John and Niko who make most progress, while Karen, Jack and George remain of concern to those supporting them.

Differentiating between young people who are different but emotionally reasonably secure within these differences and those who are more emotionally troubled can be a difficult task. The teachers and assistants need to be aware of a range of information in order to be able to pick out the students who will need additional and carefully tailored support:

- The student's behaviour in school is clearly important. Getting to know each student and how he or she copes with different situations and activities provides a wealth of knowledge that can help to identify those in most trouble emotionally.

- The progress the student is making will also provide important information concerning what additional support a student might need. Those making good social, emotional and learning progress are clearly benefiting from what they are being offered. Where progress is slow, it may be that the student needs something different in the support he or she is receiving.

The observation checklist can assist in both of these areas, guiding the practitioner in observing the behaviours that the student is displaying and offering a way of monitoring the changes or lack of change in these behaviours over time.

There is a third area of information that is also important to take into account and can help in interpreting the observations being made with the help of the checklist:

- Knowledge of the student's early and current experience will provide contextual information. What has happened and is happening at home? Are there home difficulties that have always been present, or is there some more immediate stress that the young person has to deal with?

Young people who are encountering current stress will need additional support in the school. If this stress is temporary and there is good home–school communication, the young person is likely to be relatively easily supported, and will continue to make progress over the year. Where there have been past difficulties that have impacted on emotional development and well-being, and especially when these difficulties are ongoing, the young person may need more tailored and ongoing support in the school and progress is likely to be slower. These are the students whose attachment development may have been compromised, making it harder for them to use the support of the staff and assistants in the educational setting. For example:

- Young people may have had early illnesses, compromising the development of security at home. This can include those who have a challenging birth history, prematurity, or other reasons for spending time in a special care baby unit, delaying their arrival home. Any hospitalization during the early years can compromise the development of security with caregivers, thus leading to difficulties in attachment.

- Young people may have experienced illness in a parent. A parent may have been hospitalized, or may be suffering from an illness that makes it more difficult to be available and responsive to his or her young child. Postnatal depression is an obvious example of such an illness.

- Stress within the family that is overwhelming to the parent or parents can also lead to insecurity for the young person. Any stress such as unemployment, poverty or family strife that makes the parent less responsive or available to the young person is likely to impact on the young person's attachment security and emotional development.

- Young people born with a learning difficulty may find it harder to express their needs to their parent. These parents may therefore struggle to identify these needs and thus to help the young person to feel secure.

- Parents who have their own early history of trauma and/or compromised parenting are likely to find it harder to be available and responsive to the young person.

- Parents who are actively neglectful or abusive to the young person, or whose lifestyle is impacting negatively on their parenting, are another example. Substance abuse, domestic violence, instability, changes of partner and utilization of a range of caregivers to look after the small child are all experiences that are likely to be traumatizing for the young person, sitting alongside physical, sexual and emotional abuse and neglect as experiences that have the most detrimental impact on attachment formation and emotional development.

- Young people living in foster care, adopted or living with family on a residence or special guardianship order are not necessarily emotionally distressed by their early experience, but they have all had experience of separation and loss of birth family. A significant proportion of these young people will also have experienced early traumatic care. These young people are therefore at increased risk of a range of emotional difficulties.

Understanding the development of attachments and how this impacts on the emotional development of the young person is therefore important, underpinning knowledge for supporting students with social and emotional difficulties in school.

Chapter 3 provides a summary of attachment theory and how understanding this theory can inform how we help to support young people.

3 Understanding Emotional Needs through Knowledge of Attachment Theory

In this chapter attachment theory is briefly summarized, and this working knowledge should be sufficient for the reader wanting to use the checklist. However, for those interested in a more detailed account, we provide an extended explanation in Appendix 3.

Attachment theory has been developed over many decades and is based on the pioneering work of John Bowlby (Bowlby 1973, 1980, 1982, 1998). It is a theory about the special form of affectional bond that develops between a child and a parent within which the child experiences security and comfort from the parent.

Attachment theory is therefore a theory about first relationships, and how these relationships impact on a child's journey through life. Early attachment experience influences the way children and young people develop later relationships and how they learn to rely on others for help and support. This in turn influences the way that young people develop a sense of efficacy in themselves – the belief that they can be effective in the world of relationships – and how they learn to rely on others. A secure attachment therefore promotes both dependence (the ability to use others for support) and independence (the ability to rely on self).

To start at the beginning, when children are born, they need a 'primary carer' (attachment figure) to help them feel safe and secure. If the primary carer is temporarily unavailable, a few familiar adults can substitute for this carer (secondary attachment figures). When children derive some security from their attachment figures, they feel safe enough to explore and play in the world. Children can experience worry, fear or need for comfort for a range of reasons: when something new or unknown is happening, when they are feeling tired or unwell or when they experience or anticipate that parents are not available when they need them.

If young children start to feel worry, fear or need for comfort, it is important that they have close contact with someone with whom they have developed an attachment. They need close physical contact with this person to soothe them when upset. As they get older, this can be verbal instead of physical contact, although if they are sufficiently stressed, physical contact will still be preferred.

Patterns of attachment

Patterns of attachment develop in relation to the way that attachment figures respond to the child:

- When he or she has attachment needs stemming from the experience of worry, fear or a need for comfort.

- When he or she is looking for support for exploration and play.

This will affect the child's capacity to develop relationships and ability to manage feelings as he or she grows, develops and matures.

Descriptions of attachment patterns do vary among researchers in the attachment theory field. In this book we use the more traditional A B C + D model of attachment patterns, which sets out four distinct attachment styles relating to the early experience of the children. This contrasts with the alternative Dynamic Maturational Model (DMM) developed by Patricia Crittenden (Crittenden 2008; Crittenden, Landini and Claussen 2001). In the DMM, attachment patterns are described as developing dynamically as the child matures, with increasingly controlling behaviours emerging when the child experiences a continuing lack of safety. Both models emphasize organization of behaviour in order to achieve feelings of safety, with the development of highly controlling behaviours to manage relationships that feel dangerous. The reader who would like to explore these differing models is referred to Howe (2011).

The secure pattern
SECURE ATTACHMENT PATTERN (B)

When a parent is available to meet the need for comfort as displayed by the child, and can support the child in play and exploration, a secure attachment will develop. Children with a secure attachment pattern appear confident. Whether quiet or lively, these children will appear to relish the challenges that life offers. They are confident to have a go, but will also seek help when needed.

Insecure patterns
INSECURE AVOIDANT PATTERN (A)

An insecure avoidant pattern of attachment develops out of a relationship with a carer who is distant and rejecting. The carer finds it difficult to cope with the child's emotional needs. These children start to worry when they experience strong feelings in themselves or others. They are often keen to please and to do things right. When these children do feel angry, often their anger appears to suddenly erupt. These children can mask negative feelings with false positive affect – the child who smiles whether feeling happy or sad (e.g. see Crittenden 2008).

Children with insecure avoidant patterns can appear withdrawn and quiet or more self-reliant than expected for their age. They are more focused on 'doing' than people.

They do not like to be dependent upon others and are therefore less likely to turn to adults to seek help.

INSECURE AMBIVALENT PATTERN (C)

An insecure ambivalent pattern of attachment develops out of a relationship with a carer who will sometimes meet the child's needs, but this is more dependent on his or her mood than the child's need.

Children with insecure ambivalent attachment patterns can appear attention-needing, and find it difficult to settle by themselves or with groups of children. They will sometimes talk excessively, or act as a 'clown' in order to keep adult attention. They find it difficult to concentrate on activities as they are concentrating on their need for adult attention.

DISORGANIZED/DISORIENTATED AND CONTROLLING ATTACHMENT PATTERN (D)

The disorganized/disorientated and controlling attachment pattern develops out of a relationship within which the parent is frightened of or frightening to the child. Parents can be frightened parenting a child if they had experienced being frightened when they themselves were parented. They become very unavailable and unresponsive to the child when that child is in most need of their presence and support. This is as frightening to a child as parents who are overtly frightening because they shout, punish the child, expose the child to family violence or behave oddly because of substance abuse or mental illness.

These are the children who have the hardest time feeling safe. When they feel scared, children turn to their parent or attachment figure to reduce this fear. The parent is a source of comfort. When the parent is both the potential source of comfort and also the biggest threat to them, the children are faced with a dilemma – I need you, but you are frightening me. Infants and toddlers appear disorientated and struggle to organize their behaviour in a way which helps them to feel safe in the face of this threat.

As they grow beyond toddlerhood, these children solve the problem of having a carer who is a source both of comfort and of fear by taking control of relationships. Thus their behaviour appears more organized. They become very controlling in all their relationships, developing self-reliant or coercive ways of relating with others. Some of these children appear hyper-alert, aggressive and challenging. Others appear more 'switched off' and unresponsive.

How children bring attachment difficulties into school

Children use their early attachment experience to build up a sort of template of how relationships work. This is called an 'internal working model'. This template guides them in what to expect from others and what to believe about themselves. For example, secure children will believe that they are likeable to others and that others will be available to support them. Insecure children will doubt their 'likeability' and will anticipate that others are less likely to be available to them.

When children move away from the home, they will engage in relationships outside of their family. Children will approach these new relationships based on their previous experience. We anticipate in the future what we have known in the past. A secure child will expect to be liked and that others will support him or her. An insecure child will not have this confidence.

Let us return to the examples of the children we introduced in Chapter 2. Amanda, John and Niko all experienced security of attachment. While they all approached school differently, they were all able to use their parent to support them to make the transition to school. They could all transfer this 'secure base' to the teacher or teaching assistant, and thus gain support to manage the day away from the parent. Karen, Jack and George do not have this attachment security. They are much less able to draw security from their parents. The transition to school is therefore more challenging, and they are less able either to seek support from the teacher or teaching assistant or to use this support when they have got it. This inability to use emotional support will impact not only on their feelings of security or safety while at school, but also on their emotional development. They will remain emotionally immature, making slower progress in their emotional development. This in turn affects their social development. They will feel less in tune with the other children and it will be harder for them to form and maintain friendships. It will also impact on their ability to learn. When we do not feel secure we become preoccupied with the need for safety, and this makes it much harder to face outwards to the world, to enjoy challenges, and to learn and develop new skills.

As they move through the school and into high school or similar educational settings, these insecurities are likely to continue. Whilst all children and young people mature so that they can meet the increasing expectations upon them emotionally, insecure children mature more slowly, especially in their emotional and social development. This means that they can experience more difficulty as they move through the school system. The gap between themselves and their peers widens. The gap between what they can achieve and the expectations of what they can achieve in line with their chronological age also widens. On top of this the additional developmental tasks of adolescence can add increased stress as they search for a renewed sense of identity and the need for and increased maturity of friendships takes a prominent position in their life. Past traumas and difficult experience can come back and haunt the present during this developmental stage of change and adjustment. These stresses will be displayed through the attachment needs of the adolescent. Much as toddlers and preschoolers need attachment figures in order to go out and explore the world, adolescents also need this secure base. Even if middle childhood has been a quiet time in terms of attachment needs, adolescence will generally see a resurgence in attachment needs. A secure base gives them a platform for the development of increasing independence. It is not surprising therefore for the move through high school to also be a time of additional difficulty for emotionally troubled young people. These students may need additional attachment support in school before they can achieve the level of independence expected of them.

Amanda, John and Niko will benefit from their school experience. Karen, Jack and George will need some additional support to do so. Recognizing the Karens, Jacks and Georges is therefore an important task for those working in educational settings. Observing these students, monitoring their progress in emotional and social development and being aware of their current and past experience will all be important. This information will help the teachers and teaching assistants to support the students to enjoy and benefit from the substantial amount of time they spend in school. This will in turn impact on their social and emotional development both now and in the future, providing them with the best foundation for their learning.

4 Introducing the Observation Checklist

We all need to feel safe and emotionally secure in our everyday environments. Nowhere is this more important than for a student having experience of an educational setting. Research shows that, in order for children to begin to develop their academic skills, they first need to have experienced positive early attachments. These relationships are needed before their 'learning behaviours' can begin to develop (Pianta 2006). Meeting the emotional needs of students in educational settings is therefore a priority and must precede meeting their academic needs. The observation checklist has been designed as a tool to help education practitioners with this endeavour. In this chapter the checklist is introduced alongside general guidance for using this tool.

Purpose of the checklist

As explained in the introduction to this book, this observation checklist has been designed to help to structure observations of students in schools and other educational settings, with the aim of better understanding the needs of the young people. In particular, the checklist focuses the observer on the attachment, emotional and social behaviours being displayed. Interpretation of these observations can then lead to a greater understanding of the needs of the young person in these areas. It is anticipated that this tool will be especially helpful in understanding the student with attachment insecurities or difficulties.

While this checklist can be used to increase understanding of a student, and his or her emotional needs, this is *not* a diagnostic tool. Therefore, it is important not to make a diagnosis or label a student as having a specific difficulty on the basis of these observations.

As you read through the guidance below, you may find it helpful to refer to the checklist itself, which can be found in Appendix 1. Ensure also that this chapter and Chapter 5 are referred to as the checklist is completed, because these give important guidance and prompt questions that help further reflect on how a child presents in the educational setting.

When to use the checklist

The observation checklist is useful to identify the social and emotional difficulties that a student is encountering, and to monitor the student's progress over time. It will give teachers and teaching assistants some clear targets to work towards.

This checklist is designed for students at Key Stages 3 and 4. These students are aged between 11 and 16 years.

There are a range of situations which might prompt the use of the checklist:

- Practitioners may be concerned about behaviours being displayed by a student, especially when these behaviours are challenging and disruptive. In order to successfully manage these behaviours, while also building security for the student, it is important to understand how the behaviours reflect the internal experience of the young person. The checklist will help you to focus on the emotional needs of the young person and to better understand the behavioural messages being communicated. This reflection about a student's behaviour and emotional needs helps the observer to look more closely at why a young person may be presenting in a particular way and helps him or her to view each young person with the curiosity and empathy that is so important when planning support.

- The astute practitioner will also be concerned about the student who is not overtly displaying disruptive behaviours, but is in emotional difficulty nevertheless. These young people don't cause trouble because they prefer to be 'invisible'. They rarely or never ask for help and appear very independent; they can also appear aloof or isolated from their peers. The only indications that they are having difficulty may be that they are socially inept or immature. Often these factors are not linked to their emotional needs and these students are 'missed' because their behaviours are not causing disruption in the educational setting. Additionally, their independence misleads the staff into thinking that they are coping as they should. After all, isn't that what educational settings are designed to encourage: independent, confident, self-motivated, free-thinking students? The observation checklist can help staff to rethink their opinion of this type of behaviour and to notice that the young person's emotional needs are overtaking his or her ability to make the academic progress needed to reach his or her potential.

- The observation checklist can also be a really useful reflective tool even if there are no particular problems identified; it acts as a vehicle for raising awareness of the student's needs, and of demonstrating the success of current strategies being used with the student.

- Staff can also use the checklist as a tool to monitor the student through a period of change or transition, for example when a student is moving between educational setting or class, or perhaps because of a change in his or her home situation. In this situation it can be helpful to have a checklist completed at a time when the student is settled in a familiar setting and is being appropriately supported. If necessary, previous successful strategies can be implemented again and the checklist used to monitor these if they are helping once more.

It is worth reiterating that the observation checklist is not a formal assessment and should not be used as a diagnostic tool. It is useful in understanding a student's emotional needs. The profile that is built up from the observations and contextual information can be used to help the practitioners consider a student's behaviour, presentation and underlying experience and to reflect on the young person's attachment style shown in the educational setting. A child may present very differently in different settings and at different times, and this checklist can be useful in guiding strategies and interventions to support a student.

Making observations and recording on the checklist

Figure 4.1 summarizes how to use the observation checklist.

FIGURE 4.1 USING THE OBSERVATION CHECKLIST

Who can complete the checklist?

It is recommended that the checklist is completed by a person familiar with the student. If the student is relatively new to the educational setting, the checklist can be completed by the person who is spending most time getting to know the student.

Generally where the observer is already familiar with the student, the checklist can be completed over a few days. With less familiarity, it is more likely that the checklist will be completed over a few weeks. This is a guide only; practitioners will find that the time needed will vary from student to student, and in line with the complexity of difficulties that the student presents.

In a secondary school setting within the UK a student can have a key person assigned to them – for example, this might be an appropriately supervised peer mentor, a teaching assistant, pastoral worker or teacher, or it might be a support worker from an outside agency. For looked after children within the UK Virtual School staff might provide this support. This individual has responsibility to work with a small number of children, helping them to feel safe and cared for.

The key person will develop relationships with the children and their families. This key person is therefore an ideal person to complete a checklist for an individual child. At Key Stages 3 and 4 there is currently no requirement to assign a key person, but most secondary educational settings have a pastoral worker or teaching assistant and therefore they are in a good position to take up this role. Identifying a person to build a relationship with the child will be important, however: this familiarity will provide a basis for completing the checklist. The key person model is a useful one for supporting the use of the observation checklist.

How can observations be made?

The checklist provides the observer with a tool to aid observation and reflection about an individual student. This increases understanding about the young person and his or her emotional and social needs. The checklist is completed based upon the observer's routine observations of the student together with his or her knowledge of the student. This can be supplemented by more structured observation if this is helpful. The observer might, for example, reflect upon a typical day for the student, and then supplement this with structured observations to gain further information. One teacher, for example, found it helpful to structure some observations of the student in different situations. She observed the student when there was a stranger in the room, while doing a familiar task and while doing a task that was more challenging. These observations were then integrated into the ongoing observations that were happening anyway as part of the classroom routine.

There is no right or wrong way of doing this; some of the checklist will be completed based on prior experience with the student, while other parts might be completed based on a new observation. In this way a profile is built up about the student guided by the sections of the checklist. This therefore is not a snapshot but a best fit between the observations made and the information on the checklist, based on ongoing observation and knowledge of the student.

Within educational settings, practitioners are making observations of the students on an ongoing basis. This checklist is not intended to add to this workload, but rather to guide the observer. The checklist will be completed based both on observations that are already being made during day-to-day interactions and by focusing the observations in a different way. In this way the checklist guides the observer to reflect on behaviours in a new way and to notice behaviours that might otherwise go unnoticed.

These observations can then be supplemented by the observer standing back and watching the student. For example, the observer may not have had an opportunity to notice how the student behaves while in the canteen at lunchtime. He or she may therefore choose to watch the student at lunchtime for a few days so that this part of the checklist can be completed. It can be helpful to discuss observations of the student with others. This provides multiple perspectives about the student which can enrich the information being gathered. For example, a teaching assistant might discuss his or her observations with the form teacher.

Recording observations on the checklist

Here we provide general guidance for recording observations. More detailed, section-by-section guidance can be found in Chapter 5. The observations are recorded on the checklist by ticking the box or boxes which most closely resemble the student. This can be done gradually over days or weeks, thus building up a profile of the young person. The observation period, as listed on the front of the checklist, is therefore not a set period of time. The observer can use this section to make a note of when the checklist was completed.

There are also opportunities on the checklist to record examples of the behaviours observed, and to make notes about the observations. If the observer is unsure about how to complete a section, a further few days of observation might be helpful, with this section particularly in mind.

Some young people will demonstrate different behaviours at different times, sometimes demonstrating behaviours on both ends of the checklist. These differences can be recorded by ticking more than one box in a particular row of the checklist. Again the comments section can be used to record notes about these different behaviours, perhaps noting various situations within which differing behaviours were noticed. For example, while watching a student interact with peers, the observer might notice that he or she is controlling and bossy with some but is more easily led by others. This student would get a tick at either end of the row, with a comment added about the observation, noting any differences in the peers who elicit this contrasting response: 'X is bossy with peers who are emotionally younger or more passive but is more easily led by the more mature or more confident peers in the group.'

Using the checklist to monitor progress over time

It can be helpful to revisit the checklist after an interval of time in order to monitor what progress the student is making, or to see if the behaviour changes when circumstances change. For example, a checklist might have been completed for a student and then some time later the young person's home circumstances change – perhaps parents separate or the young person moves placement. Repeating the observations can help the practitioners to see how these changes are impacting on the student in the educational setting. Alternatively the checklist might be revisited when a student moves to a new group or class, to monitor how he or she is coping with the change. In some schools practitioners might want to use the checklist at the beginning of the year so that they have a record of observations that can be used as a comparison as the student progresses through the year.

When repeating observations, the same checklist can be used for an individual student to aid easy comparison, with different-coloured ink being used to distinguish between the observation periods.

Supplementing the observation with contextual information

Contextual information can supplement and inform the understanding gained by the observations made with the guidance of the checklist. Here are some examples:

- Alongside using the checklist to observe the student within school, it is useful to have some discussions with the young person's parents or current carers regarding the young person's background, early life experiences and current functioning at home. If the student has a social worker, he or she can also be a useful source of information.

- Understanding the cultural background of the student will aid interpretation of the observations. The behaviours need to be understood against the background of any cultural differences demonstrated by the student. For example, imagine a Japanese student in a Western classroom; it is likely that this student will be a bit more self-contained and quiet compared to a Western student. This student might also demonstrate less eye-contact. If culture is not taken into account, the student might be recorded as difficult to relate to by familiar adults in the attachment section, and might be seen as overly timid when observed engaging in new tasks. These behaviours are in fact culturally typical rather than being a sign of emotional or social insecurity.

- Understanding any learning difficulties displayed by the student is important. A student with generalized learning difficulty might, for example, be at a different stage of emotional or social development, explaining some of the differences the student displays when compared to peers. For example, a student might be reluctant to engage in new activities. The observer needs to consider whether this reluctance is an indication of emotional insecurity or whether the task is too advanced for the student given his or her level of learning difficulty.

- An understanding about the impact of poor parenting upon young people will be useful background information with which to approach understanding an individual young person more deeply. In particular, understanding the attachment needs that these young people may have due to their early life experiences can provide a context for this understanding. This information can help with the shift in thinking from a focus on behaviour to considering the young person's emotional state.

With this awareness and background understanding, the observer can approach the completion of the checklist confidently, allowing a deepening understanding of the emotional and social needs highlighted.

5

Detailed Guidance for Completing the Checklist Section by Section

In this chapter we discuss the different sections that feature within the checklist and their significance. For each section of the checklist we provide information about why we have included it, followed by guidance for making the observations. We have also included illustrations for each section which provide a quick guide to help with recording observations on the checklist. These indicate the sorts of behaviours you might observe related to each side of the checklist. Whether you rate these behaviours as 'sometimes' or 'almost always' will depend upon the frequency or intensity with which these behaviours are displayed.

General behaviour

Attachment and emotional difficulties are generally displayed through behaviour (see Section 1 of checklist). Understanding behaviour in terms of underlying emotion is therefore an important part of the observation of the student.

What is student's behaviour like?

Think about the behaviour that the student is generally displaying, and how this compares to a typical young person of this age. Be aware of the 'too good' student as well as the overtly challenging one, as he or she may need additional support that hasn't been recognized.

The illustration provides guidance on observations you might make in relation to the student's behaviour that might suggest he or she should be rated towards one side or the other on the checklist.

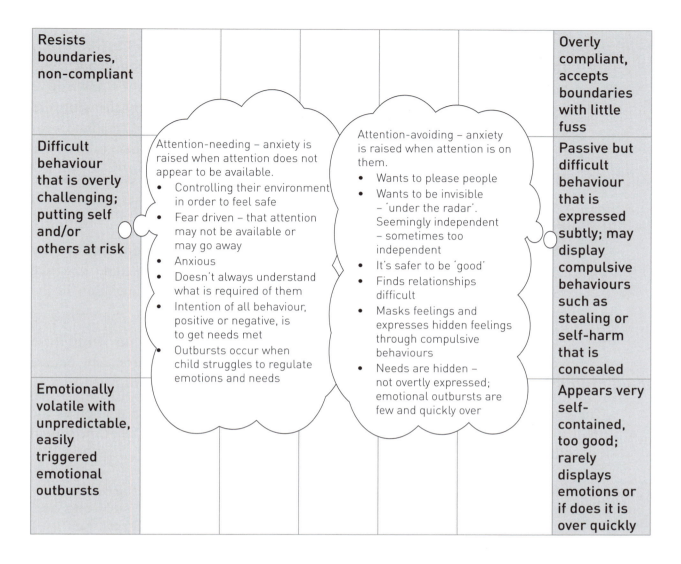

Resists boundaries, non-compliant					Overly compliant, accepts boundaries with little fuss
Difficult behaviour that is overly challenging; putting self and/or others at risk	Attention-needing – anxiety is raised when attention does not appear to be available. • Controlling their environment in order to feel safe • Fear driven – that attention may not be available or may go away • Anxious • Doesn't always understand what is required of them • Intention of all behaviour, positive or negative, is to get needs met • Outbursts occur when child struggles to regulate emotions and needs		Attention-avoiding – anxiety is raised when attention is on them. • Wants to please people • Wants to be invisible – 'under the radar'. Seemingly independent – sometimes too independent • It's safer to be 'good' • Finds relationships difficult • Masks feelings and expresses hidden feelings through compulsive behaviours • Needs are hidden – not overtly expressed; emotional outbursts are few and quickly over		Passive but difficult behaviour that is expressed subtly; may display compulsive behaviours such as stealing or self-harm that is concealed
Emotionally volatile with unpredictable, easily triggered emotional outbursts					Appears very self-contained, too good; rarely displays emotions or if does it is over quickly

Following this it is helpful to complete the section on risk-taking behaviours. This allows an understanding of specific behaviours to be gained so that these are appropriately supported as part of any actions determined as a result of the observation.

Attention, concentration and activity levels?

Young people who have had difficulties early in life often demonstrate developmental delays in ability to attend, concentrate and regulate impulses (be able to think before acting). These students may need extra support, with particular attention to the environment and how it can support these developments. Students who are overly controlled in terms of their self-management of behaviour and emotions can also be struggling, although for these students it may be less obvious.

- Does the student have difficulty regulating high arousal? Young people who when they get excited or agitated find it hard to calm themselves down have poor emotional regulation. Young people who are unpredictable, challenging and struggling with boundaries may be hyper-aroused. They may need an adult to co-regulate increasing arousal, that is, to stay with them and to help them calm down.

- Does the student have difficulty regulating low arousal? Young people who are hypo-aroused (low arousal levels) may be equally in need of co-regulation by an adult.

- Does the student have difficulty with poor concentration, attention, high activity and/or impulse control? Often these students need supervision and structure suitable for a younger child, with attention to reducing the stimulation in the environment.

- Does the student appear overly controlled and/or inactive? Less obviously these young people too may be struggling with the demands of the environment, but are trying to deal with this themselves rather than turning to adults for help.

The illustration provides guidance on observations you might make in relation to the student's attention, concentration and activity levels that might suggest he or she should be rated towards one side or the other on the checklist.

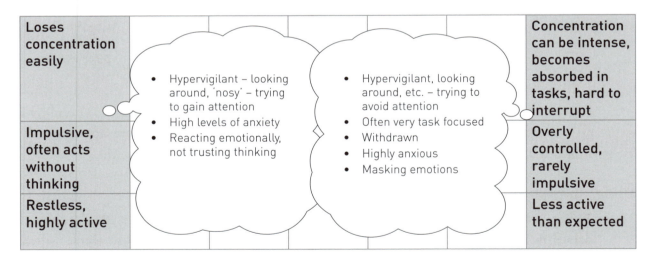

Attitude to attendance at education setting/provision

This section of the checklist provides an opportunity to observe the student's general ability to cope in the educational setting. Students rated either to the left or to the right are likely to be immature and requiring additional adult support, although the way that this is demonstrated varies from student to student.

While students who are timid or disruptive tend to be easily noticed, be careful to also notice the student who copes with insecurity by being pseudomature (rather too grown up), or 'too good to be true'. These students are also in need of additional support.

The illustration provides guidance on observations you might make in relation to the student's attitude to attendance that might suggest he or she should be rated towards one side or the other on the checklist.

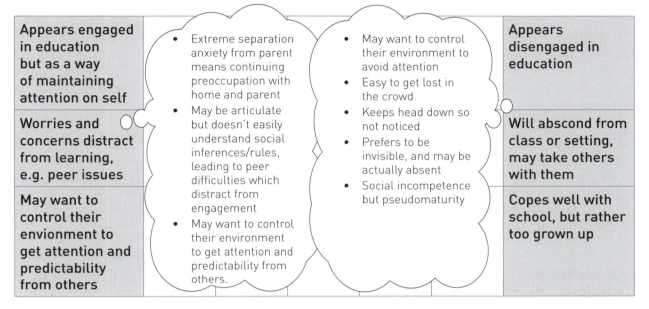

Appears engaged in education but as a way of maintaining attention on self

Worries and concerns distract from learning, e.g. peer issues

May want to control their envionment to get attention and predictability from others

- Extreme separation anxiety from parent means continuing preoccupation with home and parent
- May be articulate but doesn't easily understand social inferences/rules, leading to peer difficulties which distract from engagement
- May want to control their environment to get attention and predictability from others.

- May want to control their environment to avoid attention
- Easy to get lost in the crowd
- Keeps head down so not noticed
- Prefers to be invisible, and may be actually absent
- Social incompetence but pseudomaturity

Appears disengaged in education

Will abscond from class or setting, may take others with them

Copes well with school, but rather too grown up

Classroom-related behaviours

Section 2 of the checklist focuses on observation of the student in the classroom, considering how ready the student is to focus away from his or her need of adult support and to be able to engage with learning, including relating to other students.

Young people with attachment difficulties are generally emotionally more immature than their peers; although for some young people this is masked by an apparent pseudomaturity where they act older than their chronological age and appear too grown up. The need for attention or for self-reliance can both impact on difficulties in engaging with tasks and learning. These young people may also have immature social skills and need more adult support to work with their peers.

Behaviour with other students in the classroom/lesson setting

This element structures the observation to consider how well students are in working with their peers.

- Students who want to work with their peers, but are perhaps not competent socially to do this or whose need for attention gets in the way, will be rated more on the left-hand side of the observation checklist. They will need more structure, supervision and support to help them develop prosocial skills and learn to interact successfully with peers.

- Students who are not interested in working with their peers will be rated more on the right-hand side of the observation checklist. Consideration needs to be given as to whether these students are ready for working in large or small groups, but need additional support, or whether their level of immaturity means that they still need more help from adult relationships which will later be used to engage with peers.

The illustration provides guidance on observations you might make in relation to the student's behaviour with peers that might suggest he or she should be rated towards one side or the other on the checklist.

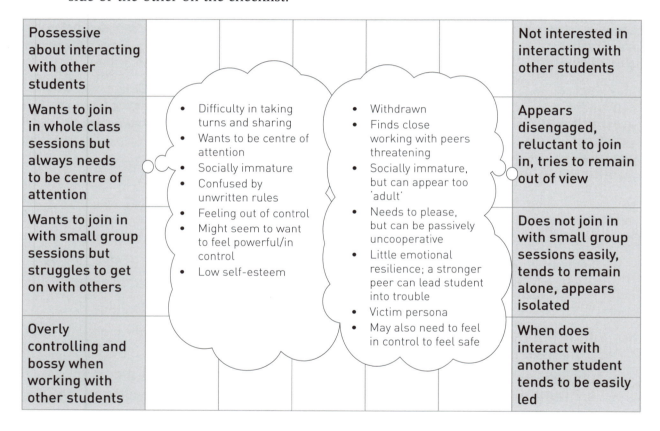

Activity-related behaviour in classroom/lesson setting

This element structures the observation to consider how well students are in engaging with tasks and learning.

- *Students who struggle to focus on tasks and activity:* the need for attention can get in the way of settling to learn. These students will be rated more on the left-hand side of the observation checklist. They will need more time and attention from the teacher in order to help reduce their anxiety about not being noticed so that they can settle to the task.

- *Students who are keen to work without help, but are quickly dissatisfied with what they have done:* these students can get very absorbed in the task, but are disengaged with peers or adults. These students will be rated more on the right-hand side of the observation checklist. These students need to be gently encouraged to engage in relationships and to use support for learning.

The illustration provides guidance on observations you might make in relation to the student's activity-related behaviour that might suggest he or she should be rated towards one side or the other on the checklist.

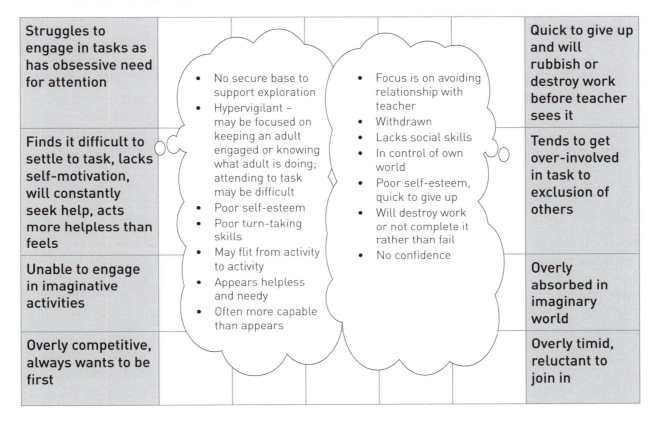

Struggles to engage in tasks as has obsessive need for attention	• No secure base to support exploration • Hypervigilant – may be focused on keeping an adult engaged or knowing what adult is doing; attending to task may be difficult • Poor self-esteem • Poor turn-taking skills • May flit from activity to activity • Appears helpless and needy • Often more capable than appears	• Focus is on avoiding relationship with teacher • Withdrawn • Lacks social skills • In control of own world • Poor self-esteem, quick to give up • Will destroy work or not complete it rather than fail • No confidence	Quick to give up and will rubbish or destroy work before teacher sees it
Finds it difficult to settle to task, lacks self-motivation, will constantly seek help, acts more helpless than feels			Tends to get over-involved in task to exclusion of others
Unable to engage in imaginative activities			Overly absorbed in imaginary world
Overly competitive, always wants to be first			Overly timid, reluctant to join in

Social relationship with peers

Section 3 of the checklist pays particular attention to peer relationships, recognizing how much this is a preoccupation of adolescence. At this developmental stage difficulties with peer relationships can dominate the student's life and will impact on learning or the ability to settle and feel comfortable within the setting.

- Students whose peer relationships dominate school life, and who frequently want to complain to adults about their problems and dissatisfaction with friendships, will be rated more on the left-hand side of the observation checklist. These students will take up a lot of adult time and attention in trying to support them with these relationships, but without some support they will struggle to settle, impacting upon any engagement with learning.

- Students who are less needy of peer relationships may not get noticed as they attend to activities well. They can appear focused in the classroom and engaged with peers outside of class, but upon closer inspection it is evident that these students are not able to form deeper, more meaningful relationships with their peers. They prefer to work alone or to engage with peers superficially. These students will be rated more on the right-hand side of the observation checklist. These students need support but are likely to reject it. Both adult and student will be more comfortable leaving the student to get on with things in his or her own way, but this will put the student at a disadvantage with poorly developed capacity for relationships in the future.

The illustration provides guidance on observations you might make in relation to the student's social relationships with peers that might suggest he or she should be rated towards one side or the other on the checklist.

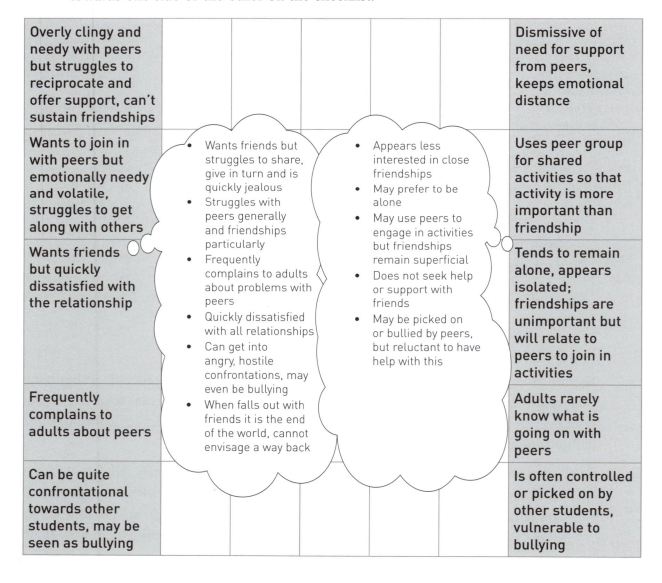

Overly clingy and needy with peers but struggles to reciprocate and offer support, can't sustain friendships		**Dismissive of need for support from peers, keeps emotional distance**
Wants to join in with peers but emotionally needy and volatile, struggles to get along with others	Wants friends but struggles to share, give in turn and is quickly jealous • Struggles with peers generally and friendships particularly • Frequently complains to adults about problems with peers • Quickly dissatisfied with all relationships • Can get into angry, hostile confrontations, may even be bullying • When falls out with friends it is the end of the world, cannot envisage a way back	Appears less interested in close friendships • May prefer to be alone • May use peers to engage in activities but friendships remain superficial • Does not seek help or support with friends • May be picked on or bullied by peers, but reluctant to have help with this	**Uses peer group for shared activities so that activity is more important than friendship**
Wants friends but quickly dissatisfied with the relationship		**Tends to remain alone, appears isolated; friendships are unimportant but will relate to peers to join in activities**
Frequently complains to adults about peers		**Adults rarely know what is going on with peers**
Can be quite confrontational towards other students, may be seen as bullying		**Is often controlled or picked on by other students, vulnerable to bullying**

Attachment behaviours

Section 4 of the checklist allows you to match observations to attachment styles of relating that the student might bring into the educational setting. Understanding the style of relating that students habitually use with adults in the educational setting can provide important information to guide ways of working with the students. Chapters 9 and 10 provide further information about attachment behaviours in school to help interpret observations in this section.

This is not an assessment of attachment difficulty or disorder but an observation of style of relating. Do not worry if observations do not match easily to one of the attachment patterns; some young people tend to relate with a single style, while others use a range of styles.

This section allows you to think about whether a student's style leans towards secure, avoidant or ambivalent (or a combination of these). Students with more serious attachment difficulties (those described as having disorganized-controlling attachment styles of relating) will also show these basic styles, but the level of the control that they exert in their relationships is greater. As a rule of thumb, students who are rated as 'sometimes' are likely to be demonstrating insecurity in their relationship style, while those who are rated predominantly as 'almost always' are likely to be demonstrating the more controlling patterns of relating.

In this section of the checklist you are guided to observe the student in a number of situations which are likely to reveal his or her habitual attachment style of relating with others.

Background
HOW DOES THE STUDENT BEHAVE WITH FAMILIAR AND UNFAMILIAR ADULTS?

Young people often generalize the behaviour they use with familiar caregivers to their interactions with other adults in their life, but this can vary depending upon how stressed or relaxed they are within these interactions. Observing students with a range of adults can therefore give some indication about both the attachment patterns they display as well as how stressful they find these interactions. Generally students will display attachment behaviours within relationships that they find more stressful.

HOW DOES THE STUDENT BEHAVE WHEN EXPERIENCING MINOR HURTS, WORRIES OR TROUBLES?

Attachment behaviours are activated when young people experience increased stress. This serves the purpose of orientating the young person towards the caregiver in order to obtain comfort and soothing. For young people with insecure attachments this reveals itself in less obvious, comfort-seeking behaviours. Self-reliance to maintain closeness, attention-needing at times of low stress and controlling behaviours are all complex ways of reducing stress in young people who find it difficult to seek comfort in straightforward ways. To observe attachment and comfort-seeking behaviours it is therefore helpful to watch students at times of increased stress. Experiencing minor physical hurts (e.g. bumps and falls) or psychological hurts (e.g. experiencing conflict with another peer) will increase stress for a student.

For each of these situations you can consider the behaviour being observed in relation to the student's attachment style. Thus:

- *Secure attachment pattern:* students will predominantly be rated as 'like any other student of the same age'.

- *Avoidant attachment pattern:* students who are self-reliant (appearing not to need their caregiver or the adults in school) are anxious to please or unusually compliant. These students will be rated on the right-hand side more than the left based on observations.

- *Ambivalent attachment pattern:* students who are clingy, attention-needing and more emotionally demanding will be rated on the left-hand side more than the right based on observations.

HOW DOES THE STUDENT BEHAVE WITH FAMILIAR ADULTS?

The illustration provides guidance on observations you might make in relation to the student's behaviour with familiar adults that might suggest he or she should be rated towards one side or the other on the checklist.

Unusually dependent, always seeking help even when doesn't need it						**Unusually independent, will actively reject offers of help**
Always demonstrating vulnerability but frequently dissatisfied with response of others						**Dislikes appearing vulnerable or in need of help**
Craves attention, stays close to adult(s), uses range of ways to gain attention						**Doesn't want attention, difficult to relate to, avoids eye-contact**
Very clingy, wants to be with adult(s) all the time, will seek attention from range of adults						**Hard to get close to, or false quality to relationship**
Overly demanding and attention-needing, talks a lot						**Overly self-reliant, undemanding, detached**
Likes to be in control/in charge						**Unusually passive, tries too hard to please**

Left thought bubble:

- Hypervigilant to adult's proximity
- Can create 'drama' to keep adults close
- Will this adult 'disappear' like others have?
- Appear dependent upon adult/adults
- Will seek help even when doesn't need it
- Clingy to adults, craves attention but rarely satisfied
- Adults always know what is going on with this student

Right thought bubble:

- Finds the intimacy of eye-contact threatening
- Greatly dislikes any appearance of being vulnerable
- May feel safer not to respond or engage with others
- Has learned to do things for self
- Appears independent from adults
- Adults often don't know what is going on with this student

How does the student behave with unfamiliar adults?

The illustration provides guidance on observations you might make in relation to the student's behaviour with unfamiliar adults that might suggest he or she should be rated towards one side or the other on the checklist.

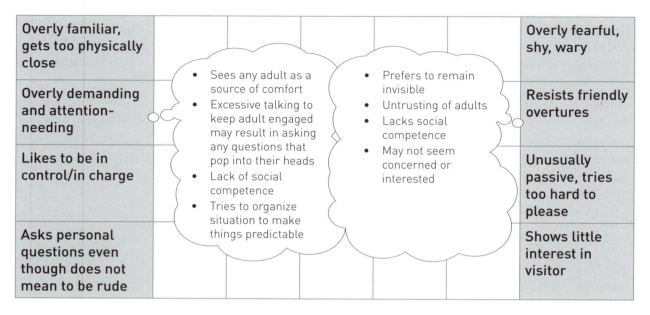

How does the student behave when experiencing minor hurts, worries or troubles?

The illustration provides guidance on observations you might make in relation to a student's behaviour when experiencing minor hurts, worries or troubles that might suggest he or she should be rated towards one side or the other on the checklist.

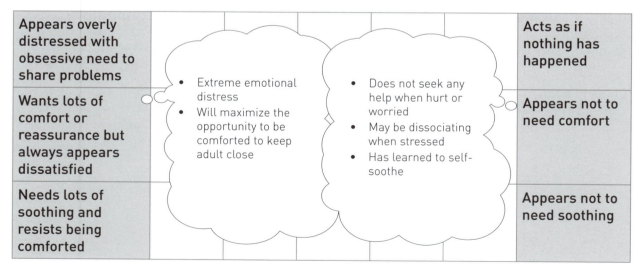

Emotional state

Section 5 of the checklist has been designed to aid observation of emotional state, and the way that this emotion is displayed through feelings.

It is likely, with the stress of being in school and the need to relate to a range of adults and peers, that the student will adopt emotional displays learnt at home with early carers. Where these early relationships are experienced as insecure or stressful, these styles of relating can place the student at a disadvantage in the educational setting.

Students with attachment difficulties are often more emotionally immature than their peers. They have learnt to display emotions in a way that is adaptive, in that it helps them to feel safer in situations where they are feeling unsafe, but can appear dysfunctional, not helpful for them and different compared to typically developing peers.

Background
CURRENT EMOTIONAL STATE, CONSIDERING ANY CURRENT CIRCUMSTANCES?

Think about the main emotional state that the student is displaying. For example, does the student appear happy, sad, worried, frightened or angry? This may be very clear from the way the student displays his or her feelings, or you may need to think about the way he or she is behaving. For example, a student who is following you around all the time may be feeling anxious, or a student who is hiding may be feeling frightened.

Take into account any relevant context. For example, if the student is new to the educational setting or has significant events happening at home, some display of anxiety or worry would be normal. Similarly a student who is generally a bit shy or slow to warm up might be expected to appear more anxious or sensitive upon arrival at the school.

Observe the student over a number of days to understand the predominant emotional state he or she is experiencing.

HOW DOES THE STUDENT DISPLAY FEELINGS?

A young person's emotional state is not necessarily displayed in a straightforward way. This section allows you to reflect on the way that the student is generally displaying his or her feelings.

Questions to consider

- Does the student appear happy, sad, angry or anxious within the educational setting?

- Does the student appear to express how he or she is feeling or do you think some feelings are hidden from view?

- Does the student find it difficult to cope with some of his or her feelings, perhaps taking this out on self or others?

- Do you think that the student's emotional displays indicate that he or she needs more emotional support than a typical young person?

- Do you think that the student's lack of emotional display indicates that he or she needs more emotional support than a typical young person?

Current emotional state, considering any current circumstances?

The illustration provides guidance on observations you might make in relation to the student's current emotional state that might suggest he or she should be rated towards one side or the other on the checklist.

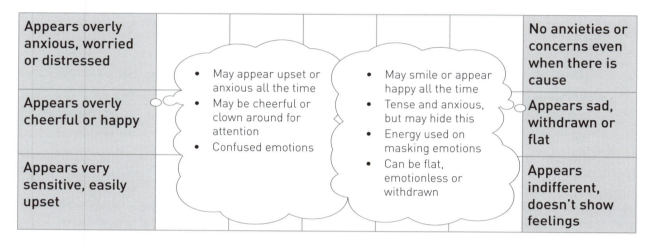

How does the student display feelings?

The illustration provides guidance on observations you might make in relation to the student's display of feelings that might suggest he or she should be rated towards one side or the other on the checklist.

It is easy to tell how the student is feeling					Tends to hide feelings away; it is difficult to tell how the student is feeling
Displays feelings only through angry, challenging or risky behaviour					Tends not to show how he/she is feeling in way he/she behaves
Will become abusive or rude if not being attended to, may alternate with charming behaviours					Will become abusive or rude if one tries to offer help or support
Hurts self obviously and in full view of others to gain attention					Hurts self secretly
May draw attention to self by humiliating or teasing peers					Tries not to draw attention to self, may hide behind peers

Thought bubble (left):
- Dysregulates easily
- Cortisol levels raised – fight, flight
- Controls situations, can be bossy
- Can be abusive or rude if not getting what one needs
- Can also be charming and appealing
- Can hurt others, to maintain feeling of control or because doesn't understand own impact

Thought bubble (right):
- Withdrawn
- Dissociates – freeze
- Safer not to show feelings
- Masking painful emotions
- Not able to verbalize feelings
- Does not want to draw attention to self
- Can hurt self as passive aggressive expression of anger

Summary: tips for completion of checklist

- It may be helpful to have a student in mind who is of similar age and developmental stage when making observations of a student. This will provide a useful guide for the observer with regard to a typical young person, that is, a young person who would be recorded in the central column on the checklist. The observed student can then be compared to this 'typical young person'.

- If a student is new to the school, the observer may be advised to wait a month to ensure that the student has had a chance to settle into the setting and that the staff are familiar with the student.

- Ideally the key person or a practitioner who knows the student well will complete the checklist. These observations can be part of the ongoing observations being made of the student. This member of staff may also need time to make additional observations of the student to inform the accurate completion of the checklist.

- Although the checklist assists the observer to make a structured observation, be careful not to simply observe the student as a 'snapshot'. It is more helpful if the checklist is used as a reflective tool. Think about a typical day for the student in the educational setting while going through each section.

- Look at each row as a whole question, with the central column as the age-typical indicator.

- The question offers contrasting examples of behaviour. Don't worry if the student demonstrates behaviour at both ends of the row. Simply tick both.

- It's useful to write some examples of behaviours, or triggers if known, in the comments space. This can be used later to identify targets for an action plan or individual education plan.

6

Worked Examples of the Observation Checklist

CAROLINE AND CARL

Following on from Chapters 4 and 5 on how to carry out the observations, this chapter has worked examples to show you how the checklist has been used for two young people, Caroline and Carl. These students illustrate adolescents with insecure ambivalent attachment patterns of relating within school. In Carl's case there is a greater degree of coercion and control within this style of relating, suggesting a disorganized-controlling pattern using the ambivalent, attention-needing strategies. This also illustrates the development of more concerning difficulties that can emerge during adolescence, and highlights the importance of intervening earlier to avoid this progression. Caroline's behaviours suggest some risk of escalating conduct problems. We might also be concerned about developing patterns of self-harming behaviours in the future. It is hoped by intervening earlier with Caroline she will not develop the more worrying behaviours that Carl is displaying.

Both of these cases are composites based on observation checklists completed for us by teachers whilst piloting this adolescent version. It was notable to us that students with ambivalent presentations were more likely to be brought to our attention within secondary settings. It is harder to miss these young people's difficulties given their attention-needing, 'in your face'-type presentations. We wonder if the more avoidant young people with self-reliant patterns of relating are more easily missed in these larger, busier educational settings, at least until their behaviour becomes of more concern due to emerging mental health problems such as self-harm, school refusal or drug and alcohol misuse. Noticing these students and intervening earlier can be an important way we can reduce the escalation of difficulties. The observation checklist provides a tool to identify these young people and to work preventively with them, improving both their mental health and academic achievement.

Caroline

Thirteen-year-old Caroline is in Year 7 at a middle school and her teachers are greatly concerned about her. Over recent months Caroline has been having difficulties at school. Caroline has been struggling with focus and attention in class. She seems to have a 'short fuse', easily becoming upset even with quiet reminders to pay attention and follow instructions, particularly when in English lessons.

When upset Caroline becomes very attention-needing. She shouts out and makes rude remarks to the teacher, disrupting the lesson. She becomes angry when reminded of expectations by her teachers. When asked to leave the lesson she refuses and does not leave the room when the head of house, Mr Welsh, comes to collect her. This has been happening more frequently of late, and following a fixed-term exclusion her teachers are considering arranging for Caroline to spend six weeks on a part-time Pupil Referral Unit (PRU) placement on a behaviour course.

Caroline, an academically bright student, had been attaining levels above those expected at school prior to the period of difficulty. Recently however her progress has considerably slowed down, and staff feel that she is not producing work of a level that reflects her ability and is not making a suitable rate of progress in school.

Caroline has also been unsettled in her foster placement and has been in trouble as she walked home, receiving a police caution for ringing people's door bells and throwing stones at buses.

With all of this happening, and the school's normal behaviour support strategies not seeming to be effective in helping to modify Caroline's behaviours, the staff at school approach the local Virtual School for Looked After and Adopted Children for help. The practitioner from the Virtual School suggests that they use the observation checklist to help them to explore Caroline's behaviours and needs more closely. They could then begin to better understand Caroline's emotional difficulties, how Caroline may be feeling and how they can successfully move forward to support her.

The school allocates a key adult to complete the tool – Mrs Foot, who has been closely monitoring her behaviour over the past weeks. Mrs Foot completes the initial checklist. Following this staff are able to consider Caroline's emotional needs in more detail and think about them from an attachment perspective. From this they are able to put an action plan together for her support. After six weeks of support via the action plan they repeat the checklist and are very pleased with the results observed.

In the following sections you can see how the checklist was completed for the first time (marked with ✔) and again after support had been in place (marked with ✘) and how this assisted Caroline's teachers and Caroline in school.

Name of student	Caroline Webb	Date of birth	21/4/2002 Year 7
Name of educational setting	Wood Forest Middle School	Start date	April 2014
		Hours attending	Full time
Special educational needs?	None – achieving above-expected levels in all areas, although rates of progress currently causing concern		
Other settings student may attend	None		
Name of parents/carers	Mr and Mrs Carr	Language spoken at home	English
Address	Big Mill Lane, Walkington		

Dates of first observation period	Symbol used	Key person	Factors affecting the observation (e.g. student's health, changes in the school, changes at home, etc.)
April 2014	✓	Mrs Foot – Pastoral Lead	C is struggling at school at the moment – persistent disruptive behaviour has led to a 1-day fixed-term exclusion. Considering PRU placement.
Dates of second observation period (if needed)	Symbol used	Key person	Factors affecting the observation (e.g. student's health, changes in the school, changes at home, etc.)
July 2014	✗	Mrs Foot – Pastoral Lead	Support from Virtual School gained – relationship-based play has been delivered and is used regularly. C has key adult with regular contact. No risk of exclusion now – PRU placement cancelled.

1. General behaviour

		Almost always	Sometimes	As student of same age or stage of development	Sometimes	Almost always	
What is student's behaviour like?	Resists boundaries, non-compliant		✔	✘			Overly compliant, accepts boundaries with little fuss
	Difficult behaviour that is overly challenging/ risk-taking (please see below to clarify); putting self and/or others at risk		✔	✘			Passive but difficult behaviour that is expressed subtly; may display compulsive behaviours such as stealing or self-harm that is concealed
	Emotionally volatile with unpredictable, easily triggered emotional outbursts		✔	✘			Appears very self-contained, too good; rarely displays emotions or if does it is over quickly
Attention, concentration and activity levels?	Loses concentration easily	✔	✘				Concentration can be intense, becomes absorbed in tasks, hard to interrupt
	Impulsive, often acts without thinking		✔	✘			Overly controlled, rarely impulsive
	Restless, highly active	✔		✘			Less active than expected

Attitude to attendance at education setting/provision	Appears engaged in education but as a way of maintaining attention on self		✓	✗			Appears disengaged in education
	Worries and concerns distract from learning, e.g. peer issues		✓	✗			Will abscond from class or setting, may take others with them
	Does not cope well with school, appears immature	✓	✗				Copes well with school, but rather too grown up

Clarification of challenging/risky behaviours including mental health difficulties

		Almost always	Sometimes	As student at same stage of development	Hardly ever	Never
Challenging/risky behaviours	Sexualized behaviours – language, gestures or body language			✓ ✗		
	Substance misuse – drugs, alcohol or other substance misuse					✓ ✗
	Verbally challenging behaviours – attitude/tone of voice	✓		✗		
	Threatening behaviour – verbally/physically		✓		✗	
	Threatening behaviour – weapon use				✓	✗
	Absconding/self-exclusion		✓		✗	
	Education refusal		✓		✗	
	Risky use of ICT – social media, games, etc.					✓ ✗

Mental health-related difficulties	Self-harm					✓✗
	Eating disorders					✓✗
	Internalizing difficulties, e.g. anxiety, depression				✓	✗
	Psychotic behaviours, hallucinations, delusions, appears out of touch with reality					✓✗
	Trauma symptoms, e.g. flashbacks, memories, easily triggered fight/flight reactions; dissociates, excessive use of fantasy; hearing voices of past perpetrators					✓✗

General behaviour: supporting evidence and comments

Caroline has been struggling greatly with focus and attention in class at present. She seems to have a 'short fuse' and easily becomes upset even with quiet reminders to pay attention and follow instructions – particularly when in English lessons.

When upset Caroline becomes very attention-seeking and will shout out and make rude remarks to the teacher, disrupting the lesson, and becomes more angry when reminded of expectations by her teachers. When asked to leave the lesson she will refuse and will not leave the room when the head of house, Mr Welsh, comes to collect her. This has been happening more frequently of late, and following a fixed-term exclusion we are considering arranging for C to spend 6 weeks on a part-time PRU placement on a behaviour course.

Caroline has been unsettled in her foster placement at the moment and has been in trouble as she walks home – recently receiving a police caution for ringing people's door bells and throwing stones at buses.

Mrs Foot now checks in briefly with Caroline each morning and attends approximately 20% of her lessons – particularly English and any led by supply teachers. Mrs Foot also leads a relationship-based play session for Caroline once per week. Caroline is now more settled in school. She is able to attend lessons without difficulty or incident and is able to devote her attention to the learning opportunities that the lessons bring. She is now far more settled and resilient in her English lessons. Her attainment in English has accelerated and she has made an excellent amount of progress in the past few weeks. Caroline has not needed to leave any lessons. She has become a little unsettled on a couple of occasions but has responded very well to Mrs Foot offering her support within the lesson. She has also visited Mrs Foot to talk about one particular problem on one occasion. Caroline's carer reports that she is a lot more settled at home now and is not getting into any difficulties on her way home from school.

2. Classroom-related behaviours

		Almost always	Sometimes	As student of same age or stage of development	Sometimes	Almost always	
Behaviour with other students in the classroom/ lesson setting	Possessive about interacting with other students		✓	✗			Not interested in interacting with other students
	Wants to join in whole class sessions but always needs to be centre of attention			✗	✓		Appears disengaged, reluctant to join in, tries to remain out of view
	Wants to join in with small group sessions but struggles to get on with others		✓	✗			Does not join in with small group sessions easily, tends to remain alone, appears isolated
	Overly controlling and bossy when working with other students		✓	✗			When does interact with another student tends to be easily led

Activity-related behaviour in classroom/lesson setting		Almost always	Sometimes	As student of same age or stage of development	Sometimes	Almost always	
Activity-related behaviour in classroom/lesson setting	Struggles to engage in tasks as has obsessive need for attention		✓	✗			Quick to give up and will rubbish or destroy work before teacher sees it
	Finds it difficult to settle to task, lacks self-motivation, will constantly seek help, and act more helpless than feels		✓	✗			Tends to get over-involved in task to exclusion of others
	Unable to engage in imaginative activities			✓ ✗			Overly absorbed in imaginary world
	Overly competitive, always wants to be first		✓	✗			Overly timid, reluctant to join in

Classroom-related behaviours: supporting evidence and comments

Caroline is struggling to maintain a positive attitude in lessons at the moment and is struggling to interact positively with her peers as she can become quite controlling of the situation.

Caroline is rarely settling to tasks at the moment apart from when she is expected to read on her own – she seems to love reading and will happily sit and read without any problems.

Caroline is now far more settled and positive in her relationships with peers whilst in lessons and outside lessons. She has not been involved in any more incidents of bullying. She still loves reading and has told Mrs Foot that she will choose to read if she feels unsettled to help her to feel better.

3. Social relationships with peers

		Almost always	Sometimes	As student of same age or stage of development	Sometimes	Almost always	
Behaviour with other students during unstructured times	Overly clingy and needy with peers but struggles to reciprocate and offer support, can't sustain friendships			✗	✓		Dismissive of need for support from peers, keeps emotional distance
	Wants to join in with peers but emotionally needy and volatile, struggles to get along with others	✓	✗				Uses peer group for shared activities so that activity is more important than friendship
	Wants friends but quickly dissatisfied with the relationship		✓	✗			Tends to remain alone, appears isolated; friendships are unimportant but will relate to peers to join in activities
	Frequently complains to adults about peers			✓ ✗			Adults rarely know what is going on with peers
	Can be quite confrontational towards other students, may be seen as bullying		✓	✗			Is often controlled or picked on by other students, vulnerable to bullying

Social relationships with peers: supporting evidence and comments

Caroline has recently been accused of bullying a peer in school using taunting and name-calling regarding the other child's hair colour as a focus. This child is also a looked after child and Caroline is aware of this.

Caroline is now far more settled and positive in her relationships with peers whilst in lessons and outside lessons. She has not been involved in any more incidents of bullying.

We can see from the above that Caroline's behaviour at the time of the first observation was causing concern. She had been exhibiting a significant level of attention-needing and challenging behaviour in school, both in the classroom and during more unstructured situations. She was highly restless and lacking in concentration, becoming controlling, bossy and competitive with other students.

In general the ticks are placed to the left-hand side of the checklist in Sections 1, 2 and 3, suggesting an ambivalent attachment style of relating at times of anxiety. This leads her to need the attention and support of adults around her to feel safe and settled. She displays a pattern of low or fragile self-esteem. When this attention is not available she becomes more anxious and hypervigilant, thus being unable to concentrate on her learning and finding the regulation of emotions difficult. If not supported this may then lead to rapid dysregulation and more challenging behaviours, as observed in the behaviour section and mentioned in the added notes provided.

We also find that her behaviour leads staff to feel that she is generally less emotionally mature than the majority of her peers. In Caroline's case we can also see that she does not display any significantly risky behaviours or mental health-related difficulties.

4. Attachment behaviours

		Almost always	Sometimes	As student of same age or stage of development	Sometimes	Almost always	
How does the student behave with familiar adults?	Unusually dependent, always seeking help even when doesn't need it		✓	✗			Unusually independent, will actively reject offers of help
	Always demonstrating vulnerability but frequently dissatisfied with response of others		✓	✗			Dislikes appearing vulnerable or in need of help
	Craves attention, stays close to adult(s), uses range of ways to gain attention	✓	✗				Doesn't want attention, difficult to relate to, avoids eye-contact
	Very clingy, wants to be with adult(s) all the time, will seek attention from range of adults		✓	✗			Hard to get close to, or false quality to relationship
	Overly demanding and attention-needing, talks a lot	✓	✗				Overly self-reliant, undemanding, detached
	Likes to be in control/in charge	✓	✗				Unusually passive, tries too hard to please

How does the student behave with unfamiliar adults?	Overly familiar, gets too physically close			✓ ✗			Overly fearful, shy, wary
	Overly demanding and attention-needing	✓	✗				Resists friendly overtures
	Likes to be in control/in charge	✓	✗				Unusually passive, tries too hard to please
	Asks personal questions even though does not mean to be rude		✓		✗		Shows little interest in visitor
How does the student behave when experiencing minor hurts, worries or troubles?	Appears overly distressed with obsessive need to share problems			✓ ✗			Acts as if nothing has happened
	Wants lots of comfort or reassurance but always appears dissatisfied			✓ ✗			Appears not to need comfort
	Needs lots of soothing and resists being comforted			✗	✓		Appears not to need soothing

Attachment behaviours: supporting evidence and comments

When Caroline is settled in school her behaviour towards all others can be excellent – cooperative, thoughtful and helpful. But when she is unsettled she becomes very demanding of attention, using generally defiant and disruptive methods to gain attention. This can be worse if she does not know or have a good relationship with the teacher in charge.

Caroline still likes attention and can be bossy, but this is much less than previously, and is no longer as disruptive. We do see some of her former behaviours when she is with unfamiliar adults.

5. Emotional state

		Almost always	Sometimes	As student of same age or stage of development	Sometimes	Almost always	
Current emotional state, considering any current circum-stances?	Appears overly anxious, worried or distressed		✔	✖			No anxieties or concerns even when there is cause
	Appears overly cheerful or happy			✖	✔		Appears sad, withdrawn or flat
	Appears very sensitive, easily upset	✔		✖			Appears indifferent, doesn't show feelings
How does the student display feelings?	It is easy to tell how the student is feeling		✔	✖			Tends to hide feelings away; it is difficult to tell how the student is feeling
	Displays feelings only through angry, challenging or risky behaviour		✔	✖			Tends not to show how he/she is feeling in the way he/she behaves
	Will become abusive or rude if not being attended to, may alternate with charming behaviours		✔	✖			Will become abusive or rude if one tries to offer help or support
	Hurts self obviously and in full view of others to gain attention			✔✖			Hurts self secretly
	May draw attention to self by humiliating or teasing peers		✔	✖			Tries not to draw attention to self, may hide behind peers

Emotional state: supporting evidence and comments

Caroline's behaviour towards teachers varies greatly between teachers – depending on the relationship she has with them. Seems to relate to the personality and teaching style of particular members of staff. With staff with whom she has a secure relationship she can be very settled, responsive and cooperative in lessons. With staff with whom she feels less secure she can become very attention-needing, oppositional and disruptive. When Caroline becomes upset when hurt or perceives that she is in trouble she can become more oppositional and angry even when approached by staff with whom she has a good relationship.

Caroline is much more settled, and we are seeing few of the behaviours we were concerned about.

Sections 4 and 5 continue to indicate that Caroline tends towards an ambivalent attachment style of relating in school, again showing that she is generally needy of adult attention in school. This leads her to talk a lot and to be demanding of adult attention within lessons. From the notes the teacher provided we can see that Caroline may become increasingly anxious when working with unfamiliar adults, with her need for the safety of a secure relationship heightening and her attention-demanding and controlling behaviours increasing.

Any other comments?

We are very concerned about Caroline, who is taking up a lot of our attention in school.

Caroline appears to be much more settled and happy in school. We can see that she does need additional support and is benefiting from this.

What works in this environment for this student?

At this time we are not finding anything that is working to support Caroline and are considering her attendance on a 6-week behaviour course at the local PRU.

We are now aware of the nature of Caroline's attachment difficulties and the impact this has upon her needs, well-being and behaviour in school. Via the initial completion of the checklist we have learned that Caroline was feeling a higher level of anxiety than we initially anticipated and that she is going to need regular support to keep her anxiety levels down. The Relationship-Based Play and 'PACE' approach has been particularly effective for Caroline as it has supported Caroline's self-esteem, resilience and feelings of enjoyment and safety in school and has deepened Caroline's relationship with Mrs Foot. Now when she is unsettled she will accept Mrs Foot's help more successfully.

Taking the overall picture from the first completion of the checklist it is clear that Caroline is frequently attention-needing in school and can often show signs of anxiety. The anxiety has been more apparent in lessons with teachers with whom she does not have a secure relationship, but the checklist also shows a more pervasive pattern of anxiety and the need for a secure attachment in school.

From the notes provided we can also see that the anxiety that Caroline is experiencing in school can spill over into her walk home as she has had difficulties with antisocial behaviours that have led to her being spoken to by the police.

Carl

Sixteen-year-old Carl, a Year 10 pupil within a local high school, is referred for support to the Virtual School as he has been experiencing significant difficulties.

Whilst Carl was attending middle school his behaviour had been very erratic. He found making friends difficult and he struggled with recognizing personal boundaries. Carl was often in trouble following disagreements with peers and he would sometimes become overly attached and overbearing with girls. Teachers reported that within relationships he could be seen as controlling and bullying, but instead of recognizing his own difficulties he perceived himself as the one being bullied. These behaviours and difficulties within peer relationships have continued into high school. When the checklist is completed it has reached the point where staff feel that they need further support to help him to settle to learn within the school.

Within the high school environment teachers also find that Carl disrupts classes if he does not understand the content being taught in a particular lesson. He loses interest quickly and is scared to try anything new or challenging. Instead of seeking help from staff he masks his anxiety by using overtly challenging behaviours and often walks out of lessons.

Carl often takes a dislike to particular teachers and refuses to take part in classroom activities with that particular teacher; however, if he is excluded from those activities he sees it as personal rejection.

Following initial conversations with the designated teacher at Carl's school the practitioners from the Virtual School ask them to arrange for a person who knows Carl best to complete the checklist so that they can think more deeply about Carl's difficulties. In this way a clearer picture of his emotional needs can be created, and from this they can identify how they could help him at this time. Mr Randle, the Pastoral Lead for the school, has been involved with supporting Carl since he started at the school, so is felt to be the best member of staff to complete the checklist.

In the following sections you can see how the checklist was completed for the first time (marked with ✔) and again after support had been in place (marked with ✘) and how this assisted Carl's teachers and Carl in school.

Name of student	Carl Linden	Date of birth	13/5/99 Year 10
Name of educational setting	South Bigley Academy	Start date	February 2014
		Hours attending	Full time
Special educational needs?	School Action – mild learning difficulties (possibly delay)		
Other settings student may attend	College placement x1 day per week – hairdressing		
Name of parents/carers	Residential placement	Language spoken at home	English
Address	Witty Tree Lane, Bigley		

Dates of first observation period	Symbol used	Key person	Factors affecting the observation (e.g. student's health, changes in the school, changes at home, etc.)
February 2014	✓	Mr Randle – Pastoral Lead	Struggling with relationships with peers and staff, not engaging in lessons, often excludes himself from lessons/goes missing.
Dates of second observation period (if needed)	Symbol used	Key person	Factors affecting the observation (e.g. student's health, changes in the school, changes at home, etc.)
May 2014	✗	Mr Randle – Pastoral Lead	

1. General behaviour

		Almost always	Sometimes	As student of same age or stage of development	Sometimes	Almost always	
What is student's behaviour like?	Resists boundaries, non-compliant	✓		✗			Overly compliant, accepts boundaries with little fuss
	Difficult behaviour that is overly challenging/ risk-taking (please see below to clarify); putting self and/or others at risk	✓		✗			Passive but difficult behaviour that is expressed subtly; may display compulsive behaviours such as stealing or self-harm that is concealed
	Emotionally volatile with unpredictable, easily triggered emotional outbursts		✓	✗			Appears very self-contained, too good; rarely displays emotions or if does it is over quickly

Attention, concentration and activity levels?	Loses concentration easily	✓		✗			Concentration can be intense, becomes absorbed in tasks, hard to interrupt
	Impulsive, often acts without thinking	✓		✗			Overly controlled, rarely impulsive
	Restless, highly active		✓ ✗				Less active than expected
Attitude to attendance at education setting/ provision	Appears engaged in education but as a way of maintaining attention on self		✓ ✗				Appears disengaged in education
	Worries and concerns distract from learning, e.g. peer issues	✓	✗				Will abscond from class or setting, may take others with them
	Does not cope well with school, appears immature	✓		✗			Copes well with school, but rather too grown up

Clarification of challenging/risky behaviours including mental health difficulties

		Almost always	Sometimes	As student at same stage of development	Hardly ever	Never
Challenging/ risky behaviours	Sexualized behaviours – language, gestures or body language	✓				✗
	Substance misuse – drugs, alcohol or other substance misuse			✓		✗
	Verbally challenging behaviours – attitude/tone of voice	✓		✗		
	Threatening behaviour – verbally/physically	✓		✗		
	Threatening behaviour – weapon use					✓ ✗
	Absconding/self-exclusion		✓			✗
	Education refusal			✓ ✗		
	Risky use of ICT – social media, games, etc.	✓				✗
Mental health-related difficulties	Self-harm		✓			✗
	Eating disorders		✓			✗
	Internalizing difficulties, e.g. anxiety, depression		✓	✗		
	Psychotic behaviours, hallucinations, delusions, appears out of touch with reality					✓ ✗
	Trauma symptoms, e.g. flashbacks, memories, easily triggered fight/flight reactions; dissociates, excessive use of fantasy; hearing voices of past perpetrators					✓ ✗

General behaviour: supporting evidence and comments

Carl is currently pushing boundaries in and outside the classroom, often refusing to take part in the lesson. He becomes disruptive within the class; his behaviour is what you would expect from a much younger child, e.g. calling out, making sounds and tormenting the others within the class. Carl struggles to keep on task and often loses concentration; he is unable to sit for long periods and moves around the classroom a lot. He is easily triggered into explosive outbursts that can result in the whole class being disrupted. When asked to leave the classroom he tries to take others with him, and instead of responding to support from staff Carl will leave the classroom area and at times abscond from school.

Carl makes sexualized comments and is often overly friendly with boys and girls within the class and on the playground. This is happening more often, and reports from other students are increasing.

When challenged he becomes very aggressive in his tone and can be physical.

At lunch time staff have noticed that Carl either gorges or eats very little, and his appearance is scruffy.

Teachers are aware that social workers are making a new search for a long-term foster care placement after he has been in residential care for 3 years, so this must be causing a lot of anxiety for him.

Carl is now pushing boundaries less within class. He is able to concentrate for longer on tasks. He is now able to seek some reassurance when he is feeling unsafe and is seeking help from the pastoral support team when needed. This has been greatly helped by the team checking in with Carl when home has communicated difficulties with them. Carl is now in lessons more often and is a lot more settled within school.

Carl is now aware of the identity of his new foster carers and introductions have been started – this has increased his anxiety, but he chooses to use the pastoral support team to help him rather than allow his anxiety to disrupt his learning.

2. Classroom-related behaviours

		Almost always	Sometimes	As student of same age or stage of development	Sometimes	Almost always	
Behaviour with other students in the classroom/ lesson setting	Possessive about interacting with other students		✓	✗			Not interested in interacting with other students
	Wants to join in whole class sessions but always needs to be centre of attention			✗	✓		Appears disengaged, reluctant to join in, tries to remain out of view
	Wants to join in with small group sessions but struggles to get on with others		✓ ✗				Does not join in with small group sessions easily, tends to remain alone, appears isolated
	Overly controlling and bossy when working with other students	✓		✗			When does interact with another student tends to be easily led

Activity-related behaviour in classroom/ lesson setting	Struggles to engage in tasks as has obsessive need for attention	✔		✘			Quick to give up and will rubbish or destroy work before teacher sees it
	Finds it difficult to settle to task, lacks self-motivation, will constantly seek help, and act more helpless than feels		✔	✘			Tends to get over-involved in task to exclusion of others
	Unable to engage in imaginative activities	✔		✘			Overly absorbed in imaginary world
	Overly competitive, always wants to be first		✘		✔		Overly timid, reluctant to join in

Classroom-related behaviours: supporting evidence and comments

Carl is struggling to take part in classroom activities. If he doesn't sit by the same person he can become bossy and reluctant to engage in tasks within the classroom.

Carl has a 1:1 teaching assistant (key adult) in the more difficult lessons and this is helping him reduce attention-needing behaviours and is helping him try new tasks set in class.

Carl is engaging more in lessons, and is receiving help with his organizational skills within school, so coursework and homework are being completed more successfully.

3. Social relationships with peers

		Almost always	Sometimes	As student of same age or stage of development	Sometimes	Almost always	
Behaviour with other students during unstructured times	Overly clingy and needy with peers but struggles to reciprocate and offer support, can't sustain friendships	✓		✗			Dismissive of need for support from peers, keeps emotional distance
	Wants to join in with peers but emotionally needy and volatile, struggles to get along with others		✓	✗			Uses peer group for shared activities so that activity is more important than friendship
	Wants friends but quickly dissatisfied with the relationship	✓		✗			Tends to remain alone, appears isolated; friendships are unimportant but will relate to peers to join in activities
	Frequently complains to adults about peers		✓	✗			Adults rarely know what is going on with peers
	Can be quite confrontational towards other students, may be seen as bullying	✓		✗	✓		Is often controlled or picked on by other students, vulnerable to bullying

Social relationships with peers: supporting evidence and comments

> He has been accused of bullying another young person within his peer group and is using social media to do this, but feels that he is being bullied and is unable to see the impact of his actions on others.
>
> This is carried on at home and Carl is struggling with the increased independence required in homework.
>
> **Carl now relates far more positively and appropriately with peers of both genders. He continues to struggle slightly with maintaining his friendships; however, instead of becoming confrontational at times of challenge, he is now able to walk away and talk to a trusted adult in the pastoral support room.**

As in the first case study of Caroline, we can see from the above that Carl's behaviour at the time of the first observation displayed a significant level of attention-needing and challenging behaviour in school, both in the classroom and during more unstructured situations. This is illustrated by his general disruption in lessons, making sounds and calling out to other pupils.

In general, although there are some exceptions, the ticks tend to be placed to the left-hand side of the checklist in Sections 1, 2 and 3, which suggests an ambivalent attachment style of relating in general. However, in comparison with Caroline, there are more ticks placed in the extreme left column, suggesting a greater degree of controlling, coercive behaviours that indicate a greater need for the reassurance, attention and support of adults and peers around him to feel safe and settled. This suggests a disorganized-controlling attachment pattern which relies on the ambivalent pattern of coercive, attention-needing behaviours.

As with Caroline, when attention is not readily available Carl becomes more anxious and hypervigilant, thus being unable to concentrate on learning and finding the regulation of emotions difficult. This may then lead him into difficulties focusing on tasks, with a lack of confidence in his ability to tackle new topics or challenges. This can escalate to rapid dysregulation. At the point when Carl becomes dysregulated staff report that he greatly struggles to accept and receive help, removing himself from classes and the school, rejecting relationships and refusing to engage with staff who reach out to help him.

We also find that Carl's behaviour in general leads staff to feel that he appears to be emotionally less mature than the majority of his peers. Carl struggles greatly with peer relationships. He shows anxiety within friendships, being very needy of the attention of friends, to the point where he may become overbearing or overly familiar or sexually inappropriate. When difficulties arise and his anxiety increases he might become very controlling of those friendships or reject peers physically or verbally, complaining to teachers about friends or being more rejecting and confrontational.

Unlike Caroline, Carl appears to be engaging in more concerning risky behaviours, showing signs of some sexualized behaviours within peer relationships – especially with girls – and also using social media such as Facebook and other sites to engage in attention-needing behaviours with others – again leaving himself vulnerable to difficulties outside school.

4. Attachment behaviours

		Almost always	Sometimes	As student of same age or stage of development	Sometimes	Almost always	
How does the student behave with familiar adults?	Unusually dependent, always seeking help even when doesn't need it		✓		✗		Unusually independent, will actively reject offers of help
	Always demonstrating vulnerability but frequently dissatisfied with response of others	✓	✗				Dislikes appearing vulnerable or in need of help
	Craves attention, stays close to adult(s), uses range of ways to gain attention	✓		✗			Doesn't want attention, difficult to relate to, avoids eye-contact
	Very clingy, wants to be with adult(s) all the time, will seek attention from range of adults	✓		✗			Hard to get close to, or false quality to relationship
	Overly demanding and attention-needing, talks a lot	✓		✗			Overly self-reliant, undemanding, detached
	Likes to be in control/in charge	✓		✗			Unusually passive, tries too hard to please

How does the student behave with unfamiliar adults?	Overly familiar, gets too physically close		✓	✗			Overly fearful, shy, wary
	Overly demanding and attention-needing	✓	✗				Resists friendly overtures
	Likes to be in control/in charge	✓	✗				Unusually passive, tries too hard to please
	Asks personal questions even though does not mean to be rude	✓	✗				Shows little interest in visitor
How does the student behave when experiencing minor hurts, worries or troubles?	Appears overly distressed with obsessive need to share problems		✓	✗			Acts as if nothing has happened
	Wants lots of comfort or reassurance but always appears dissatisfied	✓		✗			Appears not to need comfort
	Needs lots of soothing and resists being comforted		✓	✗			Appears not to need soothing

Attachment behaviours: supporting evidence and comments

When Carl is in school he requires a lot of reassurance and often checks in with the teacher, which can seem overly reliant on the adults within the room. Carl often asks questions of the adult in the room that can come across as direct, e.g. about their personal life. This has resulted in some staff members reporting his rudeness. When troubled it's hard to read him; he can either become overly distressed or will behave like nothing has happened.

Carl is responding to familiar adults, showing less anxiety. Still showing signs of anxiety with unfamiliar adults and with familiar adults he feels less attached to. Seems more resilient when experiencing troubles or worries in school.

5. Emotional state

		Almost always	Sometimes	As student of same age or stage of development	Sometimes	Almost always	
Current emotional state, considering any current circum-stances?	Appears overly anxious, worried or distressed		✔	✘			No anxieties or concerns even when there is cause
	Appears overly cheerful or happy			✘	✔		Appears sad, withdrawn or flat
	Appears very sensitive, easily upset		✔	✘	✔		Appears indifferent, doesn't show feelings
How does the student display feelings?	It is easy to tell how the student is feeling	✔	✘				Tends to hide feelings away; it is difficult to tell how the student is feeling
	Displays feelings only through angry, challenging or risky behaviour		✔	✘			Tends not to show how he/she is feeling in the way he/she behaves
	Will become abusive or rude if not being attended to, may alternate with charming behaviours	✔		✘			Will become abusive or rude if one tries to offer help or support
	Hurts self obviously and in full view of others to gain attention			✔✘			Hurts self secretly
	May draw attention to self by humiliating or teasing peers	✔		✘			Tries not to draw attention to self, may hide behind peers

Emotional state: supporting evidence and comments

Carl often shows us he is feeling unsafe by his behaviour. If there is a new teacher he will become overly challenging with them. We have also noticed that he will start to lash out at others within the class.

Carl will often become the 'class clown' and we struggle to see how he is really feeling.

Carl is more settled. Displaying and responding to feelings more normally. Resilience has grown, especially in the way he is handling and responding to forthcoming changes in his care placement.

Sections 4 and 5 continue to indicate that Carl has a disorganized-controlling presentation organized around an ambivalent attachment style of relating in school. This again suggests that he is generally needy of adult attention in school, and displays this with more extreme challenging and coercive behaviours compared to Caroline. At times, however, he will appear flat and withdrawn. Carl appears more troubled than Caroline. He becomes particularly anxious and needy of support when he is with unfamiliar staff or familiar teachers with whom he does not feel connected or attached. This is apparent when he struggles more with some teachers than others within the school.

Any other comments?

We are very concerned about Carl and are unsure how much longer we can manage him within school.

We are now much less concerned and see Carl as really making a contribution to school life.

What works in this environment for this student?

As a school we seem not to be getting it right, he is very disruptive and is at risk of exclusion, he is taking part in increasingly risky behaviours inside and outside of school and we are worried he won't sit his exams.

As a school we have now made the pastoral support team aware of Carl's difficulties, and how these impact upon his learning. Via the first checklist we have managed to put in place some strategies to help reduce his anxieties. This is an ongoing support as we need to help him regulate his emotions. Having a safe place for Carl to go when anxious is proving helpful. All the children have access to this and he appears to like the inclusion. He is choosing to take himself there more without prompting.

The PACE approach has been useful and has enabled Carl to take part in class more and has increased his self-esteem. He is now willing to have a go at new activities within school. Carl is now part of the rugby team but requires support and reassurance to do this.

Relationship-based play has had some impact; he has enjoyed 'paper punch' and bubble wrap. We tend to play these within the pastoral room at lunch times in a low-key way.

Taking the overall picture from the first completion of the checklist it is clear that Carl is frequently and overtly attention-needing in school and can often show signs of anxiety. The anxiety becomes more apparent in lessons with teachers with whom he does not have a secure relationship, but the checklist also shows a more pervasive pattern of anxiety and the need for a secure attachment in school.

From the notes provided we can also see that the anxiety that Carl is experiencing in school spills over significantly into peer relationships. His desire for attention and relationship with peers and his anxiety surrounding this can lead him into exhibiting some more tricky behaviours to manage, including the more sexualized overbearing ways of relating that he shows on occasions and his risky and inappropriate use of social media. Carl's behaviour and emotional well-being are of greater concern than with Caroline.

From the notes that the teacher provided to accompany the checklist we can see that when Carl becomes dysregulated his anxiety can escalate to the point where he becomes overwhelmed and needs to push people away and remove himself from the situation. An attachment pattern which is highly needy of attention, but also rejecting of this (pulling people in and then pushing them away), is typical of a more controlling-ambivalent style of relating which is seen within the disorganized-controlling attachment patterns.

7 Analysis of Information

INTERPRETING THE COMPLETED CHECKLIST

In this chapter interpretation of the checklist is discussed. This will consider how to interpret the profile that has been built up about a student, and how to use this interpretation to plan additional support which can meet the emotional and social needs identified.

When the checklist has been completed, it is helpful to initially look at each table's pattern of ticks before considering the observations for individual behaviours. Look at each section and consider first whether there is a pattern:

- Do the ticks lean towards a particular side – left or right?

- Are there more ticks down the centre of the page and only the odd one or two either side? Does this therefore just pinpoint some specific difficulties that can be addressed for the student?

- Alternatively, there may be a number of ticks that predominantly lean towards one side or another, with a few ticks down the central column, suggesting that the student might need more comprehensive help.

- It can be helpful to work from the outside column into the centre. Look at the 'almost always' ticks first, as the needs associated with these examples are often the most urgent to address.

- As a rule of thumb, if the majority of ticks lean towards the right of the central column look at insecure avoidant styles and strategies, and if the ticks incline towards the left look at the insecure ambivalent styles and strategies. When ticks appear on both ends a combination of strategies is likely to be helpful.

This pattern of ticks, together with notes of behaviours or triggers observed, then forms the basis of an analysis of the information. This allows a profile of the student to be developed, guiding ideas and strategies which might support the student within the educational setting.

- Return to the detailed guidance provided in Chapter 5. This will help to identify the needs shown on the checklist, and explain the relevance of where the ticks are positioned.

- Keep reading this section alongside the other chapters to plan how you are going to support the student using an attachment-led approach.

- Remember it is important to recognize the student that internalizes his or her emotions, the 'too good' student, as well as the student whose behaviour can be seen explicitly.

- Consider whether the student's behaviour would seem appropriate in a younger child, that is, is the student demonstrating immaturity? Conversely, does the student appear as an older young person, that is, is the student too 'grown up' and independent (pseudomature)?

- Consider that all behaviours are a means of communication. Reflect on what is the hidden need that the student's behaviour may be expressing.

- Within the educational setting ensure that, if possible, everyone has an understanding of the student's needs and responds consistently. This can be difficult to achieve in larger Key Stage 3 and 4 educational settings, but the communication between school staff and shared understanding of the student will be key to achieving success.

- Multiple observations can help chart the student's progress over time. One important factor to remember in completing subsequent observations is the student's home circumstances. Have there been any significant changes? Do you suspect that these changes may be having an effect on the student's behaviour?

- It can be helpful to discuss the interpretation with other people who know the student. This can enrich the interpretations being made as the profile on the checklist is considered in the context of the experience of the student by the different people.

Knowledge of attachment experience and how this can impact on the way a student relates to adults and peers within the educational setting can help in interpreting the completed checklist. It is important to note, however, that this checklist is not an assessment of the student's attachment style. It cannot be used to diagnose attachment difficulties, but it can increase awareness of the way secure and insecure patterns of attachment impact on the student's day-to-day functioning within the educational setting. This may in turn affect how a student is communicating his or her needs through his or her behaviour.

A student with an avoidant style of attachment relating may appear to be doing well, appearing as an independent young person who displays high levels of involvement in self-chosen activities and is secure in self-care skills. However, this student may miscue adults about the need for nurturing as he or she draws upon embedded self-reliant coping strategies from early life experiences. This self-reliance can look like successful independence, hiding the fact that he or she is actually feeling highly insecure.

This student may need to learn to develop relationships, and learn to be *dependent* on an adult (i.e. teacher or teaching assistant) before becoming independent. Apparent self-reliance is now seen as being 'too grown up' for the student's age (pseudomature).

A student with an ambivalent style of attachment relating may need to stay close to an adult to gain attention. The consequent behaviours that are displayed may be described by practitioners as challenging and 'attention-seeking'. The student miscues the adult, fearing the loss of attention that may come with exploration and learning. Well-meaning adults may try to encourage independence and discourage displays of dependency, failing to realize that the behaviours display 'attention-needing'. The student is demonstrating through his or her behaviour the need for reassurance that you can attend to his or her needs. Only then will the fear of abandonment reduce to the point that the student can begin to explore and learn.

Students who are showing extremes of these behaviours – appearing controlling, inflexible and rigid in their behaviours – will be observed predominantly at the extremes on the checklist. They may also have times when these behavioural strategies break down as the student 'loses it' or becomes very shut down. These fight, flight or freeze reactions indicate that these students are more disorganized and controlling in their attachment style. These are the students who struggle most to feel safe within the educational setting.

These insecure patterns of relating therefore communicate a continuing need to feel safe in the setting, and to build trust in the relationship with a teacher or teaching assistant who can help them to co-regulate their arousal levels (whether this is high or low). It is helpful in this context to understand that young people who have experienced an insecure early life may be emotionally and socially younger than their chronological age.

Keep in mind four groups of questions when interpreting the checklist:

- What age group would best relate to the behaviours being observed? This emotional age is often consistently younger than the chronological age in young people with emotional difficulties. How would you deal with a child of that age? Notice that at times of dysregulation or more extreme stress, these immature behaviours can spiral downwards, with the student's emotional age becoming much younger than the chronological age. In helping the student, the teacher or teaching assistant will need to adjust to this shifting emotional age.

- Does the student feel safe or unsafe? Think about how you are making this judgement. What triggers can you identify that increase feelings of danger or restore feelings of safety? Consider how you might increase the feelings of safety for the student.

- How well is the student fitting in with classroom expectations? Think about the 'unwritten rules' – ways of behaving that a young person is expected to know about at the age they have reached and which are therefore not made explicit.

An immature young person may need support to understand this. Has the student been specifically told about the expectations of the situation? Bear in mind, these students often have difficulties with inferences and abstract concepts and are visual learners.

- Are there any known triggers for the student being observed? Notice patterns to the behaviours that you are observing. Are there particular situations that seem to lead to habitual behaviours? Notice also exceptions to this and what has helped a student cope with a situation that he or she usually has difficulty with. Use this information to think about how triggers can be avoided or supported for the student.

Using the observations to inform an action plan

Once the observations are made and interpreted, these observations can be translated into clear targets and actions that will help to meet the needs identified. It is helpful to draw up a plan of action that practitioners might take to help the student. In this way the observations can guide the development of some clear ideas or strategies for helping the student (an action plan). Without this there is a danger that, while understanding of the student has improved, this is not translated into improvements in meeting the needs identified. Developing an action plan which helps to tailor the support to the student's needs is therefore an important part of using the observation checklist to guide practice.

Generally the person who made the observations is best placed to write the action plan, perhaps in discussion with others involved in supporting the student. For example, it might be helpful to involve the special educational needs coordinator (SENCO) or the designated teacher for looked after children.

It is important to set a review date for this action plan in order to monitor whether the actions identified are helpful, and to adapt the action plan if they are not helping or in line with the progress that the student is making. Be careful not to reduce support too quickly, however; developing security in an insecure student can be a lengthy process.

An action plan template is included with the checklist for those who want to use it, although settings may have their own action plan template that they wish to use.

In addition to the action plan, it may be appropriate to complete a plan in line with the usual recording method of intervention within the educational setting. For example, settings often develop individual education plans (IEPs), which are plans that are drawn up by the practitioner to help the school staff, together with the parent, to identify the student's needs and to ensure that particular difficulties are supported. Similar to the action plan described above, the IEP provides targets, actions for meeting these targets, who will take the action and how success will be measured. Actions that the parent can take to support the educational setting might be included in this plan. Provision maps might be used by school staff as an alternative to the IEP. This is a more succinct way of listing interventions and identifying who, where and what will be done to support the student.

Any of these plans can be used to identify targets for providing increased social and emotional support to the student, interventions that can be implemented in order to meet these targets, and ways of reviewing the targets in order to establish whether the plan has been successful or not. This can include further periods of observation using the checklist. This in turn can lead to revision of the action plan.

To support the student's continuing social and emotional development, some are also placed on 'School Action Plus' as staff seek the involvement of other services to ensure that the student's needs are met (for example, a student with identified expressive speech difficulties might be supported with the help of the Speech, Language and Communication Service). Other specialized services may also be accessed to support the educational setting in managing any specific difficulties the student may have such as smoking, drugs, self-harming or eating difficulties.

If the student's emotional and social needs are particularly severe, further funding may be sought to ensure that these needs are met. Such funding can secure the provision of input from professionals external to the educational setting, as well as providing the means to increase the staff-to-student ratio so that the student with particular difficulties can be better supported. For example, this support might enable the student's key person to build a relationship with the student so that his or her emotional needs are met. This enables the student to feel both physically and emotionally safe and able to begin to explore all the activities available in the educational setting. The structured observations informed by the checklist can provide important information to evidence this need.

Implementing the action plan

It is helpful if the action plan can be implemented by a teacher or teaching assistant working with the student, supported by other staff in the educational setting. Often the key person is already identified and has been involved in completing the checklist. However, sometimes the need for a key person to work with the student might be identified through the use of the checklist. In this case it is important to think about who in the school might be best suited to be the student's key person and how this person is going to establish a relationship with the student or in many cases how he or she can enhance a relationship that already exists. Consideration needs to be given to the level of support that the student is likely to need while in the setting, how to give the teacher or teaching assistant time to provide this support and how this can be funded. This investment in time and resources is key to supporting the student with emotional difficulties.

Putting in appropriate strategies can help to provide an environment for a student that is attuned to his or her needs, but there is no quick fix. Sometimes behaviours will continue and staff will have to take encouragement from the smallest of improvements. Additionally a strategy may work for a while but then the student changes tactics. A rethink of approach is needed. As the staff continue to understand and work with the student and are able to adjust to the student's changing needs, security will be built and slowly, over time, progress will be seen.

In Chapter 8 we return to Caroline and Carl in order to illustrate how the observation checklist can be used to provide clear ideas for interventions which will support the needs identified. Examples of completed action plans are included to provide an illustration of how the checklist can lead to specific ideas for helping the student, including details of what is needed, how this need can be met and who will have responsibility for implementing these ideas.

Consequences of implementing an action plan

One outcome of working with the observation checklist is that the teacher's curiosity about why the student behaves as he or she does, and what the behaviour is communicating, is increased. This is very helpful as it increases understanding and helps the teacher to be more in tune with what the student needs.

As the action plan is implemented, the practitioners will continue to develop a relationship with the student and to develop further understanding about this young person. For example, in observing how the student responds to the interventions that are implemented, behaviours might become better understood. Triggers to behaviours may also become more apparent. It might be noticed that when a student is more challenged by an activity his or her stress levels increase. This in turn leads to the student having increased difficulty within the peer group, perhaps because his or her controlling behaviours towards peers increase. The practitioner now understands that when the student is more controlling and less able to share and cooperate it is likely that stress has increased. Activities that reduce stress might be helpful for the student at this point. In this way strategies that work well for this student are identified and further refined.

It is important that the key person or practitioner working with the student continues to be curious and to develop a deeper understanding of him or her. Be careful, however, about asking students why they have done something. Some tentative questioning might be helpful, but generally being asked 'why' reinforces for students that they are being disapproved of in some way. This often compounds the shame felt by them, and thus can strengthen unhelpful behaviours. Wondering aloud, helping the student to make sense of his or her experience, can be more helpful than questioning about why he or she is doing something. For example, 'Jake, you are very wobbly today. I am wondering if you are worrying that your mum may not be at home when you return? Is it hard for you to trust that she will be there as she has promised?' 'Stephanie, you are very cross with Alex today. I wonder if you are unhappy because he has been chosen for a speaking part in the play and you haven't? It is hard not to have special things for yourself.'

Changes within the student over time are not always straightforward. Sometimes a student may make little progress. This may indicate that changes to the action plan are needed. The strategies being implemented are perhaps not as helpful as was hoped. For example, it may have been decided to help a young person who is arriving late to school by the parent bringing the student to the school gate each morning. However, it is noticed that the student is still late to his class as he dawdles or becomes distracted on his way in. In this case a change to the plan might be considered. Perhaps instead of leaving him at the school gate the parent could bring him to reception where the key person can meet and greet him and then help him get to where he needs to be.

It is helpful not to make changes too quickly. It may be that a particular intervention will work given additional time. The staff need to hold firm to what they have planned, allowing a longer time within which to see progress.

There are two particular situations to be mindful about. First, students who initially came across as independent, possibly withdrawn and avoidant of relationships may suddenly start presenting as attention-needing as the action plan is implemented. The student becomes more dependent, changing from one who was causing little trouble in class to one who is demanding of staff time and energy. Staff can be left thinking that they have done things wrong and created a monster! It can be difficult, under these circumstances, to recognize that the student's needs are beginning to be fulfilled. It may be tempting to stop the interventions in the hope that the student returns to his or her previous, more manageable mode of behaving. *This must not happen!* Staff will need to understand that this swing in behaviours is all part of the relationship-building, trust and feeling of safety that the student will be experiencing. As students become more able to seek relationships with adults, they start to make up for experiences they have previously missed. This increased dependency and neediness, if satisfied, will then allow them to return to an appropriate level of independence, but this time the independence will be healthy as young people develop autonomy in the context of being able to seek support when needed. If we let students down at this stage, the message to them will confirm that adults cannot be trusted, thus affecting their self-worth, self-esteem, confidence, relationships and ultimately their ability to explore and learn.

Second, remember to keep in mind the context the student is living within. Changes outside of school can have a big influence on the student in school. This will be reflected in changes on the checklist during subsequent observations, and will guide adjustments to the action plan to reflect changing needs. Without bearing in mind such a context, the different observations can present a confusing picture. For example, a checklist was completed for a student who had just come into the care system. This first observation highlighted a number of predominantly avoidant-style behaviours that this student was displaying in his primary school. As the child moved into Key Stage 3, involving a change of educational setting, he also changed placement. In a second observation, his behaviour had escalated and the student now displayed more ambivalent/disorganized-controlling attachment behaviours. This changing relationship style in school reflected his changing care arrangements outside of school alongside moving into secondary education. It is important to look at the completed checklists with caution. This student is not making the shift from independence to dependence in a healthy manner but is showing his confusion about his situation and increasingly more desperate attempts to get his needs met in school. The behaviours he was displaying were rated predominantly as 'almost always', indicating that these behaviours reflected a disorganized-controlling relationship with people in his world rather than the more healthy need for attention that a previously avoidant child can display when he realizes that adults can be a source of support.

Implementation of the action plan continues to give staff important information about the student. Reviewing this plan and revisiting targets will build up an important profile of the student and what is helpful for him or her. Additionally the checklist can be revisited to monitor progress and to provide further information. This developing understanding will underpin successful support to the student. This information can then move with the child as he or she progresses through the educational setting, ensuring good transitions and helping the student resettle and continue to benefit from the support that has been provided. New staff will want to do their own observations, but the past information will provide important context for these new observations.

Conclusion

The observation checklist can be a helpful tool for identifying the emotional and social difficulties a student is experiencing within the educational setting, and also for monitoring the progress he or she is making over time. To be of maximum use the observations need to lead to clear ideas for supporting the emotional experience of the student, helping to reduce emotional distress and to support emotional development. This in turn will impact positively on the behaviour the student is displaying and his or her ability to manage social relationships with adults and peers. It will also improve the student's readiness to learn within school.

The following chapter revisits the cases of Caroline and Carl, but before you read on, read the worked examples of the observation checklist once again and form your own interpretation of the findings – what kind of needs do you think they exhibit, and what forms of support would be appropriate? You may also want to leaf through some of the following chapters, which provide information on effective supports for young people with attachment difficulties and other developmental challenges.

Summary: developing support

Reasons for using the checklist

- Concerns about behaviour.

- Concerns about the student who is not achieving or managing socially.

- Baseline observation to compare the student to over time.

- Desire to raise awareness of needs of the student.

- Desire to monitor the student through period of change or transition.

Collecting contextual information

- Background, early experience and current functioning.

- Knowledge and observations of the student in educational setting.

- Knowledge about the impact of parenting and attachment difficulties.

Interpreting the checklist

- Look at pattern of ticks.

- Consider ticks at extreme, each side and in middle.

- Use this to build up a profile of the student.

- Relate to avoidant, ambivalent and controlling patterns of relating.

- What is the emotional age of the student?

- Does the student feel safe or unsafe?

- Is the student fitting in with classroom expectations?

- Are there any observable triggers for the student's behaviours?

- Use notes to accompany checklist for extra guidance.

- Think about the meaning underlying the behaviours.

- Relate to background information.

Developing an action plan

- Support an action plan with an IEP or provision map.

- Identify targets to increase social and emotional support.

- Develop interventions to meet targets.

- Plan how interventions will be reviewed.

- Plan further periods of observation.

- Revise action plan.

- Consider further action: placing the student on an educational health care plan (EHC), involving other services, securing additional funding.

Implementing the action plan

- Identify key person and support to build a relationship with the student.

- Implement level of support needed for the student.

- Implement strategies and monitor progress with these.

- Stay curious about the student and wonder aloud.

- Continue to support the student who becomes more attention-needing.

- Notice when there are changes for the student outside of the educational setting.

8 Worked Examples of Interpreting the Checklist and Support Plans

CAROLINE AND CARL

In this chapter we return to the worked examples of Caroline and Carl. We explore how the interpretations of the observations made on the checklist were turned into action plans with clear goals, targets and interventions, so that the student's emotional needs could be better supported.

Caroline

The action plan below shows how staff used the completed checklist, recognizing Caroline's tendency towards an ambivalent attachment style. Staff recognized that while Caroline's observable behaviour suggested that she wanted to push staff away and challenge them, her underlying need was to gain and rely upon adult attention in order to feel settled and safe in lessons. She needed a 'secure base' in the form of a key adult to provide this attention and to help her to feel more secure in her lessons. In this way she will be able to attend to learning rather than becoming hypervigilant and displaying attention-needing behaviours.

Action plan to support observation checklist

Name of student	Caroline Webb	DOB	21/4/2002 Year 7	SEN	
Dates of observation	April 2014			None	
Involved professionals	Mrs Foot – Pastoral Lead HW – Virtual School for Looked After Children				
What works well	At initial observation – nothing appears to be working well at present.	Areas for development		Tends to ambivalent attention pattern. Help with emotional regulation at times of challenge. Increase ability to seek support and self-regulate.	

Concern	Target	How will this be achieved?	Resources	Who? Where?
Fragile self-esteem, low resilience leading to rapid dysregulation and increased attention-needing behaviour in school at times of perceived challenge (particular difficulty in English lessons)	Caroline will be able to attend more than 90% of lessons positively and without use of negative attention-needing behaviours	Allocation of a key adult – adult will be trained in a PACE-based approach for working with Caroline	Key adult – Pupil Premium funded	Mrs Foot
		Key adult will take part in relationship-based play sessions led by the Virtual School and will continue to use strategies after Virtual School withdrawal	Relationship-based play intervention (1 hour per week for 8 weeks)	Virtual School
		Key adult support will be put into place in English lessons temporarily		Mrs Foot
		Awareness-raising and strategy training for all staff – PACE-based approach	Training will be commissioned from the Virtual School	Headteacher to arrange

Concern	Target	How will this be achieved?	Resources	Who? Where?
Difficulty with emotional regulation and accepting support to regulate at times of challenge	Caroline will be able to more readily accept the support of her key adult at times of challenge – leading to swifter regulation and lessened impact upon learning	Allocation of a key adult – adult will be trained in a PACE-based approach for working with Caroline	Key adult – Pupil Premium funded	
		Key adult will take part in relationship-based play sessions led by the Virtual School and will continue to use strategies after Virtual School withdrawal	Relationship-based play intervention (1 hour per week for 8 weeks)	
		Key adult support will be put into place in English lessons temporarily. Key adult will be made available at any time if the needs arise for staff to call upon her to help Caroline to regulate		

Concern	Target	How will this be achieved?	Resources	Who? Where?
Caroline has been unsettled at home most recently, particularly when difficulties in school are being discussed/raised	Caroline will be more settled at home and accept the support of her carers when discussing school-based issues	Caroline's carers will be aware of and supported to use the PACE approach used in school and to be aware of the relationship-based play strategies used via a home visit from member of the Virtual School and regular review meetings with staff at school		Mr and Mrs Carr Virtual School member of staff Mrs Foot
Review date	July 2014	**Action plan shared with**	Mrs Foot, all teachers who directly teach Caroline, senior management Mr and Mrs Carr	

Practitioners from the Virtual School for Looked After and Adopted Children supported the school to identify a key adult for Caroline (Mrs Foot) and to support the development of Caroline's relationship with Mrs Foot via the use of relationship-based play strategies. Having a person with whom she had a secure and positive attachment within the school and lessons had a significant impact upon Caroline's well-being. The second observation period revealed how Caroline's general behaviours (Sections 1, 2 and 3) on the whole became similar to a student at the same stage of development.

Again, from the second observation in Sections 3 and 4, we can see that the provision of a key adult within lessons to provide a secure base and attachment figure supported Caroline to be more settled and to engage in learning opportunities, and therefore to learn and achieve within school. This benefited Caroline, especially at times when unfamiliar adults were leading lessons (e.g. supply staff) or adults with whom she did not enjoy a secure relationship (such as her English teacher at this time).

The increased knowledge and understanding of Caroline's emotional and attachment-based difficulties helped staff to provide support to meet her emotional needs. The allocation and support of a key adult with whom Caroline was encouraged to form a secure attachment helped her to become more secure and settled in school. The key adult was able to check in regularly with Caroline, as well as attending around 20 per cent of her lessons. Caroline's ability to attend to and succeed in learning increased, and therefore her self-esteem and resilience grew. Caroline began to collect merit points in school so that she could recognize and be rewarded for her increased success. She won the prize for the most merit points collected at the end of term. She also began to make increased progress with her learning – over the first nine weeks of having a key adult in place she was assessed as making well over expected levels of progress in reading, writing and maths. The school cancelled any plans for Caroline accessing a placement at the local PRU and no further exclusions became necessary. Caroline also seemed more settled on her walk home after school. As Caroline experienced far less anxiety in school there was less likelihood that this would spill over into home, and therefore her behaviour at home settled down as well.

Carl

The action plan below was formulated for Carl following the completion of the checklist (Chapter 6). As in Caroline's case this recognized Carl's tendency towards a mainly ambivalent attachment style but with an even more intense coercive-controlling pattern. Whilst Carl's observable behaviour in school suggested that he wanted to annoy, challenge and push staff away, his underlying need was to gain and rely upon adult attention in order to feel settled and safe in school. Although older than Caroline, Carl also needed a 'secure base' in the form of a key adult to provide him with attention and to help him to feel more secure and to be able to attend to learning. This reduced his hypervigilance and attention-needing behaviours. He no longer became so dysregulated that he needed to remove himself from lessons. Carl also benefited from increased awareness of his own feelings and signs that he was becoming unsettled. It was agreed that the protective behaviours framework would be ideal for this, and it was agreed that his key adult would be best placed to work on the strategies with him once a relationship between them was established. This helped him to seek support rather than becoming dysregulated.

From the information shared by Mr Randle it was also clear that Carl's removing himself from lessons and occasionally the school was a risk to his safety. Staff realized that Carl's running from lessons was not a sign of defiance that should be prevented but a sign that he was overwhelmed and unable to regulate. Rather than stopping him from leaving lessons they needed to support him to do this safely, in this case by giving him a way to communicate that he needed to leave the lesson via a card system. They provided Carl with a safe place to go to where he would receive the support that he needed to regulate via calming activities and the availability of his key adult.

It was also determined that Carl may benefit from some specific support with peer relationships. It was felt that due to his age and sometimes inappropriate sexualized behaviour towards peers that the local Sexual Health Team would be involved to work directly with Carl to help him to form healthy and positive relationships with peers, particularly girls.

Action plan to support observation checklist

Name of student	Carl Linden		DOB	13/5/99 Year 10	SEN
Dates of observation	February 2014				Mild learning difficulties (possibly delay)
Involved professionals	Mr Randle – Pastoral Lead JR Virtual School				
What works well	At time of first observation very little seems to work well in the school setting. Carl seems to be more positive in college placement where hairdressing motivates him and the more independent nature of work suits him.		Areas for development		Tends to ambivalent attention pattern. Emotional regulation at times of challenge. Increase ability to seek support and self-regulate. Peer relationships need specific support.

Concern	Target	How will this be achieved?	Resources	Who? Where?
Fragile self-esteem, low resilience leading to rapid dysregulation and increased attention-needing behaviour in school at times of perceived challenge	Carl will be able to attend more than 90% of lessons positively and without use of negative attention-needing behaviours Carl will develop protective behaviour skills and an increased awareness of times when he feels unsafe and how support can be gained positively so that he can feel safe again and can return to learning	Allocation of a key adult – adult will be trained in a PACE-based approach to work with Carl 1x1hr per week 1:1 specific relationship-building pastoral support and mentoring session with key adult to take place each week This session also to provide support to Carl via a protective behaviours model to help him to develop self-awareness of times when he is feeling unsafe and how to manage these successfully and seek help Key adult to be closely available at times of particular difficulty for Carl – especially in lessons with teachers with whom he struggles or is unfamiliar	Key adult – Pupil Premium funded Training will be commissioned from the Virtual School	Mr Randle Virtual School

		Key adult to be available in agreed safe place during other sessions of the school day Awareness-raising and strategy training for all staff – PACE-based approach		
Concern	**Target**	**How will this be achieved?**	**Resources**	**Who? Where?**
Carl removes himself from lessons and occasionally the school, putting himself at risk	If Carl becomes dysregulated he will begin to be more aware of this and will use a card to indicate that he needs to leave the lesson. He will go to a specific safe place on all occasions rather than leaving the school	A specific safe place will be identified and the procedure for its use agreed upon with Carl. He will be given the opportunity to practise its use when settled and via the use of Social Stories™. The safe place will be part of the Pastoral Support Centre so eventually Carl sees the centre as a safe place and will use it at times of anxiety Mr Randle will be alerted via phone system in school when Carl leaves lessons and will make himself available at the agreed safe place to support Carl to regulate and return to learning as soon as he is able All staff will be made aware of Carl's needs, will respond in an appropriate PACE-based manner at times when he is becoming unsettled and will cooperate with the use of his card, enabling him to leave lessons	Safe place Regulatory activities – e.g. calm box, music station, timers, etc. Availability of Mr Randle	Mr Randle Carl

Concern	Target	How will this be achieved?	Resources	Who? Where?
Carl shows specific difficulties within peer relationships – he can be very attention-needing and overwhelming, and due to this may sometimes exhibit inappropriate sexualized behaviours, particularly towards girls Carl often posts inappropriately on social media, putting himself at risk, and may 'bully' others online	Carl will gain more settled and positive relationships within his own peer group and will maintain friendships for an increased amount of time Carl will relate appropriately to girls and will not show any inappropriate or sexualized behaviours within those relationships	1x1hr per week 1:1 specific relationship-building pastoral support and mentoring session with key adult to take place each week Local Authority Sexual Health Team will be approached to give advice to Carl's key adult to empower him to work with Carl to give him guidance and support to gain appropriate and positive friendships and peer relationships A member of the Sexual Health Team may be available to work directly with Carl to discuss appropriate sexual behaviour if appropriate at the time of support During 1:1 sessions Carl will take part in a module of work supported by CEOP to help him to develop awareness of cyber safety and appropriate use of social networking	Local Authority Sexual Health Team Protective Behaviours programme of work (online/local protective behaviours network) CEOP (child exploitation and online protection centre) resources (online) 1:1 session x1hr per week scheduled Responsive support from key adult as needed if incidents and times of difficulty occur	
Review date	May 2014	**Action plan shared with**	Carers, all staff who work with Carl via staff briefing and SIMS registration/recording system	

The action plan was implemented, and its consistent use over a period of eight weeks meant that the approach planned had been successful in supporting Carl to feel safer and behave positively in school. He was able to remain in the majority of his lessons, engage in the learning opportunities and ultimately make progress with his learning.

The key to the success in the approach planned lay in the learning and development made by both Carl and the staff. This did not just rely solely on Carl's learning and development, as often can be the case in some action plans. The shared and global understanding of Carl's attachment needs within the school and the increased use of a more attuned PACE-based approach by all staff helped Carl to take part in school life more successfully. Staff were more aware of how to meet his attention needs to prevent him becoming anxious, and on the occasions when he did become anxious they were aware of how to support him to regulate his anxiety rather than escalate it and cause shame-based reactions.

The allocation of a key adult in school helped Carl to feel safer as he had a 'secure base' within school. He also gained confidence in knowing that someone who he trusted and who understood him would be available to help him if things got tricky. When he did notice things getting tricky he had the understanding and strategies in place to intervene for himself and procedures in place to help him to remove himself safely from situations.

The use of outside agencies like the Sexual Health Team and CEOP helped staff to ensure that Carl was supported using appropriate and up-to-date strategies and information. As a result he gained more understanding of how to keep himself safe in personal peer relationships and online relationships. This is evidenced by the second observation when his peer relationships were felt to be much more successful and age appropriate.

9 Helping the Student with Attachment Difficulties in Educational Settings

This chapter provides general advice for helping students with attachment difficulties, whatever attachment relationship pattern is being displayed.

Young people with attachment difficulties are likely to have more difficulties than the typical young person in joining and attending educational settings. These young people will have experienced trauma and/or separation and loss in their early years, involving their primary carers. Whilst the young people may have had a stable time since their early difficulties, for example in foster care or in adopted homes, and may have developed some security of attachment, it is important not to assume that they therefore will be free of emotional difficulties. These young people will have an increased risk for emotional problems during adolescence.

Exploring attachment needs in educational settings

School is a source of stress for the child who is emotionally immature and not yet ready for the increased independence that attending the educational setting requires. Expectations for independence increase rapidly as young people enter the high school phase. The young person may not yet be ready for key challenges of this new educational environment:

- They may have struggled to tolerate long periods away from their attachment figure upon entering school. Now they have to also manage an increasing number of adults interacting with them. The attachment figures of primary school are not necessarily a feature within later educational settings.

- Whilst the young person might have learnt through primary school to share adult support with a group of other children, these groups of children now become larger and more diverse and the adults supporting them will change during the school day.

- Adolescence is a time of re-learning how to manage peer relationships, deal with friendships and manage conflict. Demands of friendships increase, and support with friendships reduces. There is also an increased expectation that the young person can manage reciprocal relationships; he or she is expected to be there for the friend as much as expecting the friend to be there for him or her.

- Adolescents need to cope with increasing demands for managing routines and the structured environment. The young people have additional expectations that they will be able to organize themselves within larger educational settings, with more complex timetables, and with the need to move around the school.

- The demands for developing independence and self-organization increase rapidly at this stage of education. Alongside this there will also be different expectations of how they will complete work within the classroom and manage homework.

Students with attachment difficulties are not 'good learners' (see Delaney 2009). They do not feel safe and consequently do not want to take risks. For example, writing an answer on a worksheet or completing homework carries the risk of getting it wrong. They do not have good self-esteem; they expect things to go wrong and for others not to like them. They anticipate that if they seek help they will be criticized or ridiculed. They find it difficult to concentrate as they struggle to manage frustration, anxiety or disappointment. They find it hard to bear not knowing and tend to be pessimistic, with a negative attitude towards problems. Finally some of these young people find it intolerable to wait for attention, whilst others try to disappear and not be noticed.

Louise Michelle Bombèr (2007, 2011) gives practical strategies for supporting young people with attachment difficulties in educational settings. Louise recommends that these students will need a carefully chosen key adult to be allocated to them to act as an 'additional attachment figure'. The main part of the role is to develop a relationship with the student, offering the possibility of relative dependency within which the student has the possibility for 'second chance learning'. The role of the key adult can be very powerful in adapting and changing the student's interpretation of themselves, others and the world.

Challenges faced by traumatized young people

Students with attachment difficulties need extra help because they are not yet able to fully:

- direct attention away from internal needs and focus on tasks
- trust at least one other person
- put feelings into words
- regulate strong negative emotions
- focus attention, sit and concentrate
- feel effective, confident in self
- communicate and cooperate with others
- problem-solve, and resolve conflict
- manage the shame associated with not succeeding
- consistently access learning opportunities.

What do students with attachment difficulties in educational settings need?

Safety

Until students feel safe, they will not be able to derive any positive benefit from being in education. The first priority is therefore to establish a safe environment within which the student can start to feel secure. The student will be helped by a clear structure, boundaries and routine in a relaxing environment and by having opportunities to be in a less stimulating environment at times during the day. It is important that staff are able to recognize the fear and anxiety that lie beneath behaviour so that the student can be appropriately supported. Young people feel most secure in an environment where the adults set the emotional tone, providing opportunities to co-regulate their escalating arousal. Time and opportunities for rest and relaxation will be important. Staff will also need to recognize the level of support the student needs, especially at times of transition during the school day.

Building a relationship

Young people need relationships in order to feel safe, but difficult early relationship experience can make this a difficult need to meet. A key person needs to get to know and understand the student so that he or she can begin the task of engaging the student in the relationship, helping the student to feel safe enough to trust and respond. A teaching assistant can be an effective key person. The form teacher is not necessarily the most appropriate person to fulfil this role, as this teacher also has to manage relationships with all the children in the class (for a detailed discussion of the role of the key person, see Bombèr 2007, 2011).

The key person will know the student well enough to notice not only the direct but also the distorted requests for help that he or she might make. The key person will also be aware of conditions that might throw the student, stepping in early to prevent escalating arousal. This key relationship can then be used to support the student to remain emotionally regulated, and to help the student when feelings of shame or anger threaten to overwhelm him or her. The staff member can also act as advocate or champion for the student within the school, helping other staff to understand the student and to be more fully aware of what the student needs.

Developing communication

If the relationship is central to working with traumatized students then communication is central to the relationship. Teachers and support staff need a way to connect with and relate to these students to build their sense of trust and safety. As the relationship becomes stronger the students will then be able to accept the boundaries, discipline and of course the learning that the adults also need to provide. The dyadic developmental practice (DDP) model developed by Dan Hughes (see Hughes 2011) provides some principles for connecting with young people which are equally applicable in school as within the home. Central within these is the attitude of PACE (see Golding and Hughes 2012; Hughes 2011). This provides young people with a relationship which is appropriately playful but also accepting, curious and empathic about their emotional experience of both current and past events. This attitude, alongside other DDP-informed principles, provides a framework for connecting with young people in a way that increases feelings of trust and safety. This then provides a relationship which is healing as well as educative.

DDP-informed principles for connecting and building a relationship with young people

Intersubjectivity

The heart of DDP is connecting through the intersubjective relationship. This connection is essential to our healthy development, but is a source of fear for the developmentally traumatized young person. If young people are to experience security then they need to feel safe in connection: to experience influencing and being influenced within safe and healthy relationships. Often the young person, in a state of fear, has led the adult away from connection, using controlling behaviours to influence the other without being influenced. Within DDP the adult connects with the young person, leading him or her back into connection.

PACE

If intersubjectivity is the heart of DDP then PACE helps the heart to beat. The attitude of PACE offers an unconditional relationship expressed through playfulness, acceptance, curiosity and empathy. It expresses a deep interest in the inner life of the other communicated through curiosity about and acceptance of this experience, and empathy for the struggles this experience can bring. It demonstrates the fun and joy in the relationship alongside a willingness to share and support the young person as needed.

Open and engaged

The use of PACE to connect intersubjectively is only possible if the adult can stay open and engaged. When young people become closed, defensive and/or hopeless it can be easy for the adult to join them in this closed, non-engaged state. The adults also become defensive, irritated or frustrated. All of these responses will close down the intersubjective relationship. When the adult loses the attitude of PACE and instead becomes evaluative or judgemental the relationship is damaged.

The relationship is used to help the young person with:

Safety and security

Young people who have experienced developmental trauma will have great difficulty feeling safe. Neither will they turn to adults for safety. They will stay hypervigilant, hypersensitive and hyper-reactive. They will not trust the intentions of adults, having little confidence that they want what is best for them. The adult will need to continuously monitor the young person's verbal and non-verbal communications as to whether or not they reflect safety or its absence. The adult can then increase safety by accepting and acknowledging the young person's experience with PACE, allowing the young person to take a break; move to a place of safety; or engage in activities that help regulate his or her affective state.

Co-regulation of affect

Traumatized young people are likely to have poor emotional regulation abilities. They are not good at regulating strong affective states. They are helped if their affective response to events is co-regulated by adults' affective response. The adults match the vitality and intensity of the affect whilst staying regulated themselves. They can then respond with empathy, verbally and non-verbally. This helps the young people to become more able to self-regulate or to feel comfortable seeking help from others when needed. In turn this can also help develop the capacity to mentalize (understand internal experience).

Co-constructing the meaning of experience

Young people are likely to struggle to make sense of both present and past experience. Their reflective capacities are weak and they are driven by their emotional experience. When their attention is held by adults' attentive stance the adults have an opportunity to put words to experience. The young people gradually identify and more fully express their inner life. They integrate the meaning given to the experience through the interwoven perspectives of self and other. As young people develop their reflective capacity they become more able to reflect on their experience, giving them more flexibility in responding.

Relational support for young people is helped when the adult is able to:

Use a story-telling style of communicating

To engage relationally with young people it is important to communicate with them in a way that holds their attention and maintains their open and engaged state. This will not be achieved through lecturing, reasoning or even reassuring. All of these aim to change the young person in some way rather than demonstrating a genuine interest in understanding what the young person is experiencing. Young people are more likely to be engaged by stories than by lectures. A story-telling tone of voice and rhythm is more likely to help a young person remain engaged and open to the adult.

Use affective-reflective (A-R) dialogue

The A-R dialogue brings the heart into connection with the mind, creating a rich story within which the inner lives of the young person can be explored, deepened, elaborated and made more coherent. The young person feels safe in the emotional co-regulation, allowing his or her experience to emerge in a rich story which can touch and change the experience of those witnessing it. The story-telling which emerges from the A-R dialogue provides a deepening of connection which is both safe and healing.

Use follow – lead – follow

If the young person's story is to be co-constructed, to emerge out of joint story-telling, then the adult as conductor in the telling must both follow and lead in turn. In this way the adult finds a balance between being non-directive and directive, following the themes that emerge and leading the young person to a deeper understanding. The adult sets a rhythm to the telling which allows the story to emerge.

Talk with and about

The A-R dialogue generates a new experience of events, often leading to a change in interaction patterns. This leads to increased attachment security and the development of coherent narratives. The adult will need to monitor the communication so that the young person learns to tolerate the affective experience without becoming overwhelmed by it. Talking with a young person is emotionally intense. As this threatens to become overwhelming to the young person, the adult can switch to talk *about* them. He or she might talk or wonder out loud or perhaps share a thought with another person, allowing the young person to become emotionally regulated again.

Attend to the verbal and non-verbal

Every communication is non-verbal, and some are also verbal. Noticing discrepancies between the verbal and non-verbal can help the adult more deeply understand the experience of the other and thus be more able to co-regulate that experience and reflect upon it. When the verbal and non-verbal match, the communication will be deeper and more open.

Use interactive repair

It is important that the adult notices ruptures in their relationship with the young person and repairs them. Apologizing when the young person has experienced the adult as defensive or judgemental can demonstrate the adult's deep interest and concern about the other. In this way behaviour is not seen as more important than the relationship. The relationship is not conditional on behaviour, but the adult is available to guide the young person with behaviour. The adult is responsible for repairing relationships following a rupture, whatever causes this. Demanding an apology puts responsibility for repair on the young person, which will reduce the sense of security. When the adult takes on this responsibility they will find the young person will also begin to value and attend to the relationship. Genuine remorse and apology will be given following difficult experiences. Both will see the relationship as more important than any conflict.

Mind-minded teaching

In order to connect with young people using PACE and the DDP-informed principles, teachers and teaching support staff will need to be able to be mind-minded towards themselves and the young people they are supporting. This relies on mentalization skills: the ability to recognize and respond to the internal experience of another person. The adult uses their theory of mind to understand that the young person has thoughts, feelings, beliefs and desires which are likely to be different to their own. With this understanding the adult can help the student discover his or her own mind, to organize his or her experience and eventually to help him or her put into words what he or she is experiencing. In doing this the adult will also be helping the young person to stay emotionally regulated.

Before teaching and support staff can reflect on the minds of the young people, they need to be able to reflect on their own minds. By understanding the impact a young person is having upon them the adults can stay open and engaged to that young person. Without this understanding the adult is likely to become defensive through anger, criticism or withdrawal. The following mind-minded narrative demonstrates a teacher being able to reflect on his own experience in this way.

A teacher's mind-minded narrative towards himself

It had been a long wet week and I was tired, but Friday was here at last. I was aware of Ellen, pale and thin, sitting at the back of the classroom. I did know that she had been having a tough time, moved into foster care with little notice, not knowing when she would be going back home. I am ashamed to say that this was not, however, at the front of my mind as I struggled to keep the class settled and focused for one more day. I have always prided myself on my ability to keep a class interested; but I was feeling distracted on this day. The weekend ahead was going to be difficult and my mind drifted to the worry of what might be in wait for me.

For most of the lesson Ellen had been disengaged but quiet. I paid little attention to her, but when the visitor entered the room she became noisier. I heard her banging her chair about and was irritated. I didn't want the visitor to witness me in poor control of the class. I was also aware that her key person was not available just at the moment. She had left the classroom a short while before. I felt cross; just when needed she was not around.

When Ellen finally exploded I guess my irritation, anxiety and, yes, my own anger got in the way of any understanding about what was going on for her. I strode to the back of the room aware that she was now hiding under the table. I was not going to accept this behaviour. Needless to say it did not go well.

When the teaching and support staff have good awareness of the impact young people are having upon them they are more able to stay open and engaged to the young people. They will be able to reflect upon a young person and better understand their internal experience. This understanding can then be conveyed to the young person through their empathy and understanding, as conveyed by the attitude of PACE.

We now return to Ellen's teacher. Having been able to reflect on his own experience he is now much more able to understand what is going on for Ellen and to respond to her sensitively.

A teacher's mind-minded narrative towards his student

Ellen was living with a mother who was increasingly poorly because of mental health difficulties. At 12 years old, I can only imagine how anxious and afraid this must have made her feel. Earlier in the week her mother had to go into hospital and Ellen moved to an unfamiliar foster carer. I am guessing she was afraid; who was this person and would she be kind? She must have also been worried about her mother. I guess that Ellen took care of her mother a great deal. I am wondering how it must have felt not knowing what was happening to her. Maybe she felt guilty that she had not looked after her well enough.

Now I am thinking about this, it makes sense that she would not be very focused in class. The visitor entering the classroom may have seemed like a further threat; or maybe she worried that this person was going to take her away as well. I think all these feelings erupted at once into that explosion of behaviour. Now I think about it, if I had been her I would have hidden under the table as well!

An attitude of PACE will allow staff to stay in tune with the ongoing needs of their students. Curiosity and reflection helps them to understand the young person at a deeper level; with this understanding they can accept the feelings that are leading to difficult behaviours and provide empathy and support for complex emotions. Maintaining an attitude of curiosity reduces the likelihood that staff will become angry or critical of the student, helping them to maintain a relationship with the student even at the most difficult moments. As connections deepen, the young people will experience a level of trust and safety that will help them to engage with education in a way that they couldn't whilst in a state of mistrust and fear.

Emotional development

Meeting the emotional needs of students is an important prerequisite for meeting the social and then the learning needs that the student also presents. Young people with attachment difficulties are likely to be emotionally immature and to only have fragile control of emotional arousal, whether caused by excitement or anxiety. Staff will need to be attuned to the student so that they can recognize and support feelings however these are displayed, and can step in and provide co-regulation of emotion as required. This co-regulation will be an important part of supporting the student whether or not he or she appears dysregulated. Young people who have learnt to inhibit emotion through dissociative processes may also lack these essential regulation skills. While emotional literacy is an important part of education, young people will not be able to learn to recognize their own or the feelings of others until they have experienced a sensitive, regulating relationship. Experience of emotional regulation comes before understanding.

Empathy and discipline

Young people thrive on structure and boundaries, but this is not sufficient to help them to learn to follow rules and to understand what is acceptable and unacceptable behaviour. This learning arises out of the experience of an empathic, attuned relationship. As young people learn to trust in their connection to a nurturing, empathic adult, they also experience shame at the loss of connection when their behaviour meets with disapproval. As the adult comforts and helps the young person regulate these feelings of shame, the young person is learning what is socially acceptable. Empathy is therefore an important precursor to discipline.

Remember, a young person with attachment difficulties is likely to be emotionally young and any use of structure, supervision and discipline needs to take account of this developmental age. Emotionally immature young people will need limited and simplified choices and consequences, and help to understand cause and effect.

Clear, calm discipline is important. Behavioural expectations can be provided through explicit rules with predictable and logical consequences for unacceptable behaviour. It is important to provide this in a calm and non-confrontational way, and only after regulatory support has been provided. Once the young person is fully regulated again, and if necessary, the adult can provide measured discipline alongside empathy and not anger. For example, 'I know it is really hard for you not to take my things when you are angry with me, but remember that you now have to…'

Young people with poor cause-and-effect thinking will need explicit help, much as a parent does with a toddler, to understand the links between their behaviour and the consequence and to understand the impact of themselves on others and others on themselves.

With this approach to discipline it is easier to maintain a positive emotional rhythm within the classroom and to avoid getting pulled into confrontation and anger.

Controlling students can present a particular challenge; entering control battles is rarely successful. Learning to step aside from confrontation and allowing students to experience a safe sense of being in control under the overall supervision of the adults will be helpful to them. From this they will develop trust in the adults. By providing an appropriate time for the student to feel in control, the student will be supported to trust in and enjoy the adult being in charge.

Meeting emotional needs provides a foundation for social and cognitive development:

- developing capacity for enjoyment
- developing social awareness
- developing reflectivity, the ability to notice and understand experience.

Summary: what do students with attachment difficulties need?

Safety

- Until students feel safe, they will not be able to derive positive benefit from being in the educational environment.

- Establish a safe environment within which the student can start to feel secure.

- Provide clear structure, boundaries and routine in a relaxing environment.

- Recognize the fear and anxiety that lie beneath behaviour so that the student can be appropriately supported.

- Set the emotional tone, providing opportunities to co-regulate the student's escalating arousal.

- Reduce stimulation and provide opportunities for relaxation, talking and reflection.

- Support during times of transition during the school day.

Building a relationship

- Students need relationships in order to feel safe.

- A key person gets to know and understand the student and begins engaging the student in the relationship, helping the student to feel safe enough to trust and respond.

- The key person will know the student well enough to notice distorted as well as direct requests for help.

- The key person will be aware of conditions that might throw the student, stepping in early to prevent escalating arousal.

- This key relationship will support emotional regulation, and help the student when feelings of shame or anger threaten to overwhelm.

- The key person can also act as advocate or champion for the student.

- An attitude of curiosity and reflection will allow the key person to stay in tune with the on going needs of the student, accepting the feelings that are leading to difficult behaviour and providing empathy and support for complex emotions.

Developing communication

- Communication is central to developing relationships.

- Teachers and support staff need a way to connect with and relate to these students to build their sense of trust and safety.

- As the relationship becomes stronger the students will then be able to accept boundaries, discipline and teaching.

- The DDP model provides some principles for connecting with young people.

- Central within these is the attitude of PACE. This provides young people with a relationship which is appropriately playful but also accepting, curious and empathic about their emotional experience of both current and past events.

Mind-minded teaching

- Teachers and teaching support staff will need to be mind-minded towards themselves and the young people they are supporting.

- This relies on mentalization skills: the ability to recognize and respond to the internal experience of another person.

- This helps the young people to organize their experience and to help them to put into words what they are experiencing, also contributing to emotional regulation.

- It is important to reflect on one's own mind before the young person's in order to stay open and engaged to them.

- As the adults reflect upon a young person they can better understand their internal experience and convey this using PACE.

- As connections deepen, the young people will experience a level of trust and safety that will help them to engage with education in a way that they couldn't whilst in a state of mistrust and fear.

Emotional development

- The emotional needs of the student need to be met when meeting social and learning needs.

- Students with attachment difficulties are likely to be emotionally immature and to have only fragile control of emotional arousal, whether caused by excitement or anxiety.

- Co-regulation is an important part of supporting students whether or not they appear dysregulated.

- Students who have learnt to inhibit emotion through dissociative processes may also lack these essential regulation skills.

- Students will not learn to recognize their own or the feelings of others until they have experienced a sensitive, regulating relationship.

- Experience of emotional regulation comes before understanding.

- Attune to the student to recognize and support feelings, however these are displayed.

- Step in and provide co-regulation of emotion as required.

Empathy and discipline

- Provide regulatory support before discipline or expecting reparation.

- Discipline with empathy and not anger.

- When learning to follow rules, understanding what is acceptable and unacceptable behaviour arises out of the experience of an empathic, attuned relationship.

- As the adult comforts and helps the student regulate the feelings of shame, the student is learning what is socially acceptable.

- Students with attachment difficulties are likely to be emotionally young.

- Students will need limited and simplified choices and consequences, and help to understand cause and effect.

- Provide explicit rules with predictable and logical consequences for unacceptable behaviour in a calm and non-confrontational way.

- Support understanding of behaviour and its consequences and the impact of themselves on others and others on themselves.

- Avoid getting pulled into confrontation and anger.

- By providing an appropriate time for the child to feel in control the student will be supported to trust in and enjoy the adult being in charge.

How can we meet these needs in educational settings?

(For further detail about meeting emotional needs, and especially the role of the key adult, the reader is referred to Louise Michelle Bombèr (2007, 2011).)

All emotionally troubled students, whatever attachment pattern they display, will benefit from the following:

- The use of activities that involve relationship-based play is really important for children of all ages. This allows us to model healthy adult–child relationships and has a positive impact on the young people we work with. These ideas have been successfully adapted for adolescents, so that they too can get an experience of fun, playful and empathic interactions which help them to build stronger relationships. It focuses on the here-and-now relationship and allows the young people to be in the moment within a non-threatening relationship. Activities such as hand massage, painting nails, seeing how quickly you can pop all the bubbles on bubble wrap, blow football, shove penny and paper punch have all worked well with older children, providing experience of adults engaging them in safe relationships which can be safely nurturing, challenging and structured.

- Help to regulate high levels of excitement, anger or anxiety. 'Time in' rather than 'time out' can be used to provide the student with time away from activities and time with a supportive adult. In particular, following difficult behaviour, the adult sits with the student and helps him or her with the feelings that underlie the behaviour.

- Help to feel safe in school, with special attention to times of transition, changes of routine and when visitors attend the classroom.

- Ensure predictable and consistent routines and structure. When these routines and structures have to be disrupted because of planned or unplanned events, the student is likely to need time to adjust to the change. Simple explanations sometimes accompanied with a visual cue to remind the student about the change, and more attention to supporting the student during the change, can be helpful.

- Think younger. Students who need a high level of emotional support tend to be emotionally immature, even if they are generally bright with a good ability to learn. These students often struggle with expectations typical for their age group but respond well when expectations are adjusted to a younger emotional age and additional support is provided.

Allocation and role of a key person

One of the ways in which these benefits can be provided is by allocating a key person.

Creating a secure base

The key person can ensure that a secure base is created for the student.

- The key person is an active presence, not an observer. This role is an important tool in the student's social and emotional education.

- The key person and the student need time to spend together, to connect and begin to build a relationship. This ensures that the key person is tuned in and available to the student.

- The key person will initiate and supervise games, activities and conversations between the student and his or her peers, supporting the development of social skills and friendships.

- The key person's aim is to become a secondary attachment figure for the student while he or she is away from the primary attachment figures.

- The key person helps the student to learn to become dependent, a necessary developmental stage before he or she is able to become an independent learner.

The key person will provide consistency and be able to recognize triggers and signals that indicate that the student is beginning to struggle with his or her emotions.

Providing emotional support

The key person can ensure that emotional support is provided for the student.

- Give the student the experience of feeling safe and respected. All young people deserve to be cared for, regardless of their ability to conform.

- Support and build relationships with the student at the emotional age he or she is displaying rather than the chronological age.

- Set the emotional tone for the student. The adult stays calm and nurturing, especially at times when the student is becoming dysregulated. Staying calm does not necessarily mean being quiet; an intense but calm tone which matches the intensity of the student's feelings will more quickly help the student to regulate. This is called affect matching. The adult matches the vitality and intensity of the expression of emotion by the student. If the student is sad, the adult will be quieter and softer. If the student is angry, adults need to be more intense in tone without becoming angry themselves.

- Acknowledge, reassure and provide security for a student in a physical, verbal or feelings-based way (emotional containment).

- Provide a calm area in the school for cooling off, reflection and relaxation when anxiety levels seem to be rising.

- Provide a calm box with sensory activities when anxiety levels seem to be rising.

- Tune in to the student's behaviour in the context of the underlying emotion.

- Pay attention to interactive or relationship repair, re-establishing a positive relationship with the student following a disruption to this relationship.

- Allow processing time between chunks of information.

- Be prepared to repeat, repeat, repeat: 1. The student hears. 2. The student absorbs information. 3. The student acts.

Providing behavioural support

The key person can ensure that behavioural support is provided for the student.

- Reflect on the possible underlying causes of a student's non-compliance. This may be a signal that the student feels anxious, perhaps fearful of change or endings. These feelings need supporting.

- Choose the battles. Ignore, pre-empt, redirect and distract, as you would for a younger child.

- Plan ahead. Think about what you will do when an outburst occurs. Practise what strategies you will use, such as taking the student to a calm area with sensory activities.

- Be clear while being supportive and empathic. Use a warm, matter-of-fact tone.

- Try not to confront, as this can lead to an increase in anxiety and can escalate behaviour.

- Think about the effect of 'time out' on a student who has already experienced rejection.

- Use 'time in' to calm the student and reduce his or her anxiety.

- Think about the effect of praise and rewards on a student who doesn't believe him or herself deserving of love and treats. Short, descriptive praise and rewards for very specific behaviours (e.g. 'You really helped Jake to feel welcome in our school') might be easier for the student to accept than more global praise and rewards (e.g. 'Great job today showing Jake around').

- Wonder aloud to make sense of behaviour (e.g. 'I think you might be feeling a bit angry because you didn't make the team...'). Use sentences such as: 'I know this is hard for you...'; 'I am wondering if you are feeling...'; 'I guess you are really feeling...'

Providing learning support

The key person can ensure that learning support is provided for the student.

- Prepare the student for any change in routine in advance. Change can be scary.

- Routines and boundaries are important to help a student feel safe, but not too rigid. Be flexible and adapt to the student's needs.

- Help the student to remember that he or she is being 'kept in mind' by his or her parent throughout the day, to reduce feelings of abandonment.

- Model and initiate good social interactions with peers and adults.

- Provide specific safe places within school that the student can go to during unstructured times, when they are not coping without structure and routine.

- You may need to give the student short periods to practise independence.

- Give consistent, clear and simple instructions.

- Use a visual timetable to reinforce instructions. This can help the student to understand what is going to happen next when he or she is too anxious to hear properly or understand.

- Look for opportunities to build self-esteem. It is important for students to feel good about themselves. Celebrate success and good choices. For example, use photographs to reinforce and evidence these. These can be shared with the student regularly.

Looking after the key person

The key person can ensure that they look after themselves.

- Talk to colleagues and seek support. This is hard work!

- Be prepared for the long haul. Change takes time.

- Make good use of supervision and opportunities to reflect with others about the student.

- Notice small signs of progress, and hold on to these during the more difficult times.

- Try not to take behaviours directed towards you personally. Remember, the student does not know how to manage angry feelings. Young people tend to target those they feel safest with when they have feelings they can't otherwise manage.

- Have a back-up key person to support you. This person will also need to develop a relationship with the student.

Summary: the role of the key person

Creating a secure base

- Ensure that the key person has an active presence.

- Help the student to become dependent before becoming independent.

- Tune in (attunement) and be available.

- Develop capacity for enjoyment.

- Let the student know he or she is being kept in mind (mind-mindedness).

- Initiate and supervise games, activities and conversations between the student and his or her peers.

Providing emotional support

- Acknowledge, reassure and provide security in a physical, verbal or feelings-based way (emotional containment).

- Set the emotional tone (affect matching).

- Provide relationship repair following times of rupture.

- Give the student the experience of feeling safe and lovable.

- Provide a calm area for rest and relaxation.

- Provide a calm box with sensory activities.

- Support and build relationships with the student at the emotional age he or she is displaying.

Providing behavioural support

- Avoid confrontation.

- Reflect on the possible underlying cause.

- Be clear, while being supportive and empathic.

- Use 'time in' rather than 'time out'.

- Ignore, pre-empt, redirect and distract.

- Wonder aloud.

- Don't take projections personally.

Providing learning support

- Provide predictable and consistent routines and structure.

- Prepare the student for any change in routine in advance.

- Provide boundaries to help the student feel safe.

- Be flexible and adapt to the student's needs.

- Give the student short periods to practise independence.

- Give consistent, clear and simple instructions.

- Use a visual timetable to reinforce instructions.

- Look for opportunities to build self-esteem.

- Celebrate success and good choices, e.g. photographs.

Looking after the key person

- Seek support.

- Anticipate that change will take time.

- Use of supervision and opportunities for reflection.

- Notice and value small signs of progress.

- Remember behaviours directed at you are often not personal even if they feel that way.

- Use a back-up key person who also has a relationship with the student.

The importance of support

Supporting a student with attachment difficulties is hard work. It is therefore important that adults are well supported. Time for reflection is important – to be able to step back from the situation and think with others about what is going on for the student, and understand the relationship that is developing.

Networks and multi-agency working

Young people with attachment difficulties can have complex networks built up around them. Good communication and working together within these networks is an important part of supporting the student. By working together, professionals will develop a shared understanding about the student and what the student needs. It is also an important part of avoiding splitting within the network. Young people with attachment difficulties can have very concrete and immature thinking abilities; finding it difficult to hold on to different perspectives, they view others and experiences as 'all good' or 'all bad'. Without good multi-agency working, networks get pulled in to these immature thinking processes so that parts of the network become the all-good rescuers while other parts become the all-bad persecutors.

Support for the adults

The staff working directly with the student with an attachment difficulty will need good support, training and opportunities for high-quality supervision which facilitates reflection and planning.

The risks of secondary trauma when working with traumatized young people are high (Cairns and Stanway 2004). Good supervision can ensure that early signs of secondary trauma are noticed, with appropriate and timely support provided.

The key person will become a transitional attachment figure to the student, but will need to avoid the student forming a secondary attachment to the adult which is at the expense of the primary attachment to the carer. Helping the student know that his or her parent or carer is thinking about him or her during the school day, and symbolically receiving from and handing back to the primary attachment figure at the beginning and end of the day, is an important part of the support that is provided. This can be done, for example, by checking in with the student as he or she arrives at school. How were things at home? Is there anything he or she is worrying about today? A similar conversation can be held at the end of the school day, acknowledging that the student is now going home to parents who care about him or her.

We have all encountered a range of relationships in the past – some rewarding and some more difficult. Working with a student with attachment difficulties can remind staff of their own early attachment experience, interfering with their ability to relate to the student in the present and to experience empathy for the student. In working with students with attachment difficulties, it is therefore important that staff have a good understanding of their own attachment and past relationship experience. This will then allow them to stay truly in the present with the student in front of them.

Conclusion

Secure attachment gives the student the opportunity to feel safe, to trust, to relate, to be dependent and to be independent. The student with attachment difficulties has not had this experience. These students bring their fear, their lack of trust, their difficulties with relationships, their unfulfilled dependency needs and their struggles with independence into school. We need to provide school environments within which we can help the student to feel safe and secure – meeting his or her emotional needs and providing the foundation for learning. The starting point for this is close working together, leading to a shared understanding of the student and what the student needs.

10
Helping the Student with Different Attachment Styles in Educational Settings

Following on from Chapter 9, which provided a general exploration of how schools can meet the attachment needs of students with emotional difficulties, this chapter provides more specific advice for helping students in relation to the different attachment patterns of relating that they might display and the attachment state of mind that they might hold. Not all young people fit neatly into these patterns, but may show combinations of these styles. In this case combinations of the tailored advice might be helpful.

Attachment during adolescence

At early adolescence the parents are still the principal attachment figures for young people, and in fact can become more prominent again in providing a secure base for the young person's gradually extending exploration of themselves within a growing world. Young people may not want to know it, but they need their parents more than ever as they enter this new phase of their life! However, the journey towards adulthood is also a slow shift from parents as principal attachment figure to friends, and then romantic partners. The young person will gradually learn to turn to friends and partners for comfort and support, whilst also learning how to give comfort and support in turn. Adolescence is a time of developing the capacity to be the attachment support for another. Parents remain important but friends and intimates move alongside them, and eventually overtake them as their main source of security. It is not hard to understand how difficult this must be for the young person who is emotionally maturing more slowly whilst the expectations upon him of parents, friends and intimate relationships increase.

Alongside this shifting use of attachment figure is the development of an attachment state of mind. During childhood children will hold multiple models of attachment as they learn to relate to a range of caregiving adults. Adolescence is a time of organizing these models into a more sophisticated attachment state of mind. For example, the child may hold a model of available mother who loves him or her, whilst also holding a model of cold grandmother with expectations that are difficult to live up to and a father who is good for practical support. The journey of adolescence will be one towards holding a model of self and other which suggests that the young person is lovable but not always able to meet expectations and is able to rely on friends for practical support. The attachment pattern of relating learnt in childhood finds its best fit in an attachment state of mind ready for adulthood (see Howe 2011).

Helping the student with insecure avoidant patterns of relating and a developing dismissive attachment state of mind within the educational setting

Students with insecure avoidant patterns of relating tend towards being self-reliant within the educational setting. They experience difficulty seeking or using help from adults. Thus when the student feels insecure or in need of assistance he or she is reluctant to seek this support. As these young people develop during adolescence they learn to become dismissive of their attachment needs or of emotional support from others. They defend against memories of feeling rejected or unloved by downplaying the importance of caring relationships and not engaging with issues that raise the spectre of emotional need and dependency. Their personality becomes infused with the need for self-reliance and a dislike of appearing vulnerable or in need of help. This impacts on their developing friendships as well as with their relationships with adults.

In the classroom, as Delaney (2009) notes, these students will focus on learning when on their own or when in a group with a task as the main focus, but will struggle if needing support from the teacher or from peers within the group to accomplish the task. When help is offered they reject it rather than engaging in the relationship, fearing that they will be rebuffed.

The goal of the teaching staff is to help these students feel more secure within the setting so that they are more confident in using the support on offer.

The student can be helped in achieving this goal by providing a high level of structure and routine. Geddes (2006) suggests that the task can provide needed structure which then helps the student to experience safety in the relationship with the adults. These students may find it easier to be in a small group as this can help them cope with proximity to the adult. Additionally older students can be buddies for younger children.

Students with avoidant styles of relating benefit from having some choice in the content of the activity. The adults gradually help students to build their confidence in seeking and using help. It is helpful to let the student experience being thought about and held in mind – for example, 'I thought about you this weekend when...'

Helping the student with an insecure avoidant attachment

These students tend to miscue the adults regarding their need for nurturing. When they need emotional closeness, they act as if they don't need the adult. Help the avoidant student by taking care of hurts, however minor, and listening to worries, however small.

Find opportunities to nurture them and encourage them to accept reassurance when distressed. These students need help to focus on and express their feelings. They also need help to feel good about themselves, to cope with not being the best and sometimes getting things wrong.

Helping the student who withdraws

Some students will dissociate when stressed. This is a cutting off from emotion. These students may display little emotion or may move quickly from one emotion to another. This makes it difficult to feel emotionally connected to them. These students need help to stay with their feelings. Reflect back feelings that they may be experiencing – for example, 'If I were you I would be feeling really angry right now.' If they are very 'switched off', try to encourage them 'back to the present'. Remind them of who they are, where they are and who you are.

Summary: insecure avoidant attachment pattern of relating

Attachment pattern develops out of a relationship with a parent who is distant and rejecting. These students need help to focus on and express their feelings and to feel comfortable seeking and receiving comfort and support (see Delaney 2009).

Insecure avoidant profile	Interventions
• Rely on knowledge and ignore feelings to guide behaviours • Withdrawn and quiet • Generally appear more self-reliant and independent than expected for their age • Will try to work alone even when don't know what to do. Prefer known tasks and give up quickly with a new or more open-ended task • May appear more focused on activities than on people • Reluctant to turn to adults when they need help; show apparent indifference to teacher, e.g. may ignore teacher and avoid eye-contact. If talked to, likely to shrug, or say they don't care. Do not like the teacher to be close to them. Reluctant to engage and discuss a problem • Resistant to help from the adult but also lack confidence in their own ability, e.g. may rip up their work or proclaim that it is rubbish before teacher can look at it • Focus more on what they can't do rather than what they can do. Fear of failure means they won't take a risk with learning – thus will not take creative opportunities to learn • Underachieve because won't let adult help • May try to take care of the adult • Can appear happy or settled but, if stressed, may show a sudden and apparently inexplicable tantrum which is quickly over • Relatively isolated as they lack emotional engagement with peers or with adults; avoid intimacy • Act with indifference to new situations • Distress is denied or not communicated • Anxious but may not show this; however, can develop compulsive behaviours, e.g. stealing, self-harm, to increase feelings of control	• Find opportunities to nurture, support and comfort. Student will be uncomfortable with this, so need to build up very slowly • Help student to experience trust in the relationship with the teacher. Gradually build student's ability to accept help • Support in coping with the proximity of the adult • Help the student to experience being thought about and held in mind: 'I thought about you this weekend when...' • Encourage accepting the adult taking care of hurts, however minor, or listening to worries, however small. Again have to build this slowly • Help to feel good about themselves and to cope with not being the best, and sometimes getting things wrong • Organize small groups and a task or project to focus on as the student may find this easier. Gradually increase importance of relationships and working cooperatively, i.e. use task to develop relationship • Student will find projects that focus on product rather than process easier. Have achievable goals • Start with tasks that student enjoys and which can be self-directed • Stay at one remove when offering support, e.g. 'I wonder what would happen if...' rather than 'Now try...' • Similarly ask student to focus on tasks that are one removed using story and metaphor rather than speaking about themselves, e.g. use TV, films and videos to help describe characters' emotions • Arrange for older students to be buddies for younger students • Allow some choice in content of activities • Use questions that are factual and precise • Help student to stay regulated through concrete, mechanical tasks, sorting, organizing, categorizing • Use 'writing frames' – filling in boxes, completing sentences and writing brief sentences in defined spaces can help with the anxiety of 'spilling out' onto a blank page • Initially avoid games that are about winning and losing but focus on games that are simply about having fun • Think about how you use language, and try not to impose the relationship on the student by talking about self, e.g. 'I think you should'; 'Let me help you with that', etc. Try to focus more on the student. 'What do you think you should do?' 'What would you like to happen next?', etc.

Expressed need	Hidden need
I will do it by myself. I fear my need of you. I will push you away.	I will not show my need for comfort and protection.

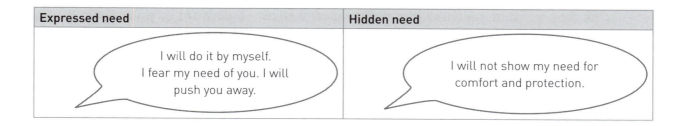

Helping the student with insecure ambivalent patterns of relating and a developing preoccupied-entangled state of mind within the educational setting

Students with insecure ambivalent patterns of relating tend towards being attention-needing and clingy. It is difficult for these students to focus on the activity because all their focus is on checking out the availability of the adults. They quickly feel anxious when they experience a degree of separation and therefore behave in ways which restore the connection with the adult again. As these young people develop during adolescence they become preoccupied with memories of inconsistent and unreliable caregiving from the past. The memories and associated unregulated emotions invade the present so that their earlier feelings of uncertainty, neediness and dissatisfaction become attached to current relationships. Their emotional neediness and entanglement with peer and adult relationships mean that it is hard to develop independence. They both need friendships and are quick to feel dissatisfied with these. They are emotionally volatile and demanding, meaning that friendships are difficult to sustain. They want support but cannot provide it in turn. Equally they are demanding of the attention of the teacher; they struggle to work independently because this does not give the needed reassurance that the teacher still has them in mind. They can behave as if they are more helpless than they actually are in order to get this attention. Teachers can be very frustrated by these behaviour patterns as they have increased expectations through the school that the young people will become more self-motivated and independent learners.

In education the goal is to help the students feel confident enough in the availability of the adult that they can reduce their focus on this in order to attend to the activity. The adults can be helped in reaching this goal by providing highly predictable, structured routines, and visual timetables to help the students to follow the routines. Turn-taking with the adult can help the student achieve some independence in activities.

Geddes (2006) recommends differentiating tasks into small independent steps and using a timer to help the student cope with brief independent times away from the adult. Additionally transitional objects (looking after something for the adult) can help a student to cope with times apart. The student needs to experience being noticed by the adults frequently during the day. They can use comments to let the student know that they are thinking about him or her. Special attention needs to be given to transition times when these students feel particularly anxious.

These students are helped if the adults provide reliable and consistent support, facilitating a gradually increasing separation and attention to activities. It is important not to reduce these supports too quickly; allow the student to develop more independence slowly.

Helping the student with an insecure ambivalent attachment

These students tend to miscue the adults about their need for attention. They will be reluctant to signal that they don't need you close at the moment because they will fear that you might not be close when they do need you.

These students need lots of attention, support and nurturing while also being encouraged to cope with short periods without your constant attention. These periods can then be gradually extended. These students need help to understand behaviour and its predictable consequences ('When I do this, this happens; when you do this, this happens'). They also need help to regulate strong emotions. Support them in calming down so that they can learn how to calm themselves down.

Summary: insecure ambivalent attachment pattern of relating

Attachment pattern develops out of a relationship with a parent who is inconsistent and unpredictable.

The students need lots of attention, support and nurturing while also being encouraged to cope with short periods without your constant attention. These students especially struggle to make the steps to independence expected in secondary settings (see Delaney 2009).

Insecure ambivalent profile	Interventions
• Tend to make their presence known with highly dependent, attention-needing behaviours that can feel manipulative because they coerce the other to attend	• Need to meet need for attention without overly reinforcing dependency. Student will need increased support, but with opportunities for small periods of independent working which are gradually built up
• Preoccupied with relationships, alert to the availability of others, and in constant need of reassurance	• Provide some empathic but clear boundaries which increase confidence when not getting attention and with frequent check-ins so the student does not feel abandoned
• Will monopolize favourite teacher with constant need to share problems or gain reassurance. This can lead to inappropriate boundaries with teachers, with the student wanting to share personal information or be too close to the adult	• Provide highly predictable, structured routines; use visual timetables; and don't reduce supports too quickly
• Overly focused on the relationship with the teacher or teaching assistant at the expense of learning	• Differentiate tasks into small steps, and encourage turn-taking to help achieve some independence in activities
• Find it difficult to settle by themselves or with groups of students; unable to take independent action	• Use a timer to help calm anxieties during short, timed independent tasks
• Will not want to go out at unstructured times, look for reasons to stay with the teacher	• Gradually increase duration of independent tasks with a clear structure, letting student know when adult will be back to check in with them, i.e. clear time frames
• Sometimes talk excessively, or act as 'class clown' in order to maintain the focus of adult attention. Skilful use of language to maintain teacher's attention	• Be dependable by coming back when agreed, or if that is not possible apologizing and acknowledging how difficult that must have been
• Concentrating and focusing on tasks is difficult as they remain hypervigilant to what the adults are doing and are easily distracted	• Provide special transitional objects to take place of teacher for a short while: 'Please look after this for me for a while'
• Very focused on feelings	• Notice the student frequently during the day. Use comments to let student know you are thinking about him or her
• Find it difficult to attend to the rules and structure of the classroom	
• Find it difficult to follow rules and to learn from consequences	• Encourage responsibility for tasks
• Rely on feelings rather than knowledge to guide their behaviour	• Use stories around issues of separation, identity and independence
• Poor understanding of cause and effect. Find it difficult to take responsibility for behaviour and learning	• Allow the student to develop more independence slowly
• Can escalate confrontation in order to hold the attention of others	• Provide reliable and consistent adult support
	• Gradually increase separation
• View the teacher as either all good or all bad, and may oscillate between these depending on their immediate feeling	• Support understanding of their behaviour and the predictable consequences: 'When I do this, this happens; when you do this, this happens'

Insecure ambivalent profile	Interventions
• Find it hard to maintain friendships and can be clingy and possessive • Highly anxious and oversensitive to signs of rejection • Quick to become abusive or rude if they feel they are being ignored	• Pay special attention to transition times, plan beginnings, separations, endings • Support the anxiety of the unknown • Support them in regulating strong emotions and in calming down so that they can learn how to calm themselves down • Give 'permission' cards – these can be used by student to 'bank' if the teacher is busy and can't give the student attention immediately. The student can use them to 'book' a prearranged time later on • Plan calming and regulating activities involving physical resistance and deep pressure touch to help ground them • Build up frustration tolerance by not over-helping, but acknowledge and empathize with anxiety and frustration
Expressed need	Hidden need
I can't trust in your availability. I need you to attend to me.	I will not show my need to separate and explore. I will pull you in and push you away.

Helping the student with disorganized-controlling patterns of relating and a developing unresolved-disorganized state of mind within educational settings

Students with disorganized-controlling patterns of relating feel highly unsafe and tend towards being angry, aggressive and highly controlling with the adults and their peers. It is difficult for these students to focus on the activity or on the availability of the adult because all their focus is on checking out and trying to ensure their safety. They quickly feel anxious when they experience any unpredictability, uncertainty or the unexpected, and work hard to force the environment to be predictable again.

As these young people develop during adolescence they struggle to manage the growing challenges of regulating emotions and managing relationships. With poor stress tolerance and over-sensitized nervous systems these young people are poorly equipped to manage the additional stresses of adolescence. They have however learnt to manage without attachment figures because of the fear they generate. This means that they struggle to develop independence without the support of trusted adults. Emotional volatility is high as painful and unresolved memories of fear and stress associated with relationships makes it hard for them to trust in either peer friendships or adult support. Increasingly coercive and/or controlling behaviours are developed to try and manage these difficulties.

At adolescence these students can display a range of erratic, risky and disruptive behaviours, putting self and others at risk. Extreme behaviours seem to come from nowhere as triggers are difficult to spot. It is difficult to maintain them within the classroom. The goal for the adults is to help the student feel safe within the school. Because these children have very poor stress tolerance, stress needs to be kept to a minimum while they slowly build up their ability to manage it. The adults can be helped in reaching this goal by providing highly safe and predictable environments, reducing the unexpected or the unplanned to a minimum. Adults need to help the student to feel physically safe and contained by providing high levels of calm, non-confrontational responses, empathy and understanding to help the student feel emotionally contained. Be aware of the emotional level the student is functioning at; provide activities and experiences matched to this level. Adults can develop safety routines and plans to be engaged when the student is very distressed. Think about the place (quiet, non-stimulating) and provide time with the key person.

Geddes (2006) suggests that concrete, mechanical and rhythmic activities can help soothe an over-aroused student. Rhythmical physical exercise and music can also help an aroused student to calm down. Permission cards can be used when he or she needs to go to a safe place without need for explanation.

Helping the student with a controlling pattern of relating

When students are displaying a lot of controlling, manipulative and aggressive behaviour or overly compliant and withdrawn behaviour, they are signalling that they are feeling anxious, distressed and insecure.

They will need a period of reduced stress and high security. This includes reducing excitement and providing a calm, predictable and low-key routine. As they relax they will be open to accepting care and support, leading to a reduction of the controlling behaviours.

Summary: disorganized-controlling attachment pattern of relating

Attachment pattern develops out of a relationship within which the parent is frightened of or frightening to the child.

When students are displaying a lot of controlling, manipulative and aggressive behaviour or overly compliant and withdrawn behaviour, they are signalling that they are feeling anxious, distressed and insecure (see Delaney 2009).

Disorganized-controlling profile	Interventions
• May be either quiet and withdrawn or loud and aggressive, can explode in temper for no obvious reason • Controlling within peer relationships. May want friendships but immaturity impedes this, can be very abusive to other students in the class • Anxiety may be expressed as controlling, omnipotent, knowing everything already • Demonstrate a diminished range of emotions, lacking the contentment and joy in activities of other young people • Frequently afraid but tend to mask anxiety through more aggressive or powerful behaviours. May provoke, bully or challenge others to maintain feelings of control • May have poor stress tolerance, detracts from learning • Can be highly disruptive in school. They can run around uncontrollably, run out of class unexpectedly • Abscond from classes and will bully other students into leaving the school with them • Tend to be anxious and inattentive • May demonstrate highly compulsive or obsessive behaviours which allow them to hold on to rigid control • May appear compliant but resist attempts to be helped or comforted • Some students portray a pseudomature caregiving role within the classroom • Others may demonstrate more obsessive preoccupations with being noticed through a combination of aggressive and coy behaviours. Can rubbish the teacher and be very abusive but will then switch to appeasing and trying to win teacher around • Hypervigilant to what is going on around them, making it difficult to concentrate or attend to a task • Their early brain development has developed over-responsive fight–flight reactions, leaving a diminished capacity to concentrate or think	• Provide a period of reduced stress and high security • Reduce excitement and provide a calm, predictable and low-key routine • Provide highly safe and secure environments with reliable and predictable routines which help reduce stress. Avoid sudden change. Provide warning when change is going to happen and acknowledge how difficult this can be for student • Help the student to feel physically safe and contained with attention to where sitting in classrooms and how getting around school • Use calm, non-confrontational responses, empathy • Help the student feel emotionally contained. A 'safe' area/activity/object helps with this • Be aware of the emotional, social and developmental level the student is functioning at and provide activities and experiences that match to this • Plan concrete, mechanical and rhythmic activities to help soothe an over-aroused student, e.g. word searches, card games, doodling and some computer games such as Tetris • Use rhythmical physical exercise and music to help an aroused student calm down • Develop safety and/or calming routines for when the student is very distressed. Think about the place (quiet, non-stimulating) and provide time with the key person • Wherever possible, give positive comments about achievement, whether about behaviour or in terms of task • Try to address the class/group generally rather than directly to student • Depending on concentration span – engage in short task interspersed with mechanical tasks, e.g. computer or 'safe' activity, in order to calm the brain • Give 'permission' cards – these can be used by student to 'bank' if the teacher is busy and can't give the student attention immediately. Student can use them to 'book' a prearranged time later on

Disorganized-controlling profile	Interventions
• Although hyper-aroused, some cope with excessive feelings of stress by dissociating – appearing 'switched off', and they can oscillate quickly from agitation and demanding attention to switching off and telling adults to go away • Strong feelings are overwhelming, and very little tolerance for frustration. Demonstrate frustration through extreme behaviours such as banging head against wall • May find it hard to understand, distinguish or control emotions in themselves or others • Immaturity and rigid, controlling style of relating to peers can lead to social isolation • Likely to be underachievers and possibly at a very immature stage of learning • May be unable to accept being taught, and/or are threatened by others knowing more than they do, as this triggers overwhelming feelings of humiliation • Struggle in relatively unsupervised settings such as the playground or moving between lessons	• Carefully plan transitions and endings • Important to have good level of support and helpful supervision for yourself
Expressed need	**Hidden need**
I will not need you. Needing you is dangerous. I must be in control.	I can't explore the world. I am too busy ensuring I am safe.

Disciplining the student with attachment difficulties

Clear, calm discipline is important, but will only be successful once the student is regulated again. In other words provide regulatory support before behavioural support. Behavioural expectations can be provided through explicit rules with predictable and logical consequences for unacceptable behaviour. It is important to provide this in a calm and non-confrontational way. Discipline with empathy, not anger, and begin with understanding the student's experience before helping him or her to understand this from someone else's point of view.

With this approach to discipline, it is easier to maintain a positive emotional rhythm within the setting and to avoid getting pulled into confrontation and anger.

Students with poor cause-and-effect thinking will need explicit help, much as a parent does with a toddler, to understand the links between their behaviour and the consequence and to understand the impact of themselves on others and others on themselves.

Disciplining students with attachment difficulties

- Provide regulatory support.
- Understand the student's experience and let him or her know you get it.
- Help the student to think about other people involved.
- Think together about what the appropriate consequences might be.
- Support the student to implement these consequences.

For example, Gregory has physically attacked Tony following an incident when Tony was laughing at him for not making the school team. The teaching assistant, Jill, separates the boys and ensures that Tony is being taken care of. She then spends time with Gregory, helping him to calm down. Jill has to prepare some materials for the teacher and gets Gregory to help her. She allows him to use the guillotine, knowing that the deep pressure he will need to cut through the card will help him regulate further. She then gets him a drink and snack whilst they sit down to figure out what happened. Jill lets Gregory know that she gets that he was angry with Tony for teasing him. She validates this anger, expressing that she would have been angry too if her friend teased her like this. She acknowledges that Gregory was disappointed that he hadn't made the team and hurt that his friend would not be supportive about this. She then wonders why Tony had reacted in this way, and Gregory admits that he had been teasing Tony first and his friend had been upset with him too. Gregory is now able to acknowledge that hitting Tony was wrong, however upset he was. Jill wonders how Gregory can make amends. Gregory decides to text Tony, telling him he is sorry. He draws out his mobile phone, and Jill, choosing to ignore the fact that he is using his phone in school, helps him to compose the text. She suggests he doesn't begin the text by pointing out that Tony should not have laughed at him for not being on the team! Gregory is able to let this go and sends a suitable apology.

11

Supporting the Emotional Needs of Students with Attachment Difficulties

Generally there are two aspects to providing support that staff need to consider when individualizing support tailored to a student's emotional needs. First, there will be a range of support already present which could be helpful for the student, but staff need to find ways to help the student access this support. For example, regular outside activities can help a child who struggles with focus and concentration. The more active exercise can help the student to relax and release some tension. The student might have difficulties making the transition from indoors to outdoors, however, or may struggle to use this relatively unstructured time. A key adult will need to provide some additional support to help the student make best use of this activity.

This can be challenging because the student with attachment difficulties has a basic distrust of adults. The student needs to be helped to build up security with a trusted adult, who can then help the student to use the support on offer.

Second, students may benefit from some innovative practice tailored to their needs. This will place more demands on staff but can be highly effective for some students. Again supporting the student to access this support will be key to its success.

For example, a student might be displaying excessive attention neediness from the key adult. This might make it very difficult for this student to cope with the gentle challenge of managing an activity without this close attention, or coping when the adult takes a break. The use of a transitional object, holding on to something that belongs to the adult, might be a way to help the student 'hold on' to that adult in his or her absence.

Challenges in supporting the emotional needs of students with attachment difficulties

There are a range of challenges which can face staff when they try to develop a plan for supporting an individual student, as described below.

Managing need for dependency versus independence

One important aspect of school life relies on students having some degree of independence. They will be most successful if they can manage without a parent figure around and if they become increasingly independent as they progress through the school. When a student's identified needs are for increased dependency, this can seem at odds with a key objective for the student. Staff might be tempted to push the student to be more independent, believing that this will serve him or her better in the future. This can be unhelpful. The route to independence is via dependency. It can be a mistake to try to move students too quickly to more independent activities when they are not yet ready for it. Understanding the emotional age of the student and gearing support to this emotional age is a key part of supporting the emotional needs of the student with attachment difficulties.

This can be a double challenge when supporting students who have learnt to deal with their emotional distress through self-reliance. An apparent 'pseudomaturity', appearing more mature than they actually are, can mask the dependency needs of some students. Staff need to hold on to an assessment that a student needs to be more dependent, and to support the student to accept dependency when he or she distrusts reliance on others. This can be additionally challenging when it appears counter to the objective of the school to help students be more independent.

Maintaining high boundaries and high warmth

Research has shown that all children and young people do best in an atmosphere of authoritative parenting (Hetherington and Parke 1993). This is parenting that provides a high degree of warmth while both encouraging autonomy and providing clear and consistent boundaries. Young people with attachment difficulties need and thrive best on this same combination of autonomy, boundaries and warmth in schools. The boundaries provide consistency, predictability, routines and clear consequences. The encouragement of autonomy, but matched to the student's capacity, provides the gentle challenge that moves the student forward, and the warmth provides nurturing support.

Maintaining high warmth can be difficult. For example, starting with empathy and concern for a student can feel like being soft, or giving in to him or her. If students are to benefit from consequences and behavioural guidance they will need support for their emotional insecurity. This is what the warmth and nurture provides. Students with attachment difficulties often have a core belief in their own badness. Without a high degree of warmth from supportive adults, they are much more likely to enter a state of shame. Experience of shame tends to further cut young people off from the relationships that they most need while reinforcing the maladaptive relationship strategies that are maintaining their insecurity and emotional distress.

Managing behaviour while supporting emotional development

A school is a social environment with its own set of expectations and values. We want the students within the school to conform to these. The challenging behaviour of the student with complex emotional needs can oppose our expectations and values. The usual response to such behaviours is to discourage these behaviours and encourage alternative behaviours. This is the basis of behavioural management programmes. We use rewards and consequences to help the other come in line with our expectations. Thus we reward a behaviour we want to increase and provide a negative consequence for a behaviour we want to reduce. In this way we provide a 'correction' for the behaviour. While this might be an effective way to manage behaviour, it is not a helpful way to influence emotional development. Emotional development thrives on connection, not correction. In other words, when we connect emotionally to a young person, recognizing and understanding the emotional experience which has led to the behaviour, we are also helping that young person to develop emotionally. Young people need both connection and correction. An example of this approach was given at the end of the last chapter. Young people with attachment difficulties are at particular risk of missing out on connection. This is because their difficulties make them distrustful of emotional connection with another and because the behaviours can be especially difficult, leading to a focus on these rather than on the emotional experience of the young person. When developing support tailored to the emotional needs of the student, it is vital that attention is given to how the adults can emotionally connect to the student before they manage the behaviour that the student is presenting, that is, connection before correction.

Supporting students with shame-based difficulties

Many young people with attachment difficulties will struggle with the experience of shame. The development of shame is influenced by the early relationship experience of the young person. The experience of shame emerges at a time in the child's development when he or she is becoming more mobile. It is part of the socialization process. When parents tell their children 'no' or discourage them from particular behaviours, the attunement experienced by the children with their parents is temporarily disrupted. This break in attunement is experienced as a sense of shame, therefore discouraging the behaviour the child was engaged in. Sensitive parents will then 'repair the relationship', re-establishing attunement with the children by letting them know that they are still loved and that any disapproval of the behaviour does not affect the relationship the parent has with the children.

When children experience little attunement with parents, when discipline is harsh, punitive or inconsistent and when parents do not attend to relationship repair, children will experience overwhelming and unregulated shame. This experience of shame becomes tied up with the child's developing sense of identity. The child no longer experiences him or herself as having done a 'bad thing' but as being a 'bad person'. Instead of the healthy development of guilt – an emotion which drives us to make amends, to connect with the person wronged and put it right – the child gets stuck in shame. This emotion leads to a desire to hide away from other people, preventing the ability to make amends.

Students bring this early experience of shame and guilt into the classroom. Healthy development means that students can take responsibility for their behaviour, experiencing guilt and being able to make amends, with the support of the teacher or teaching assistant. Students with shame-based difficulties react more defensively. They cannot respond to the other because they are too busy defending against the feelings of shame in themselves. They put up a 'shield against the shame': they lie, minimize and blame others, or when all else fails they rage (see Figure 11.1).

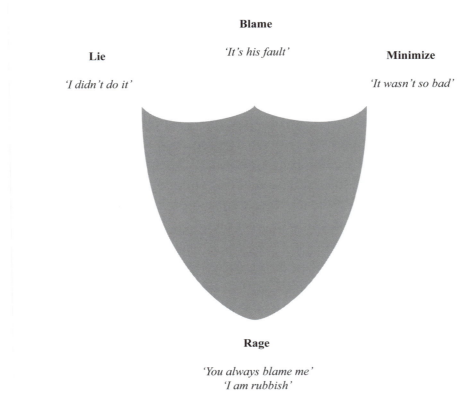

Blame

'It's his fault'

Lie

'I didn't do it'

Minimize

'It wasn't so bad'

Rage

'You always blame me'
'I am rubbish'

FIGURE 11.1 SHIELD AGAINST SHAME [IN GOLDING & HUGHES, 2012]

Teachers and teaching assistants are advised to recognize the shame that underlies these behaviours. Too much attention to the behaviours will only increase feelings of shame and thus reinforce the shield. If instead teachers and teaching assistants help the student to regulate the feelings of shame with empathy and understanding, the shield will weaken and the behaviours will reduce. The student is now on a path towards the development of guilt, and the ability to respond to consequences and to make amends. Again connection has to precede correction; only in this way will the student be able to take responsibility for behaviour instead of becoming overwhelmed by this behaviour.

Summary: challenges in supporting the emotional needs of students with attachment difficulties

Managing need for dependency versus independence

- Don't be tempted to push the student to be more independent.

- The route to independence is via dependency.

- Understand the emotional age of the student and support at this age.

- Apparent 'pseudomaturity' can mask dependency needs of some students.

- Support the student to accept dependency.

- This can be challenging when it appears counter to the objective of the setting to help students be more independent.

Maintaining high boundaries and high warmth

- All students do best in an atmosphere of authoritative education support.

- This provides warmth, support for autonomy and appropriate boundaries.

- Boundaries provide consistency, predictability, routines and consequences.

- Warmth provides nurturing support, encouraging autonomy.

- If students are to benefit from consequences and behavioural guidance, they will need support for their emotional insecurity.

- Students with attachment difficulties often have core beliefs in their own badness.

- Without a high degree of warmth from supportive adults, students are much more likely to enter a state of shame.

- Experience of shame tends to cut students off from relationships.

Managing behaviour while supporting emotional development

- The challenging behaviour of the student with complex emotional needs can oppose our expectations and values.

- Behavioural management programmes respond in a way which discourages the inappropriate behaviours and encourages alternative behaviours.

- We provide a 'correction' by rewarding a behaviour we want to increase and provide a negative consequence for a behaviour we want to reduce.

- Emotional development thrives on connection, not correction.

- When we connect emotionally to a student, we recognize and understand the emotional experience which has led to the behaviour.

- Students with attachment difficulties are at particular risk of missing out on connection as their difficulties make them distrustful of emotional connection with another.

- When developing support tailored to the emotional needs of the student it is vital that connection precedes correction.

Supporting students with shame-based difficulties

- The experience of shame is part of the socialization process, via breaks in attunement leading to shame and behaviour inhibition.

- Attunement, breaks and relationship repair are healthy for students.

- When discipline is harsh, punitive or inconsistent and when relationships are not repaired, students will experience unregulated shame.

- If the healthy development of guilt does not develop – an emotion which drives us to make amends – the student gets stuck in shame.

- These students learn to put up a 'shield against the shame', leading to defensive behaviours such as lying, minimizing, blaming others and raging.

- Too much attention to the behaviours will only increase feelings of shame and thus reinforce the shield.

- By helping the student to regulate the feelings of shame with empathy and understanding, the shield will weaken and the behaviours will reduce.

12

Supporting Students with Multiple Difficulties

Many of the students who especially concern us in schools have complex emotional needs stemming not only from attachment difficulties but also from neurodevelopmental difficulties. These difficulties originate in a combination of early experience and genetic vulnerability. Difficult early experience can impact on neurodevelopment: the brain develops within a social environment and therefore is vulnerable to poor development when the social environment is poor.

Additionally difficult early experience can exacerbate genetic difficulties that the student was born with. All of this can be difficult to unpick, and teachers and teaching assistants are often left struggling to know whether they are supporting a student with attachment difficulties, developmental difficulties or both. An educational psychologist can be helpful in advising on further assessment and providing advice about support for these students.

Fortunately many of the ideas for supporting students with attachment difficulties are also helpful for students with neurodevelopmental difficulties. Likewise ways of supporting students with neurodevelopmental problems can be helpful for students with attachment difficulties.

Students with generalized learning difficulty

The experience of a generalized learning difficulty can increase the difficulty that students have in building and maintaining relationships. Thus the risk of attachment difficulties is increased and the subsequent difficulties in attachment and relationships can cause emotional distress, leading to the development of challenging behaviours. In addition, the difficulties that the students have may make them less responsive, or less clear, in what they signal. This can affect the communication between adult and student. Learning difficulties may slow down the process of learning about relationships, and in adjusting to change and new routines.

These students may therefore have more difficulty in adjusting to and feeling secure in school. They may take longer to respond to the consistent and nurturing care that the school is providing, and they may find it difficult to communicate their distress because of both the attachment difficulty and the learning difficulty.

With these students it is important to focus on reducing emotional distress, increasing security and building relationships. As the emotional distress is reduced and relationship development is facilitated, the behavioural difficulties will also reduce (e.g. see O'Driscoll 2009).

Students with autism

Peter Hobson (2002) has identified how problems within the child or within the environment can lead to 'autistic' difficulties. Children need the mental equipment (nature) and experience of other people (nurture) to allow them to experience interpersonal relations with others.

Many children with autism do develop secure attachments in early life. For example, in one research study 50 per cent of children with autism were shown to have developed a secure attachment to their mother (Koren-Karie *et al.* 2009). However, it can be more difficult for carers to interpret signals from the children because of their social difficulties. Thus risk of attachment difficulty is increased. It might be that children with autism are more vulnerable in families where parenting difficulties are already high.

Students with attachment difficulties are similar to students with autism in responding well to a highly structured environment, with predictability and lots of preparation for change. Therefore, the use of visual calendars and Social Stories™ can be helpful whether the emotional difficulties the student is presenting are due to neurodevelopmental or attachment difficulties, or a combination of both.

Students with sensory integration difficulties

Young children depend on adults to provide for their sensory needs and thus to foster the development of the nervous system. Children with attachment difficulties may have missed out on important experiences, usually occurring during nurturing care, which help the sensory systems to develop and to work in an integrated way. Similarly exposure to trauma during pregnancy or early infancy can alter the way the infant's brain develops and how he or she organizes sensory experiences. Eadaoin Bhreathnach (2006) highlighted that children who have a history of separation, loss, abuse and neglect are more likely to present with both attachment and sensory processing difficulties.

This is therefore another difficulty that emerges out of a combination of genetic and environmental factors. Sensory integration is the ability of the central nervous system to organize and process input from different sensory channels to make an adaptive response (Ayres 1972). Students with difficulties in this area are not able to use sensory information easily to plan and carry out actions. This makes everyday experiences unpleasant or overwhelming. For example, a student may struggle to sit comfortably surrounded by other students, or may not be able to sit still on a chair. These difficulties can have a significant impact on a student's emotional regulation and learning.

Some students may have difficulty modulating their responses to sensory input, which means they may over- or under-respond to certain sensory experiences. These students may present with either hypersensitivity or hyposensitivity to a greater or lesser degree.

Hypersensitivity

The hypersensitive student has a low threshold for sensory input and is therefore quickly overwhelmed, leading to a strong emotional response and defensive reactions. These students may struggle with auditory or visual stimulation. Such students may, for example, respond aggressively when touched unexpectedly; they may dislike certain textures or fabrics or certain smells, or they may avoid messy tasks or areas which are visually stimulating. Similarly they may become overwhelmed quickly in noisy environments or in response to unexpected noise, and may make noise themselves to drown out these noises.

If the vestibular system is hypersensitive, students will struggle with balance and heights. They may avoid physical education and similar activities.

Hyposensitivity

The hyposensitive student has a high threshold for sensory input and therefore ignores or is relatively unaffected by sensory stimuli to which most people would respond. These students often seek out intense sensory experiences, and are therefore described as sensory-seeking. Such students may, for example, be unaware that they have been touched, be constantly touching or smelling things, or seek out rough-and-tumble play excessively. They may sit close to the television or prefer bright, flashing toys. They may seek out loud noise, preferring noisy activities, and they may talk loudly themselves.

Students who have low sensitivity to proprioception may appear uncoordinated with low muscle tone. They seek out activities that involve heavy resistance – pushing and pulling or climbing, for example.

If the vestibular system is hyposensitive, the students may have exaggerated movements and seek out activities such as spinning and climbing.

Alongside the checklist observations, notice the types of movement the student is engaging in. Advice about how to help these students can be found in a range of books by Carol Stock Kranowitz and colleagues (e.g. Koomar *et al.* 2001; Kranowitz 2005). Advice can also be sought from the local paediatric occupational therapy service.

Students who demonstrate extreme non-compliance and explosive behaviour

There are a group of students who are fragile neurodevelopmentally because they have difficulties not only with compliance to adult demands but also with regulation of their behaviour. These are also examples of difficulties that can arise within the development of attachment difficulties, although at its extreme it is likely to be the result of both genetic and environmental factors. Ross Greene (2010), in his book *The Explosive Child,* describes these young people as being developmentally delayed in the skills of flexibility and in being able to tolerate frustration.

The root of this difficulty is poor executive functioning. Executive functioning skills are governed by frontal and prefrontal areas of the brain. Brain development in this area can be particularly influenced by lack of good early parenting experience, although some children are born genetically more at risk of these difficulties.

Difficulties in executive functioning can lead to emotional distress and frustration which is displayed through non-compliant and/or explosive behaviour. These students can have difficulties in the following areas:

- *Cognitive shifting:* this means they find it difficult to mentally adjust to changing circumstances. Imagine a student who is told to go to the library ready to read with a mentor. The mentor doesn't arrive and the student then has to deal with a quick change of plan. The student is ready for reading and cannot quickly adjust to not reading after all.

- *Organization and planning:* students have increasingly sophisticated abilities to form a plan of action and to use this plan to solve a problem based on the ability to organize and plan. A student with this difficulty might find it hard to work out what to do when a problem presents itself. For example, a girl who is asked to take a message to the office, but when she arrives finds the office empty, may not have the ability to work out what to do in this situation.

- *Self-regulation:* students need to be able to regulate their emotional reaction to an event well enough to be able to plan and behave in a way that reaches a goal. When you can emotionally manage a problem, you will be able to think and thus solve the problem. A boy wants to join his peers in a game of football, for example. There is no obvious pause in the game so that he can join in. He needs to think about how to reach his goal of joining the game. This might be asking the others if he can join in, or waiting until a natural break occurs. If his emotional reaction to the lack of an opening, such as anxiety or frustration, is not managed, the student will not be able to think through how to reach this goal.

- *Problems with attention and impulse control:* these difficulties can make it difficult for a student to manage his or her initial impulsive reaction to a problem, in order to focus on the problem, and to attend to the important things needed to solve this problem. The student cannot filter out the unimportant so that he or she attends to what is important. A boy picks up a pencil just as a girl is reaching for it. The girl needs to inhibit her first impulse – probably to snatch the item or to push her peer. She can then focus on the problem that she has lost access to the pencil. If she cannot inhibit this impulse, she won't be able to engage in the problem-solving. These students benefit from being supported by a key adult who knows them well. This adult can spot difficulties as they arise, stepping in early to support the child, and helping him or her to develop the missing skills in the process.

Students with ADHD

Some students demonstrating the difficulties described in the previous section are diagnosed as having attention deficit hyperactivity disorder (ADHD). This is also a problem with faulty executive functioning, leading to poor attention span and impulse control, combined with excessive activity levels. As with the previous difficulties, it is hard to sort out cause from effect with these students, especially when there are known home difficulties for them. Did genetic difficulties with activity and attention contribute to poor early parenting experience or did poor early parenting experience impact on the development of these students, leading to or exacerbating the activity and attention difficulties?

These students need to attend classrooms that are adapted to the difficulties that they are displaying. They need to be supported by teachers and teaching assistants who know them well, with opportunities to get outside and 'run off steam'. Research suggests that exercise, especially rough-and-tumble games, can be beneficial for these students, improving their ability to focus and concentrate (Panksepp 2007). Appropriately supervised time outside can help the student to be more successful with indoor activities.

Further advice about supporting students with attention and attachment difficulties can be found in Randy Comfort's book, *Searching to be Found* (Comfort 2008).

Students with FASD

Foetal Alcohol Spectrum Disorder (FASD) is an umbrella term describing the range of effects that can occur in an individual. It is a lifelong disability that can severely affect development because of a mother drinking alcohol during pregnancy. There is no known safe amount of alcohol use during pregnancy or while trying to get pregnant. Alcohol in the mother's blood passes to the baby through the umbilical cord. Drinking alcohol during pregnancy can cause miscarriage, stillbirth and a range of lifelong physical, behavioural, social, emotional and intellectual disabilities.

Each young person with FASD is affected differently. Some have more difficulties and challenges than others. The primary disabilities associated with FASD are difficulties with attention, filtering sensory information, language, memory, planning and initiating activities, regulating emotions and life skills. Often these students have normal intelligence but have difficulty using the information they have in an organized fashion.

FASD is often referred to as the invisible disability. Due to the fact we cannot see the disability it often goes misdiagnosed or undiagnosed. If those diagnosed with FASD are not properly understood and supported at home, at school and in the community they can develop secondary characteristics such as poor school experiences, trouble with the law, drug or alcohol addiction, problems with employment and mental health disorders.

Young people with FASD might have the following characteristics and behaviours, although the extent and severity of such issues vary significantly from young person to young person:

- sleep and sucking problems as a baby

- low body weight

- abnormal facial features, such as a smooth ridge between the nose and upper lip

- small head size and shorter-than-average height

- vision or hearing problems

- problems with the heart, kidney or bones

- poor coordination and dexterity

- hyperactive behaviour

- learning disabilities and speech and language delays

- difficulty with attention, suffering from lapses in concentration and being easily distracted

- poor memory, leading to difficulties in following instructions and retaining information

- poor reasoning and judgement skills

- difficulty in school, especially with Maths, and understanding abstract concepts such as money and time

- social difficulties leading to peer relationship problems, including being bullied, being easily led, or engaging in bullying behaviours

- behavioural difficulties, especially defiant behaviour when frustrated

- intellectual disability or low IQ.

FASD lasts a lifetime. There is no cure for FASD, but research shows that early intervention treatment services can improve a child's development.

To support these students, educational staff will need time and understanding. Students might benefit from being located in a quiet part of the classroom and they will need support with organization and increased structure. This will include warnings that a lesson is soon to finish, repeating instructions and going over individually instructions that have been given to the class or that are written on the board. They are also likely to need considerable support with their peer relationships both within and outside of the classroom.

In recent years there has been more interest in understanding and identifying young people affected by foetal alcohol, although information and guidance has been around since the late 1990s. For example, Diane Davis wrote a handbook for teachers in the 1990s (Davis 1994) which provides a lot of useful guidance.[1]

Conclusion

Students can therefore have a range of developmental difficulties alongside the difficulties more directly stemming from poor early attachment experience. The observation checklist provides structured observations of the social and emotional abilities and difficulties of the student. This information used sensitively alongside an understanding of other neurodevelopmental difficulties that the student is experiencing can help to build up a profile. This will guide staff about the special needs of the student and how to meet these. It will also prompt staff when external advice might be helpful.

Summary: working with students with multiple difficulties

Students with generalized learning difficulty

- The risk of attachment difficulties is increased, and the subsequent difficulties in attachment and relationships can cause emotional distress, leading to the development of challenging behaviours.

- Students may be less responsive, or less clear, in what they signal, leading to communication difficulties between adult and student.

- Learning difficulties may slow down the process of learning about relationships, and in adjusting to change and new routines.

- Students may take longer to respond to the consistent and nurturing care that the educational setting provides.

- It is important to focus on reducing emotional distress, increasing security and building relationships.

Students with autism

- Young people need the mental equipment (nature) and experience of other people (nurture) to allow them to experience interpersonal relations with others.

- Many young people with autism do develop secure attachments in early life.

---

1   The most current information and resources on FASD for educators can be found at www.fasdtrust.co.uk

- However, it can be more difficult for carers to interpret signals from the children because of their social difficulties – thus risk of attachment difficulty is increased.

- It might be that young people with autism are more vulnerable in families where parenting difficulties are already high.

- Students with attachment difficulties are similar to students with autism in responding well to a highly structured environment, with predictability and lots of preparation for change.

- The use of visual calendars and Social Stories™ can be helpful, whether the emotional difficulties the student is presenting are due to neurodevelopmental or attachment difficulties, or a combination of both.

Students with sensory integration difficulties

- Students with attachment difficulties may have missed out on important experiences, usually occurring during nurturing care, which help the sensory systems to develop and to work in an integrated way.

- Exposure to trauma during pregnancy or early infancy can alter the way the infant's brain develops and how he or she organizes sensory experiences.

- Young people who have a history of separation, loss, abuse and neglect are more likely to present with both attachment and sensory processing difficulties.

- Sensory integration is the ability of the central nervous system to organize and process input from different sensory channels to make an adaptive response.

- Students with difficulties in this area are not able to use sensory information easily to plan and carry out actions.

- Everyday experiences are unpleasant or overwhelming, e.g. sitting still.

- These difficulties can have a significant impact on a student's emotional regulation and learning.

- Some students may over-respond (hypersensitivity) or under-respond (hyposensitivity) to certain sensory experiences to a greater or lesser degree.

Students who demonstrate extreme non-compliance and explosive behaviour

- These are difficulties that can arise within the development of attachment difficulties, although at its extreme it is likely to be the result of both genetic and environmental factors. Brain development in this area can be particularly influenced by lack of good early parenting experience.

- These students are developmentally delayed in the skills of flexibility and in being able to tolerate frustration.

- The root of this difficulty is poor executive functioning leading to emotional distress and frustration, which is displayed through non-compliant and/or explosive behaviour.

- These students can have difficulties in cognitive shifting; organization and planning; self-regulation; and attention and impulse control.

- These students benefit from being supported by a key adult who knows them well.

Students with ADHD

- Faulty executive functioning leads to poor attention span and impulse control, combined with excessive activity levels.

- It is hard to sort out cause from effect with these students, especially when there are known home difficulties for the student.

- Genetic difficulties with activity and attention may contribute to poor early parenting experience.

- Poor early parenting experiences impact on the development of these students, leading to or exacerbating the activity and attention difficulties.

- Education environments need to adapt to the difficulties that they are displaying.

- These students benefit from being supported by workers who know them well, with opportunities to get outside and 'run off steam'.

- Rough-and-tumble activities can be beneficial for these students, improving their ability to focus and concentrate.

- Appropriately supervised time outside can help the student to be more successful with indoor activities.

Students with FASD

- This is a lifelong disability that can severely affect development because of a mother drinking alcohol during pregnancy.

- Drinking alcohol during pregnancy can cause miscarriage, stillbirth and a range of lifelong physical, behavioural, social, emotional and intellectual disabilities.

- Each child with FASD is affected differently. Some have more difficulties and challenges than others.

- The primary disabilities associated with FASD are difficulties with attention, filtering sensory information, language, memory, planning and initiating activities, regulating emotions and life skills.

- Often these young people have normal intelligence but have difficulty using the information they have in an organized fashion.

- If not properly understood and supported at home, at school and in the community, students can develop secondary difficulties including school problems, trouble with the law, drug or alcohol addiction, problems with employment and mental health disorders.

- Students with FASD will benefit from understanding and support which helps them to organize themselves and manage instructions. They are also likely to need increased support with peer relationships.

Appendices

Appendix 1
OBSERVATION CHECKLIST

Name of student		Date of birth	
Name of educational setting		Start date	
		Hours attending	
Special educational needs?			
Other settings student may attend			
Name of parents/carers		Language spoken at home	
Address			

Details of observations

The student will be observed over a few days (observation period) by a person who knows him or her well (e.g. teacher or teaching assistant). This key person might make some observations for this tool or might rely on observations that are being routinely made anyway. Further observation periods can be used to monitor progress after implementing an action plan. Different colours for different observation periods will allow ease of monitoring.

Dates of first observation period	Colour used	Key person	Factors affecting the observation (e.g. student's health, changes in the setting, changes at home, etc.)
Dates of second observation period (if needed)	Colour used	Key person	Factors affecting the observation (e.g. student's health, changes in the setting, changes at home, etc.)
Dates of third observation period (if needed)	Colour used	Key person	Factors affecting the observation (e.g. student's health, changes in the setting, changes at home, etc.)

1. General behaviour

		Almost always	Sometimes	As student of same age or stage of development	Sometimes	Almost always	
What is student's behaviour like?	Resists boundaries, non-compliant						Overly compliant, accepts boundaries with little fuss
	Difficult behaviour that is overly challenging/ risk-taking (please see below to clarify); putting self and/or others at risk						Passive but difficult behaviour that is expressed subtly; may display compulsive behaviours such as stealing or self-harm that is concealed
	Emotionally volatile with unpredictable, easily triggered emotional outbursts						Appears very self-contained, too good; rarely displays emotions or if does it is over quickly
Attention, concentration and activity levels?	Loses concentration easily						Concentration can be intense, becomes absorbed in tasks, hard to interrupt
	Impulsive, often acts without thinking						Overly controlled, rarely impulsive
	Restless, highly active						Less active than expected

Attitude to attendance at education setting/ provision		Almost always	Sometimes	As student of same age or stage of development	Sometimes	Almost always	
	Appears engaged in education but as a way of maintaining attention on self						Appears disengaged in education
	Worries and concerns distract from learning, e.g. peer issues						Will abscond from class or setting, may take others with them
	Does not cope well with school, appears immature						Copes well with school, but rather too grown up

Clarification of challenging/risky behaviours including mental health difficulties

Challenging/ risky behaviours		Almost always	Sometimes	As student at same stage of development	Hardly ever	Never
	Sexualized behaviours – language, gestures or body language					
	Substance misuse – drugs, alcohol or other substance misuse					
	Verbally challenging behaviours – attitude/tone of voice					
	Threatening behaviour – verbally/physically					
	Threatening behaviour – weapon use					
	Absconding/self-exclusion					
	Education refusal					
	Risky use of ICT – social media, games, etc.					

Mental health-related difficulties	Self-harm					
	Eating disorders					
	Internalizing difficulties, e.g. anxiety, depression					
	Psychotic behaviours, hallucinations, delusions, appears out of touch with reality					
	Trauma symptoms, e.g. flashbacks, memories, easily triggered fight/flight reactions; dissociates, excessive use of fantasy; hearing voices of past perpetrators					

General behaviour: supporting evidence and comments

2. Classroom-related behaviours

		Almost always	Sometimes	As student of same age or stage of development	Sometimes	Almost always	
Behaviour with other students in the classroom/ lesson setting	Possessive about interacting with other students						Not interested in interacting with other students
	Wants to join in whole class sessions but always needs to be centre of attention						Appears disengaged, reluctant to join in, tries to remain out of view
	Wants to join in with small group sessions but struggles to get on with others						Does not join in with small group sessions easily, tends to remain alone, appears isolated
	Overly controlling and bossy when working with other students						When does interact with another student tends to be easily led

Activity-related behaviour in classroom/ lesson setting	Struggles to engage in tasks as has obsessive need for attention						Quick to give up and will rubbish or destroy work before teacher sees it
	Finds it difficult to settle to task, lacks self-motivation, will constantly seek help, and act more helpless than feels						Tends to get over-involved in task to exclusion of others
	Unable to engage in imaginative activities						Overly absorbed in imaginary world
	Overly competitive, always wants to be first						Overly timid, reluctant to join in

Classroom-related behaviours: supporting evidence and comments

3. Social relationships with peers

		Almost always	Sometimes	As student of same age or stage of development	Sometimes	Almost always	
Behaviour with other students during unstructured times	Overly clingy and needy with peers but struggles to reciprocate and offer support, can't sustain friendships						Dismissive of need for support from peers, keeps emotional distance
	Wants to join in with peers but emotionally needy and volatile, struggles to get along with others						Uses peer group for shared activities so that activity is more important than friendship
	Wants friends but quickly dissatisfied with the relationship						Tends to remain alone, appears isolated; friendships are unimportant but will relate to peers to join in activities
	Frequently complains to adults about peers						Adults rarely know what is going on with peers
	Can be quite confrontational towards other students, may be seen as bullying						Is often controlled or picked on by other students, vulnerable to bullying

Social relationships with peers: supporting evidence and comments

4. Attachment behaviours

How does the student behave with familiar adults?		Almost always	Sometimes	As student of same age or stage of development	Sometimes	Almost always	
	Unusually dependent, always seeking help even when doesn't need it						Unusually independent, will actively reject offers of help
	Always demonstrating vulnerability but frequently dissatisfied with response of others						Dislikes appearing vulnerable or in need of help
	Craves attention, stays close to adult(s), uses range of ways to gain attention						Doesn't want attention, difficult to relate to, avoids eye-contact
	Very clingy, wants to be with adult(s) all the time, will seek attention from range of adults						Hard to get close to, or false quality to relationship
	Overly demanding and attention-needing, talks a lot						Overly self-reliant, undemanding, detached
	Likes to be in control/in charge						Unusually passive, tries too hard to please

How does the student behave with unfamiliar adults?	Overly familiar, gets too physically close						Overly fearful, shy, wary
	Overly demanding and attention-needing						Resists friendly overtures
	Likes to be in control/in charge						Unusually passive, tries too hard to please
	Asks personal questions even though does not mean to be rude						Shows little interest in visitor
How does the student behave when experiencing minor hurts, worries or troubles?	Appears overly distressed with obsessive need to share problems						Acts as if nothing has happened
	Wants lots of comfort or reassurance but always appears dissatisfied						Appears not to need comfort
	Needs lots of soothing and resists being comforted						Appears not to need soothing

Attachment behaviours: supporting evidence and comments

5. Emotional state

		Almost always	Sometimes	As student of same age or stage of development	Sometimes	Almost always	
Current emotional state, considering any current circum-stances?	Appears overly anxious, worried or distressed						No anxieties or concerns even when there is cause
	Appears overly cheerful or happy						Appears sad, withdrawn or flat
	Appears very sensitive, easily upset						Appears indifferent, doesn't show feelings
How does the student display feelings?	It is easy to tell how the student is feeling						Tends to hide feelings away; it is difficult to tell how the student is feeling
	Displays feelings only through angry, challenging or risky behaviour						Tends not to show how he/she is feeling in the way he/she behaves
	Will become abusive or rude if not being attended to, may alternate with charming behaviours						Will become abusive or rude if one tries to offer help or support
	Hurts self obviously and in full view of others to gain attention						Hurts self secretly
	May draw attention to self by humiliating or teasing peers						Tries not to draw attention to self, may hide behind peers

Emotional state: supporting evidence and comments

Any other comments?

What works in this environment for this student?

Action plan to support observation checklist

Name of student			DOB		SEN	
Dates of observation						
Involved professionals						
What works well			Areas for development			
Concern	Target	How will this be achieved?		Resources		Who? Where?
Concern	Target	How will this be achieved?		Resources		Who? Where?
Concern	Target	How will this be achieved?		Resources		Who? Where?
Review date		Action plan shared with				

Appendix 2
Adolescent Development

In Western society there is a clear transition in schooling coinciding with the onset of adolescence. In the UK this transition is marked by the move from primary to secondary education, although in some areas a middle school is used to help make this transition less abrupt. This is generally a move from a small to a much larger school, from classroom-based education to complicated timetables and movement around the school, and from having a class teacher who stays with their pupils through much of the school day to a large number of teachers interacting with the students at different times and in different places. The adolescent is considered to be at a stage of independence that can manage all these changes, alongside the increased expectation for organization and self-learning. This shift in the organization of education assumes that the student will have a reduced need for adult emotional support.

Adolescence is also a developmental stage of huge change and biological reorganization, of the inner drive to be more independent and of the increase in the importance of the peer group over the adults in the young person's life.

The move from primary to secondary education will be a challenging one for all young adolescents. It is going to be especially challenging for the more emotionally immature young people whose development and adjustment is impacted upon by early relational trauma.

In this appendix a brief overview of adolescent development will be provided before in the next two appendices we consider attachment theory and how to support vulnerable young people at this developmental stage make the change to and then progress through their secondary education.

Adolescence as a life stage

Childhood has been viewed differently in different ages and across different cultures. It is very much an adult invention, and is re-invented for different generations. Thus the length of childhood can alter depending on ideas about schooling, childhood employment and other adult-imposed practices (Cunningham and Morpurgo 2006). As childhood became extended, with protections around children working and the legal age for attending school moving later, a new developmental stage was constructed to describe the time between childhood and adulthood. Adolescence was invented and teenagers had arrived.

In all cultures there are biological changes which are associated with a child growing up; the cognitive, social and emotional changes which are also emerging will, however, vary between cultures, as a consequence of the expectations, education and parenting of the young people. Graham Music (2011) notes how the transition into adulthood is later, slower and more piecemeal in modern Western cultures. He suggests that there is less adult involvement than in some other cultures and less clearly defined expectations and endpoints. Whilst there are some markers of transition – for example, leaving school, taking a gap year – Western culture does not have the rituals of some non-Western cultures.

Music (2011) also notes how adolescence can be considered a second chance, with new opportunities for resilience as developmental changes occur. Even young people who have struggled up to this point might emerge more resilient if they get good-quality adult support during this stage. This is an important message for educational staff who might be focused on learning and education but with a broader focus could have a big influence on emotional and social development as well. Adding emotional and social resilience can in turn ensure that the young people make the most out of their educational opportunities.

> When I was a boy of 14 my father was so ignorant I could hardly stand to have the old man around. But when I got to be 21, I was astonished at how much the old man had learned in seven years.

This popular quote, attributed to Mark Twain but probably anonymous, reveals how Western culture views adolescence as a distinct developmental stage, one in which young people appear to hide their uncertainties and confusions behind a mask of knowing it all! As we have moved into the current century it appears that this adolescent developmental stage is starting earlier, and lasting longer. Thus children are entering puberty earlier, whilst at the other end young adults are remaining with parents, or returning to live with parents, following time at university or college, well into their twenties.

Within this chapter the focus will be on adolescence within Western cultures, exploring the development which is occurring alongside the move to secondary education.

Biological changes
Hormonal and chemical changes

For many people it is the hormonal and chemical changes that are really seen as the beginning of adolescence; the teenage years are signalled by moodiness and behavioural changes. Body changes are the most obvious signal of this developmental stage as distinctively different male and female bodies emerge. In girls this is especially marked by the beginning of menarche: an event which has been occurring earlier alongside improvements in Western diet and standard of living. The onset of puberty also appears to be influenced by experience. Thus puberty emerges later for adolescents who have lived in harmonious families, where a father is present and, for girls, where there is a good father–daughter relationship. Poor early experience on the other hand appears to correlate with an earlier onset of puberty in girls. For example, high infant stress and, being adopted from abroad have both shown this correlation. This has been explained as a biological push to reproduce early when the early environment indicates likelihood of danger and therefore a prediction of a shorter lifespan (Music 2011). Whilst this might make biological sense, it seems an added burden for families and schools alike. Young girls who are emotionally immature also have to cope with these earlier biological changes and the behavioural consequences of these.

Patterns of sleeping

One of the biggest frustrations for families, and educational staff wanting to start the school day at 9am, is the biological changes in sleep patterns at adolescence. Teenagers generally need more sleep, and therefore sleep longer and are on a different internal time clock to other family members. The changes in the way melatonin, the biological trigger for sleeping and waking, is released means that adolescents wake on average two hours later than adults. Frustration levels rise for parents trying to get their young people up, and also for teaching staff being faced with barely awake students in the morning, whilst we continue to expect the adolescent to fit in with our time clocks. Starting school later has been shown to lead to increased school performance (Danner and Phillips, cited in Music 2011), but it is difficult to make these adjustments within a culture that is organized around a 9 to 5 working day.

Brain development

Whilst many of the difficulties of adolescence are blamed on hormones, this is a misunderstanding of the biology of adolescence. Changes in chemistry are only one side of this biological coin. To fully understand the differences in adolescence, changes within the brain must also be taken into account.

The human brain is highly immature at birth, with its maturation being heavily influenced by environmental experience. This maturation is marked by increased myelination, the fatty sheath which builds up around neurons, allowing these nerve cells to transmit information up to 100 times faster and thus to increase the complexity of brain functioning. This myelination process begins from the bottom upwards such that the cognitive areas of the brain are myelinated later in childhood and adolescence, with the last area, the dorsal-ventral area of the cortex, not occurring until the mid-twenties.

Executive functioning, the brain's control centre, is maturing during adolescence, but is not yet fully developed. This provides the coordination needed to plan, problem-solve, manage impulses and regulate emotions. The limbic system in contrast is very active, allowing adolescents to take the risks needed to explore their growing independence in the world. Adolescence is a time of much emotionally driven behaviour, with impulsivity and pleasure-seeking both more intense. The active limbic system promotes the search for risk and reward whilst the top-down control of the executive functioning is underdeveloped. A bit like having the accelerator but without the brakes, adolescence is a time of exploration, which can be alarming for the adults around them.

Alongside this there is also a massive reorganization occurring in the adolescent brain marked by the process of synaptic pruning. The brain prunes out many connections that have been underused so that the total number of synaptic connections decrease. Alongside this the popular neuronal paths become hardwired. This prepares the brain for increased specialization. Needed skills can be honed in preparation for adulthood, whilst those skills not needed are reduced. The expression 'use it or lose it' is particularly apt during this developmental stage. During this process young people can be more unpredictable and withdrawn, and a degree of cognitive impairment is apparent (Golding *et al.* 2006). Fortunately these are just temporary states, but the loss of eye-contact, the range of grunts denoting an apparent inability to speak and the other changes of behaviour in adolescence which can be so unsettling for parents are explained by this brain re-organization.

The increased importance of the peer group at adolescence is also matched by changes within the brain. Thus areas involved in social understanding are reorganizing and increasing in synaptic connections, helping the adolescent to learn to negotiate more complex relationships. The social brain works differently in adolescents compared to that of adults. Thus the amygdala is more active and more involved in processing of social cues than the prefrontal cortex (see Music 2011). This can mean that the adolescent is over-reactive to strong facial signals, leading to rapidly triggered fight and flight responses. The over-reactions and eruptions which can be a feature of the teen years is probably understood by this bias within brain functioning. Music (2011, p.188) describes how teenagers 'respond with amygdala-led and other sub-cortical reactivity rather than the as yet underdeveloped prefrontal cortex, which only in time will regulate emotionally reactive brain regions'. Teenagers are driven by more immediate emotional stimuli and are more easily distracted. Research has shown that this is even more marked in fearful and anxious adolescents who have more over-reactive and dysregulated amygdalae (see Music 2011). This might explain why some parents report calm and relatively easy transitions through the teen years whilst others have a much more difficult time. This is especially relevant for adolescents who have experienced a poor early parenting environment, leading them to be hypervigilant for signs of danger. These young people will see an angry face even in neutral expressions, and their increased hypervigilance will mean that they have many more difficulties in concentration and attention to the task in hand.

Emotional and social development

We have already considered that the brain organization of adolescence can make emotional functioning quite challenging, and popularly adolescence is considered, at least within our culture, as a time of emotional upheaval. Alongside this adolescents are trying to figure out who they are and how they fit in with their peers. They are much influenced by the peers they are associating with, and despite parental and other guidance these peer influences are not always the most beneficial!

This can lead to an increase in novelty-seeking and risk-taking alongside efforts to be less dependent upon adults. The adolescent is learning how to leave the safety of home and parents and to make his or her way in the world. Understanding emotional and social development is therefore an important part of understanding the functioning of the typical adolescent.

Social development and peer relationships

Young people's relationships with peers change dramatically during adolescence as their social understanding and ability to reflect on self and others matures. Young people are developing a more mature understanding of the behaviour and emotional experience of their peers and are more able to take into account their feelings and point of view. In particular these young people are learning how to develop and maintain close, reciprocal friendships with varying degrees of intimacy. David Howe (2011) explores how the play of childhood becomes less central in friendships as adolescents use their relationships for emotional exploration and regulation. Thus the amount of self-disclosure increases, and as young people become more aware of their emotional vulnerability they are also more able to share this with friends and to offer mutual support.

Early adolescence is a time of experimentation. Friendships and partnerships can be unstable, frequent changes in best friend or in boyfriend/girlfriend are typical and there is much forming of in groups and out groups. These friendships and peer groups become more settled as the adolescent matures.

Young people who have experienced abuse and neglect earlier in life are particularly vulnerable within their peer relationships (see Music 2011). For example, they have been shown to be more attracted to peer groups involved with delinquency and drug use.

Adolescent identity

Adolescence is a time of re-appraising identity. Young people during this development become more aware of global issues, with a growing political and moral conscience. Additionally they consider what their aspirations are, as the future opens up for them. This can lead to anxiety and uncertainty, but nearer home their growing autonomy, coupled with a degree of egocentricity and as yet underdeveloped perspective-taking skills, can lead to feelings of grandiosity. Adolescents often think they know better than others.

Peer groups exert most influence in helping the adolescent to establish a new sense of identity separate from the family. The young person tries on different roles and ways of being, as evidenced by the experimentation with different hairstyles, fashions and even personality styles typical of this age group.

If this wasn't enough to cope with, the adolescent is also establishing a sexual identity and the drive for sex and romance is high. Adolescents spend a large amount of time thinking about romantic relationships, whether real or in fantasy, and anxiety around these potential relationships can be high. With strong moral principles around sexual encounters having reduced in Western cultures, and an earlier onset of puberty, the age of first sexual encounters is now earlier. Young people are trying to manage the emotional intensity of these experiences whilst still being relatively immature and with a sexual identity newly forming.

Parental and peer influence are both features of adolescence, but these influences are different, with parents having more influence on academic and career-related matters, an influence that seems to be greater for girls than boys. Peers, on the other hand, assume the ascendancy for the development of identity and social aspirations (see Music 2011).

Emotional health and well-being

Given the many developmental challenges of adolescence, biologically and culturally, and the rapid biological changes not always in step with these challenges, it is not surprising that emotional and mental health is vulnerable during this stage of development. Adolescence is associated with low mood and increased rates of depression and anxiety (see Music 2011). This is the stage when eating disorders, antisocial behaviour and psychotic illnesses can all become apparent. Worryingly, levels of self-harming behaviours appear to be on the increase within this age group, and there is ongoing concern about risks of alcohol, drug use and sexual and criminal exploitation.

The most vulnerable groups to all of these difficulties will be those who have experienced the most difficult experience during childhood. Abuse, neglect, family disruption, loss and separation will all increase the risks of emotional ill health as the young person takes on the additional challenges of adolescence.

Attachment development

The development of attachment relationships is an important part of early child development. During middle childhood, if these relationships are successful, attachment will take a back seat to learning and exploration. However, the formation of the early attachment relationships will continue to have an influence on the child, and this becomes especially prominent again during adolescence. Toddlers use their attachment relationships as a secure base in order to explore the world. In a similar way, but on a bigger world stage, adolescents are also driven to explore, extending their exploration and preparing for the independent life ahead.

Whereas infants and children demonstrate multiple patterns of attachment with different caregivers and close supportive adults, by adolescence young people have developed an integrated strategy for approaching attachment relationships. This pattern predicts behaviour in new attachment and caregiving relationships; thus it influences the young people's search for peer and intimate relationships as well as their ongoing relationships with parents and supportive adults. Multiple models in childhood provide flexibility and adaptability, but the cognitive task moving towards adulthood is for specialization – hence this cognitive reorganization of attachment representation.

Once again the security of attachment will be an important influence on how well this search for independence goes. Howe (2011) describes how parents are the steady and continuous backdrop for adolescents' search for independence. The relational templates formed and the experience of closeness and intimacy that parents have provided will impact on the way adolescents approach new relationships, including romantic relationships.

Good relationships with parents are associated with relationship success in adolescence. For example, experience of a secure attachment has been associated with greater autonomy, flexibility and open communication styles in adolescence. In romantic relationships these young people have a greater capacity for intimacy, demonstrate more warmth and display less hostility.

When attachment needs have not been satisfactorily met during childhood the young people will have more difficulties in the range of relationships they are engaging with. In addition the renegotiation of their relationship with their parents is made more difficult as the need to separate from parents activates the insecure attachment system at the same time as they are seeking independence. It can be very confusing when the need for attachment security from parents occurs at the same time as there is a strong drive for independence (see Howe 2011).

Disorganized attachment experience in the early years unsurprisingly poses the most difficulty. This early experience predicts a greater risk of mental health difficulties in adolescence (Music 2011). As in many areas of development, very early experience has a long-lasting impact.

Whilst not a necessary feature of adolescence, conflict with parents can increase during this developmental stage. The adolescent often wants more independence than the parent is comfortable with, and influence by the peer group overtakes the influence of parents. However, increased maturity also means that the young people can more easily discuss, negotiate and thus resolve this conflict. Young people whose life experience has led to developmental immaturities will be at a disadvantage, being heavily influenced by peers and often getting into conflict with parents, but not having the skills to resolve these conflicts easily. As with younger children, secure attachment provides a healthy dependency which makes the development of independence more straightforward.

An understanding of attachment in adolescence would not be complete without consideration of the attachment to peer groups that is such an important part of this life stage, replacing to some extent the security that parents have so far offered. The group becomes a new secure base, reducing the fear that might be experienced as the young people move out into the world. The support and encouragement from these group relationships facilitates exploration and discovery about self and others.

Brisch (2009) describes how different attachment styles develop in relation to groups much as they do in dyadic child–parent relationships.

Securely attached adolescents will be able to develop stable new attachments outside of the family and comfortably move between family and peer attachments. These young people will be sensitive and emotionally available to others, demonstrate mutual respect and cooperation and are able to take responsibility within the group, seeking prosocial solutions to conflict.

Insecure-avoidant group attachment is marked by the use of the group for shared activities and exploration but not to engage in emotional relationships. These young people will often leave the family prematurely in favour of peers but avoid emotional closeness. They prefer to use their own resources rather than rely on friendship when experiencing emotional needs.

Insecure-ambivalent group attachment is distinguished by intense fluctuations between group and individual activities as the young person oscillates between a need for closeness and an avoidance of this. These young people find it difficult to reconcile their need to separate from their family with their continuing need for security from the family. They want to join groups but remain highly dependent on family.

As would be expected, this all becomes much trickier for those young people traumatized by their past experience and who developed disorganized patterns of relating with early attachment figures. These young people will replicate this disorganized-controlling pattern within the groups they join. Thus they might idealize the group as providing protection, a sense of safety and a sense of power and agency whilst also experiencing intensely hostile, aggressive and frightened feelings towards other group members. This can be reflected in a range of ways; for example, Brisch (2009) highlights how some young people will avoid group membership whilst others demonstrate quickly changing allegiances. Some young people will use provocation and aggression towards peers outside of the group in order to secure group support or might develop difficulties (e.g. eating difficulties, self-harming) in order to maintain the attention of other group members. These young people are unpredictable and constantly seeking demonstrations of allegiance, but are rarely satisfied. Peers are viewed as either all good or all bad, making the sustaining of relationships difficult.

Adolescence is therefore a time of using earlier relationship templates to explore an expanding range of peer and adult relationships. Whilst early experience can be replicated, it is also a time of opportunity. Brisch (2009) describes how the support of new adult or peer attachment figures from outside of the family can move young people who are insecure onto a more secure track.

Cognitive development

Maturing intellectual abilities during adolescence lead to more complex and profound thinking abilities. This is aided by enhanced working memory and improvements in managing competing information (see Music 2011). In particular adolescents have a developing ability for abstract thought which allows them to build on their experience and to develop problem-solving skills. The increased expectations for learning, organization and independence at adolescence is helped by this cognitive maturation.

Early patterns of attachment can influence a young person's ability to process information throughout life. Again it is the children with the poorest early experience who are most vulnerable moving into adolescence. Cognitive maturation happens more slowly, whilst biological maturation continues or is even advanced. These young people will struggle to meet increased expectations by adults and peers. They have difficulties regulating intense emotions, and weaker abilities to reflect on their experience and thus process this. Their perspective-taking skills are poor, and therefore they struggle to understand or take into account the experience of other people. Core cognitive skills for comprehending, organizing, planning and taking action are compromised because of poor executive functioning, especially in young people who suffered severe neglect early in life. Whilst their intellectual ability might be average or above, their capacity to utilize this intellectual potential is compromised because this 'central control panel' in the brain is underfunctioning. This can be frustrating for others who see an intellectually able young person and fail to recognize the emotional and cognitive deficits beneath the intellectual ability. It can be difficult to find services to help these young people, when services are so often available on the basis of global intellectual ability rather than on assessment of adaptive functioning. Vostanis (2014) describes how these young people continue to think concretely rather than abstractly, and experience difficulty predicting routine social interactions or anticipating how to resolve everyday challenges. Expectations of them can be unrealistic, especially when apparent lack of conformity to norms and expectations are viewed as wilful rather than due to immaturity and a lack of skills.

Substance misuse

As we have explored earlier in this chapter, adolescence is a time of much change and reorganization within the brain. This represents both an opportunity and a risk. It is an opportunity to give the adolescent some good experiences which can help to shape the brain reorganization: healthy relationships, learning opportunities and good peer experiences will all help to make a resilient brain. The risk, however, is that the adolescent will engage in experiences which will be harmful to this brain reorganization. The risk-taking of adolescence, with less openness to adult support and guidance, is a damaging cocktail for the vulnerable brain. Substance misuse is high on the list of the more damaging experiences that young people can engage in. Music (2011) provides a description of some of the impact that this can have on the brain. For example, the hippocampus can be damaged, affecting memory formation and retention; marijuana use has been associated with memory loss and difficulties with planning and attention; whilst smoking will lead to increases in nicotine receptors in the brain. Young people are vulnerable to the addictive qualities of drugs like cocaine; these will lead to an increase in dopamine levels which are already altered during this life stage. Cannabis use has been shown to increase risk of the development of psychotic symptoms.

Alongside the physiological consequences of substance misuse the young people will be susceptible to increases in risk-taking behaviours. The influence of peer group is strong, and vulnerability to exploitation by older group members can lead young people into crime and antisocial behaviours, as they try to fit in and belong.

Conclusion

Adolescence is a stage of active, purposeful flight away from earlier attachment relationships. It represents the transition to increased autonomy, and a reduced reliance on parental support. It prepares the young person for the adult relationships and tasks ahead.

In order to achieve this, young people will have to renegotiate their relationships, moving away from parental attachment relationships to a wider range of emotionally reciprocal relationships. This shift from parents to long-term friends for security means that attachment needs are transferred and transformed from hierarchical attachments, where parents offer security to the child, to non-hierarchical friendships, where young people give and receive care and support.

A highly active exploratory system motivates adolescents to develop independence, a task which is easier to do if they have secure attachment relationships to return to when needed. Thus autonomy is most easily established from a base of secure relationships that will endure beyond adolescence. Adolescents can explore living independently from parents because they know that they can turn to parents in cases of real need.

These developmental challenges of this life stage are made easier when adolescents have mature emotional, social and cognitive functioning. The ability to think flexibly, to hold multiple perspectives in mind, to plan and organize, to regulate emotionally and to establish reciprocal relationships with peers will all make for a smoother transition through adolescence. This will allow the young people to successfully explore peer, friendship and sexual relationships; to feel comfortable with intimacy and to cope with distance from attachment figures; to appraise childhood experiences and explore the wider world; and to build a strong sense of self and identity. By the end of adolescence the young person will be ready to move from being a receiver of care from parents to being a partner and potential caregiver to their own progeny.

Insecure attachment relationships lead to difficulties in the adolescent renegotiating their relationship with parents and other supportive relationships. This can lead to an activation of the attachment system at the same time as the young person is attempting to become more independent, a potentially confusing and troubling experience.

Young people with severe attachment difficulties will be less able to cope with transition and change, be emotionally younger than their peers with less mature thinking abilities, and less able to feel safe and secure. This means they will have greater difficulty focusing attention on social or learning tasks. Whilst in need of increased support from adults they will be less able to trust in or use this support and they will be at increased risk of mental health difficulties, including eating disorders, self-harm, risk-taking, depression and anxiety. They will be more likely to seek relief in drugs and alcohol, increasing risk physiologically and socially, and can be vulnerable to becoming involved in antisocial behaviour or to sexual or criminal exploitation.

These more vulnerable young people will need increased social and learning support in school, but their challenging behaviour will mean that they will be difficult to support and they will quickly alienate others. They will need adults around them with a good understanding of these difficulties, a willingness to understand the lived experience of the young person, and sufficient 'stickability' to hang on in there even when the young person is doing their best to push them away.

Summary

Adolescence as a life stage

- Transition from childhood to adulthood.

- Marked by move from primary to secondary education.

- Cultural differences in adolescence as a consequence of differing expectations, education and parenting.

- 'Second chance' to build resilience underpinned by brain reorganization.

Biological changes

HORMONAL AND CHEMICAL CHANGES

- Onset of puberty.

- Distinctly different male and female bodies develop.

PATTERNS OF SLEEPING

- Biological changes in sleep patterns.

- Wake later, sleep longer and have a different internal time clock.

BRAIN DEVELOPMENT

- Myelination of the cognitive structures of the brain facilitates maturation of thinking processes continuing into early adulthood.

- Synaptic pruning leads to reorganization of the brain with increased specialization and reduced flexibility.

- Executive functioning is maturing, leading to improved abilities to plan, problem-solve, manage impulses and regulate emotions.

- Limbic system is very active, increasing risk-taking and emotionally driven behaviour. Impulsivity and pleasure-seeking are more intense.

- Driven by more immediate emotional stimuli and are more easily distracted.

- Areas involved in social understanding are reorganizing and maturing, but more driven by amygdala and less by prefrontal cortex compared to adults. Biases brain to be vigilant to social threat and to quickly triggered fight/flight responses.

Emotional and social development

SOCIAL DEVELOPMENT AND PEER RELATIONSHIPS

- Peer relationships change as social understanding increases.

- More able to take into account feelings and point of view of peers.

- Developing and maintaining close, reciprocal friendships including intimate relationships.

- Friendships used for emotional exploration and regulation.

- Experimentation in friendships and peer groups, including in groups and out groups; becoming more stable and continuous as adolescent matures.

ADOLESCENT IDENTITY

- Experimentation and formation of new sense of identity.

- More aware of global issues, with a growing political and moral conscience.

- Start to look to the future and have ambitions and aspirations.

- Confusion and uncertainty but also feelings of grandiosity, of knowing better than others.

- Peer influences for development of identity and social aspirations, whilst parents continue to be an influence on academic and career decisions.

- Establishing sexual identity, with high drive for sex and romance, and earlier-occurring sexual experiences.

EMOTIONAL HEALTH AND WELL-BEING

- Increases in low mood and rates of depression and anxiety.

- Onset of eating disorders, antisocial behaviour and psychotic illnesses.

- Increases in self-harming behaviours, alcohol, drug use and sexual and criminal exploitation.

Attachment development

- Developing integrated strategy for approaching attachment relationships which predicts behaviour in new relationships.

- Previous attachment experience influences peer relationships as well as ongoing relationship with parents and supportive adults.

- Good relationships with parents facilitates relationship success, achievement of autonomy, flexibility and capacity for intimacy.

- Conflict with parents can increase alongside increasing influence of peer group.

- Increased ability to discuss, negotiate and resolve conflict.

- Secure attachment provides healthy dependency, making development of independence more straightforward.

- Peer group is new secure base; secure attachment experience predicts success within peer group, whilst insecure attachment experience will lead to adolescents who struggle with aspects of peer relationships avoiding emotional closeness or struggling with conflicting needs to join peer groups and not to separate from families.

- Opportunities for wider relationships with adults and peers to help young people move from insecure to secure.

Cognitive development

- Maturing thinking abilities.

- Developing ability for abstract thought and executive functioning.

Substance misuse

- Increase of risk-taking combined with vulnerable, reorganizing brain can lead to risks from lure of drugs and alcohol for some adolescents.

- Risks to hippocampus affecting memory.

- Risks of marijuana for memory loss and planning and attention difficulties.

- Smoking increases nicotine receptors in brain.

- Vulnerable to addiction from dopamine-increasing drugs.

- Cannabis use associated with increased episodes of psychosis.

The disadvantaged adolescence

Experience of early relational trauma impacts on development and adjustment in the following ways.

BIOLOGICAL DEVELOPMENT

- Earlier onset of puberty in girls.

- Brain development is sensitized for danger with over-reactive and dysregulated amygdalae; hypervigilant for signs of danger; and reduced concentration and attention to task in hand.

SOCIAL DEVELOPMENT

- Struggle to meet expectations of adults and peers.

- Difficulties in range of relationships with peers and adults.

- Heavily influenced by peers, increased conflict with parents and poorer ability to resolve conflicts.

- Vulnerable within peer relationships and more attracted to peer groups involved with delinquency and drug use.

- More likely to engage in substance misuse and antisocial behaviour, and vulnerable to sexual or criminal exploitation.

EMOTIONAL DEVELOPMENT

- Emotionally immature.

- Difficulties regulating intense emotions.

- Less able to cope with transition and change.

- Increased risks to emotional ill health, with increased vulnerability to mental health difficulties.

ATTACHMENT DEVELOPMENT

- Struggle to renegotiate relationship with parents as driven to separate and search for independence whilst continuing to need parents for attachment security.

- Disorganized attachment increases risk of mental health difficulties, and will impact detrimentally on friendships and peer group participation, increasing both idealization and hostility towards peers.

COGNITIVE DEVELOPMENT

- Cognitive maturation is slower, and reflective abilities are weaker.

- Poor executive functioning leads to difficulties comprehending, organizing, planning and taking action; adaptive functioning can be poor, even in intellectually able children.

- Continue to think concretely rather than abstractly.

- Poor perspective-taking skills means struggle to understand or take into account the experience of other people, and reduced social understanding means they struggle to predict routine social interaction or anticipate how to resolve challenges.

Appendix 3
Attachment Theory and Educational Settings

In this appendix we expand on Chapter 3 to provide a more in-depth overview of attachment theory and discuss its relevance for those caring for students in educational settings. An understanding of this theory of relationship development will help education staff better understand the emotional needs of the students in their care.

What is attachment theory?

Attachment theory was first proposed by John Bowlby (see Bowlby 1973, 1980, 1982, 1998) and expanded with the work of Mary Main (see Main and Solomon 1986) and Mary Ainsworth (see Ainsworth *et al.* 1978). Attachment theory is essentially a theory of how children develop, with a particular focus on the influence of early relationships. The theory describes the impact this early experience has on the way the child approaches later relationships and how this influences social, emotional and cognitive development.

Attachment theory suggests that infants are born biologically predisposed to form attachment relationships with their parents and carers. In this discussion we will use the term parent to describe those who are currently parenting the children. These parent–child relationships are used by the children not only to elicit security and comfort, but also as a secure base from which to explore and learn in the world. Innate drives to attach and to explore are both present within the child. When children feel safe and secure, they will explore. If, however, their feelings of safety are threatened, the desire to explore reduces and the children will seek comfort from their parents. In this way the parent becomes an attachment figure, available to the child to provide security when needed.

The young child therefore develops a set of attachment behaviours which serve to keep the parent close when the child is experiencing increased stress. These are:

- *Proximity seeking:* the child moves closer to the parent.

- *Separation protest:* the child protests at separation from the parent by crying.

- *Secure base effect:* the child derives comfort from the presence of the parent.

> ## Attachment and exploration
>
> Imagine Lucy and her mum visiting the classroom for the first time. When they first arrive Lucy is wary, remaining close to her mum. Her attachment needs are high in this new environment.
>
> Gradually Lucy begins to feel confident and she starts to explore the room. She 'homes in' on the dressing-up corner and moves over to watch the children putting on the costumes. Her exploration needs are high now. At this point the school bell rings. This is mildly alarming for Lucy, who wasn't expecting it. This triggers the attachment system. Lucy returns to her mum in order to feel secure again.
>
> Like a see-saw, the attachment and exploration needs rise and fall; as attachment needs rise, exploration falls, and vice versa.

These behaviours are triggered by anxiety, fear or need for comfort; for example, when:

- there is actual or threatened separation from the parent at a time when the child is experiencing insecurity

- there are alarming conditions within the environment, such as the presence of someone unfamiliar

- the carer is rejecting or psychologically unavailable to the child

- the child is feeling tired and unwell.

As children grow older they become more confident in the world. The attachment behaviours become less obvious as they get on with the job of learning and exploring in the wider world they are encountering. However, at times of increased stress they will again seek support and comfort from their attachment figures. Adolescence brings a whole new set of stressors – emotional, social and biological. The adolescent is also managing changes of educational setting, with all the additional demands and expectations that this brings. Given all these changes it is not surprising that attachment behaviours become prominent again at this developmental stage. The adolescent, however, can find this difficult; the drive towards independence and concern about what peers might think can mean that seeking support from parents presents its own challenges.

School transfer: Lucy

Lucy is now 11 years old and will be transferring to the local secondary school in the autumn. As she struggles with emotional difficulties it is decided that she will need some additional visits to her new school during the summer. As the time of these visits approaches, Lucy becomes more challenging at home. She gets cross quickly with her brother and becomes more non-compliant when asked to do things by her parents. There is a noticeable increase in door slamming! When Mum wonders if she is worried about leaving her school and moving to the new school, she angrily denies this and retreats to her bedroom. Mum leaves her for a while and then takes her up a cup of hot chocolate. Tearfully Lucy snuggles in to her mum and admits that she is feeling scared about the new school. She knows there is a visit coming up and she is worried about how this will go. There have been some stories going around the class about what the older children do to the 'new kids'. Mum asks Lucy if she would like her to come on the visit with her. Lucy would like this but she thinks the other children will tease her if she has her mum with her. Mum agrees to talk with her teaching assistant about her worries so that they can plan the visit together.

Sheila, the teaching assistant, talks through the impending visit with Lucy. Sheila will take her and will be available to support her during the visit. Together they draw up a visual calendar of what will happen on the day and make a map of the school. They plan where the teaching assistant will be if Lucy needs her and arrange a time and place to meet at intervals during the visit. The visit goes well, and Lucy gets on well with her buddy who shows her around the school. She is relieved to see Sheila at their prearranged times. That night Lucy talks enthusiastically about her new school to her mum. She especially likes the gymnasium and looks forward to being able to do an individual programme instead of competitive sports.

Children and young people of all ages need to know that their attachment figures are available and able to sensitively meet their emotional needs. This is about the parent being not only physically present but also psychologically available – ready to respond to the child or young person when needed.

Young children are dependent upon close contact with an attachment figure. This may be their parent, substitute carer or someone involved in providing nurture, such as a child-minder. When children are upset or distressed, they need physical contact to soothe them. As they grow older, they will still need to draw security from attachment figures, but they will be able to tolerate longer periods away from them. They will also be calmed by the presence of the parents, through verbal reassurance, as well as by physical contact. At adolescence the young person continues to need support but does not always signal this in a straightforward way. Parents need to be good at recognizing the emotional need underneath the behaviour so that they can give the support and comfort needed.

From their early experience within attachment relationships, children develop a cognitive model of how relationships work (called an internal working model). This means that they have a memory of relationships, which influences how they respond in later relationships. Their later experience will influence and modify this model, but children remain strongly influenced by their early experience. The quality of the relationship with parents will influence children's social and emotional development.

During adolescence these internal working models become organized into a state of mind-informing expectations about self and others. Memories of past relationships influence the way that the young person creates a mental representation of who they think they are and what they expect from other people. This influences their developing peer relationships as well as their ongoing relationships with parents and other supportive adults. The emerging personality is heavily influenced by these mental representations as the differing relationship experiences from the past become coordinated into a set of expectations in the present. Relationships become self-fulfilling and assumptions about self become self-confirming as these expectations guide how the young person responds to different situations, and people in turn respond to the young person in line with the expectations held about how they will behave. In this way new relationships have a habit of repeating old relationship patterns, and the personality becomes formed in the light of this experience. Only when another actively resists conforming to expectations will the young person be able to modify their mental representations, opening up new possibilities for them.

The quality of earlier relationships will therefore impact on young people when they are at school. This will influence the degree to which they can trust other adults and therefore feel safe at school. It will also influence the degree to which they can focus away from their attachment needs and attend to learning. Prior experience will strongly influence the way a young person approaches high school, and as their expectations influence peers and school staff, history can indeed repeat itself. There is, however, also an opportunity here for sensitive, supportive adults to respond differently and to help the young person adjust their expectations at a critical point of their development when internal working models are becoming more organized and more defined.

School transfer: Jack

Jack has struggled through his primary school years and has got a reputation for being disruptive and difficult. He tends to form friendships with peers who take advantage of his vulnerability and thus lead him astray. Adults have tried various behavioural strategies to bring him to order but with little success.

As Jack moves into the high school he again falls in with a less-than-helpful peer group who involve him in some absconding and petty shop-lifting. He is rude and uncooperative with the adults, who increase the sanctions they give him in an effort to turn him around.

Jack is moved into Mr Wilson's form. He is an experienced teacher who has a reputation for turning some difficult pupils around. Mr Wilson expresses an interest in getting to know Jack, but Jack is suspicious and distrustful. He becomes ruder in an effort to put Mr Wilson off. Expecting the usual sanctions, Jack is rather puzzled when Mr Wilson continues to be friendly, accepting and encouraging. When Jack is absent from school Mr Wilson makes an effort to reconnect with him upon his return and to find out what has been going on for him. When Jack has to be interviewed by the police because of his latest shop-lifting, Mr Wilson supports him as the responsible adult.

Very gradually a tentative trust develops and Jack discloses small bits of information about himself. Mr Wilson discovers that Jack has an interest in the guitar and so brings his own guitar into school. By the end of the school year Jack is staying in school more often and is getting into less trouble. Jack will be in Mr Wilson's form the following year and they plan to start a guitar club together. Mr Wilson has in mind a couple of boys to involve in this who he hopes will be a positive influence for Jack. Slowly Jack is beginning to experience himself as likeable and to adjust some of his expectations of others.

What are the different patterns of attachment that a child might display?

Children will develop different behavioural styles of relating to attachment figures depending upon their early experience. These are called attachment patterns and they develop in response to the sensitivity of the parenting they have received, in particular how able and willing the parent is to understand the behaviour and emotions of the child from the child's point of view. When parents can do this, they will provide an attuned relationship with the child which provides comfort at times of distress and facilitates exploration and an interest in the world when attachment needs have been met. This experience is important for the child's emotional development, enabling him or her to learn to regulate feelings and behaviour and to be able to reflect on experience. These capacities for regulation and reflection will be a strength for the young person, positively influencing emotional development during childhood and through adolescence.

Parenting

Parenting lies on a continuum between sensitive and insensitive, depending on how able the parent is to recognize and respond to the needs that the child signals. This will vary from day to day, but if parenting is sensitive enough of the time, the child will feel secure.

Tom falls over and cries, and his sensitive parent comforts him until he is ready to return to his play. Jake falls over, but gets up unconcerned; his sensitive parent gives him a quick check over and then lets him return to play. If the parents told Tom not to make a fuss and to get back to his play or tried to excessively cuddle and comfort Jake, they would be demonstrating insensitivity.

This can be broken down further according to whether the parent is one of the following:

- *Accepting–rejecting*: how able the parent is to accept that the child has his or her own needs. The accepting parent can recognize the signals that the child is giving and accept that this is how he or she is feeling. Tom's parent accepts he needs comfort, while Jake's parent accepts his need to get on with playing.

- *Cooperating–interfering*: how able the parent is to respond to the child's signals, helping the child to feel comforted or to explore in line with the needs being expressed. Tom's parent provides comfort, while Jake's parent facilitates play.

- *Accessible–ignoring*: how able the parent is to remain alert and available to the child, noticing the signals that the child gives out. An accessible parent is able to engage with the child when the child needs it rather than when the parent wants to. Both Tom and Jake's parents are accessible, meeting the needs as signalled by the boys.

For more information on these patterns, see Ainsworth *et al.* 1978)

As children mature through childhood, the sensitive parent continues to be accepting, cooperative and available to the child, providing comfort and facilitating exploration as needed. They become very attuned to the child's needs and are able to recognize when the child needs a bit more support or has the confidence to go further with help. This provides a strong platform for adolescence. Signals can become more complex as the young person struggles between his or her continuing need of supportive parents and the drive towards independence and going it alone. The parents who have a good understanding of their young person and who can recognize the emotional need beneath the behaviour will be in a good position to support the young person through this developmental transition to adulthood. Insensitive parents will tend to repeat earlier patterns of caregiving, thus perpetuating the young person's style of relating. Through adolescence the pattern of hiding and expressing needs becomes strengthened as the young person continues to miscue the parent about what he or she needs in line with the expectations of the parent. This can lead to complicated relationships, as the challenges of adolescence are increased by these complex patterns of attachment relationships.

Patterns of attachment

Psychologically children develop a strategy to help them experience closeness and psychological engagement with their parents. This allows them to feel safe, to expect protection when in danger and to receive comfort when distressed. This pattern will be adaptive for the child in relation to the parent's behaviour and degree of sensitivity. This will then reflect the quality of the attachment relationship and the way the internal working model develops. These patterns of relating therefore influence the way children respond to later relationships, including those relationships they form as they enter nursery and later at school. Children will have experienced a number of relationships before they enter school. This means that they may have a range of styles of relating, showing combinations of the patterns described below.

Perhaps confusingly there are contrasting models of the development of the attachment patterns. In this book we describe the patterns using the more traditional A B C + D model (see Figure A3.1), rather than the alternative Dynamic Maturational Model (DMM) developed by Crittenden (Crittenden 2008; Crittenden *et al.* 2001). This latter model does not recognize a disorganized pattern, preferring a focus on organization and adaptation to conditions of fear and danger. However, in both models the development of controlling behaviours to deal with perceived threat is emphasized, and it is these controlling behaviours which will be most apparent within school. (A useful discussion of these differing models can be found in Howe 2011.)

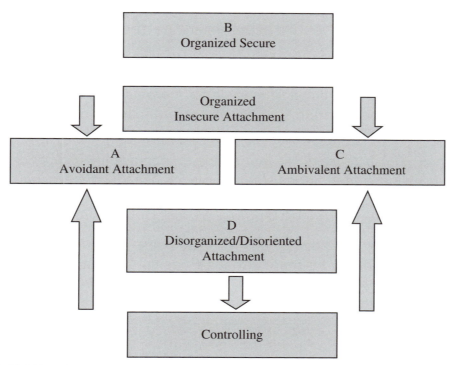

FIGURE A3.1 SUMMARY OF PATTERNS OF ATTACHMENT

The Secure Attachment pattern
Secure attachment pattern (B)

A secure attachment develops out of an attuned relationship. The parent is sensitive to the child's signals, accessible when needed, accepting and supportive of the child. Secure relationships allow children to develop trust in others and appropriate self-reliance in themselves. Securely attached children have positive expectations of themselves and others and approach the world with confidence. When these children are faced with potentially alarming situations, they will tackle them effectively or will seek help to do this.

At adolescence these secure young people will continue to seek support when they feel emotionally troubled, but will also be developing some independence, allowing them to make their own decisions and sort out their own problems. They achieve a balance between managing by themselves and seeking support when needed. Alongside this there is a gradual move from parents as primary attachment figure to friends assuming more importance for emotional support. Parents remain important, but the young people are now able to provide and seek support from peers and will preferentially seek this in favour of parents. Their parents remain available for advice and guidance through this developmental stage but will take a back seat until needed.

Sophie displays a secure attachment pattern

Sophie is a quiet but confident six-year-old who enjoys playing with her friends. She likes Mum to be around, but is able to amuse herself. She likes drawing and playing with her dolls. She was a bit alarmed when a wasp flew into the room, however, and ran to Mum for help. Mum made sure the wasp was gone. Sophie, feeling safe, readily returned to her playing.

When Sophie reaches ten years, she is increasingly independent, keen to walk to school and to attend sleepovers with her friends. In school she works both independently and as an active participant within group work. She is usually very responsive to teacher instruction.

At 15 Sophie is a popular girl with her peers and with her teachers. She enjoys being a buddy for more anxious students and is active as a prefect and representing the school in music. She has a steady group of friends and is actively engaged in making choices about her future.

Secure attachment in educational settings

Young people with a secure attachment pattern appear confident. Whether quiet or lively, they will appear to relish the challenges that the educational setting provides. They are confident to have a go, but will also seek help from the adults when needed.

Socially these young people can draw on the full range of cognitive and emotional information to make sense of the social world. They are able to make friends and mix well with their peers.

They have a good understanding of their own and others' feelings. They are developing a sense of self-efficacy, self-confidence and social competence. They can trust others and will approach others for help. They can resolve conflicts and demonstrate self-reliance. They cope with stress and frustration. They are also comfortable seeking support when needed.

These students achieve success in school. They enjoy learning tasks suitable for their age and ability. They gain satisfaction in achievement and can cope with not knowing. They are able to use the educational staff for support as needed. These students enjoy engaging with learning tasks, both on their own and supported by the adults. The students relate well to adults and engage fully with activities.

Secure attachment can be promoted by working in partnership with parents (see Figure A3.2).

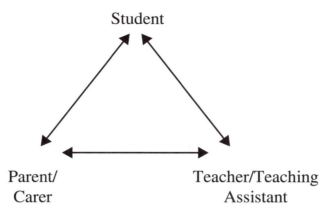

FIGURE A3.2 PARTNERSHIP WORKING TO SUPPORT A CHILD

Insecure attachment patterns

Research has demonstrated that around 60 per cent of children have a secure attachment, while 40 per cent of children develop insecure attachments (Van IJzendoorn and Sagi 1999). It should be noted therefore that insecure attachment does not necessarily mean that problems will follow. Rather, insecure attachment is a risk factor for later emotional and developmental difficulties, while secure attachment is a protective factor. However, when children have experienced early adverse environments including abuse or neglect, it is likely that they will develop more extreme insecure attachments and therefore will be at greater risk of emotional and developmental difficulties that can continue through adolescence.

INSECURE AVOIDANT PATTERN (A)

An insecure avoidant attachment develops out of a relationship with a parent who is distant and rejecting. The parent finds it difficult to cope with the child's emotional needs and therefore is not sensitive to these needs. Overt expression of emotional distress from the child tends to lead the parent to withdraw further. As a consequence the child becomes anxious when experiencing strong feelings. The child learns to minimize attachment behaviour to maintain closeness to the parent. This is expressed through undemanding behaviour with limited displays of emotional distress. Additionally, when these children experience parents as hostile, they will demonstrate compulsively compliant behaviour, being anxious to please and to do things right. When these children do feel angry, they often express this through short-lived loss of control with anger suddenly erupting. Alternatively they might show this anger through passive-aggressive behaviour. This is indirect behaviour: the child displays anger through an action that is carried out behind the adult's back.

In adolescence the developing young person works hard to ignore issues related to their emotional needs, anxiety and dependency. They do not want to acknowledge need for emotional support and will be dismissive about parents or supportive adults, either idealizing them but without depth to this experience, or by denigrating them and dismissing their importance to them. Behind all this is a young person who wants to keep early memories of rejection, hurt or demonstrations of lack of loveability out of awareness. By dismissing emotional neediness they can also dismiss the relevance of past experience. This does mean however that they are poorly equipped to deal with conflict or relationship difficulty in the present, as they cannot draw upon their past experience to help them. The young person trusts in his or her own self-reliance, clinging to this even when they are in need of support. These young people take fewer risks than their other insecure peers but also withdraw from meaningful social experience generally. They will explore intimate relationships and experiment sexually but will generally have less commitment to these relationships. They may also experiment with drugs and alcohol as a way of managing uncomfortable emotional experience as they try not to appear vulnerable or in need of support within friendships or from adults.

Mark displays an avoidant attachment pattern

Mark is an independent six-year-old who makes few demands of his father. Mark will play alone, giving Dad a bright smile when he comes in. He is also keen to help his dad, frequently checking he is OK and helping him with little jobs. When Mark sees a wasp fly into the room, he keeps a wary eye on it but continues playing.

At school Mark follows the rules and routines, making few demands on staff. He approaches other children but tends to hang back, waiting to be invited to join in. He enjoys running around at the fringes of their games in the outdoor area. Sometimes he falls over, but generally just picks himself up and continues with the game. Mark prefers to work on his own. He lacks confidence but does not like to be helped. If working in a group he is quiet, tending to follow the lead of the other children. Staff rarely see Mark upset, but occasionally when he is very frustrated with something he will 'explode' with anger. He resists staff attempts to help him and is quickly back to normal.

When Mark reaches ten years, he remains seemingly independent within the classroom and his work output is usually the minimum required. Mark will just sit rather than ask for help from school staff. He continues to experience seemingly 'untriggered' outbursts from time to time.

At 15 Mark does just enough not to get noticed, trying to stay under the teachers' radar. His homework is completed, but never his best. He still will not seek help or ask for advice. He has few friends but will rub along with his peers. He can be seen at the back of the queue in the canteen and does not volunteer for activities or responsibilities.

Insecure avoidant patterns in school

These students can appear withdrawn and quiet. They rely on knowledge and ignore feelings to guide behaviours. They will generally appear more self-reliant and independent than expected for their age, and will be reluctant to turn to adults when they need help. Distress is denied or not communicated. They may try to take care of the adult staff. These students can appear happy or settled much of the time. If stress builds up, the student may show a sudden and apparently inexplicable tantrum which is quickly over.

Although they appear friendly, careful observation can reveal that these students are relatively isolated as they lack emotional engagement with their peers or with adults. They avoid intimacy and are confused and uncomfortable with their developing need for social relationships. They can withdraw socially or may become aggressive in socially demanding situations.

These students may appear more focused on activities than on people. They can focus on learning to avoid relationships. While achievement can lead to some sense of accomplishment, they fear failure. They can therefore focus more on what they can't do than what they can do. They resist help from the teacher but also lack confidence in their own ability. The student finds it easier to engage with activities than to relate to adults. These students are less able to use the teacher or teaching assistant to support and help them with the task.

INSECURE AMBIVALENT PATTERN (C)

An insecure ambivalent attachment develops out of a relationship with a parent who is inconsistent and unpredictable. These insensitive parents will sometimes meet their children's needs, but this is more dependent on their mood than the children's need. The child learns to maximize attachment behaviour to elicit care. This is expressed through coercive, demanding and clingy behaviour. Emotional distress can be extreme and there is a resistance to being soothed and comforted.

Adolescence is a time for increased preoccupation with fears of not being good enough or acceptable to others, increasing the young person's attention-needing behaviours as they seek approval from others. In contrast to the adolescent with an avoidant attachment, these young people are haunted by their attachment-related childhood memories, which leaves them feeling angry, dissatisfied, jealous and needy but unable to manage this heady mix of emotion. Their negative view of self and anger at the perceived disregard of others can lead to emotional distress, anxiety and low, but volatile, moods. They may also engage in risky behaviours often as a way of ensuring the attention of others. These young people have entangled, demanding relationships with their parents, which makes the shift to independence hard to make. They oscillate between aggression and helplessness as they continue to coercively demand that parents pay attention to them.

Within peer relationships this neediness is equally apparent as the young person demands support but is unable to reciprocate. They perceive slights and feel a sense of abandonment or rejection by others too readily and are thus emotionally volatile and demanding. This often leads to the withdrawal of others, confirming their worst fears, as they redouble their attempts to keep others engaged with them.

Kelly displays an ambivalent attachment pattern

Kelly is a needy six-year-old who has not yet learnt to play alone. She follows her parents around the house, rarely settling to anything. If a visitor arrives, Kelly tries to insert herself between her parents and the visitor. Sometimes Mum, exasperated by this behaviour, will insist that Kelly play by herself for a time. When Kelly sees the wasp fly into the room, she screams and shouts. When Mum arrives, Kelly clings to her. She will not settle even when Mum shows her that the wasp has now gone.

Kelly is not confident when brought to school. She tends to cling to her parents and does not want to be left. Once they have gone, Kelly 'attaches' herself to a member of staff. She is demanding and 'attention-needing'. She talks constantly, often asking questions repetitively but not paying any attention to the answers. She likes to stay close to the staff member, not wanting her to go out of sight. She is possessive and jealous when other children want to talk to this member of staff.

Kelly will not work independently, always seeking assistance even when she does not need it. If working in a group Kelly quickly falls out with the other children as she tries to stay the centre of attention. If she falls or bumps herself, Kelly is inconsolable, clinging to the staff member who comes to help her.

By the time that Kelly has reached ten years, she has developed skills in drawing funny pictures and making jokes, and uses this to make her peers laugh and get adult attention – whatever the cost. At breaktimes she finds excuses to stay in the school and 'help' staff rather than mix with her peers.

These behaviours have become more exaggerated by 15 so that Kelly is always at the centre of disruption and trouble. She is constantly making and falling out with friends, having a new best friend every week. She flirts with the boys in her form, always claiming one or other of them as her latest boyfriend. She will flout the school rules, wearing unsuitable clothes, make-up and jewellery so that teachers are constantly pulling her up about these.

Kelly finds it difficult to engage with school work, rarely starting a piece of work without the teacher helping her. She makes a drama over the simplest tasks, and will volunteer for activities but is unreliable about turning up to take part in them. Teachers are running out of energy to keep supporting Kelly.

Insecure ambivalent pattern in school

These students tend to make their presence known. They are preoccupied with relationships, alert to the availability of others. They therefore have an obsessive need for adult attention. They will therefore appear attention-needing, and find it difficult to settle by themselves or with groups of peers. They will sometimes talk excessively or act as a 'class clown' in order to maintain the focus of adult attention.

Concentrating and focusing on tasks is difficult as they remain hypervigilant to what the adults are doing. These students are very focused on feelings and therefore find it difficult to attend to the rules and structure of the classroom. They therefore find it difficult to follow rules and to learn from consequences. They have poor understanding of cause and effect.

These students rely on feelings rather than knowledge to guide their behaviour. They need attention and approval to feel secure. This leads to enmeshed and entangled relationships. They constantly keep others involved in the relationship through coercive behaviours. They can escalate confrontation in order to hold the attention of others. They view the teacher as either all good or all bad, and may oscillate between these depending on their immediate feeling.

Learning is difficult as they have poor concentration to tasks and are easily distracted. They are highly dependent and therefore need a lot of attention. They remain overly focused on the relationship with the teacher or teaching assistant and this can be at the expense of learning. The students find it difficult to engage with the activity because they are busy making sure the teacher or teaching assistant is noticing them. These students find it difficult to engage in activities without adult support.

DISORGANIZED/DISORIENTATED AND CONTROLLING ATTACHMENT PATTERN (D)

A disorganized/disorientated and controlling attachment develops out of a relationship within which the parent is frightened of or frightening to the child. Parents can be frightened of their children when they have their own history of trauma associated with being parented. The act of parenting their child triggers memories of their own fear, and they become absorbed with this memory and thus unavailable to the child. This is as frightening to the child as more overt acts such as hitting or shouting at the child.

In this pattern the parent is both the source of fear and the potential for safety. This dilemma causes extreme anxiety in the children, which is demonstrated in young children through bizarre behaviours such as freezing, approaching with the head turned away or unusual movements. Whilst children will have organized strategies to engage with their parents, at times of extreme stress they are unable to organize their behaviour in a way that allows them to obtain emotional support.

As they grow older, disorganized children solve the dilemma of having a parent who is a source both of comfort and of fear by taking control of the relationship. They do not trust in the parent so they become controlling in their behaviour. This forces the other person into a predictable, although sometimes angry, pattern of responding. The child feels both powerful and frightened.

These controlling patterns of behaviour continue through adolescence, increasing in line with the extra stress and challenges of this developmental stage. They have limited skills to manage relationships or to regulate emotion, with control taking over as a way of feeling some sense of competence, but any feelings of achievement are quickly dispelled, leading to unstable patterns of escalating control of others. Their oversensitized nervous systems mean that they struggle to manage the transitions and change of this developmental stage. Past trauma is unresolved and lives in the present with them so that they are in a constant state of fear, expecting the worst. In desperate attempts to feel some sense of agency the young people engage in risky behaviours, engaging in early sexual relationships, alcohol, drugs, self-harming behaviours and falling in with peer groups where antisocial behaviour and criminality are the norm. Boys and girls are vulnerable to sexual exploitation, gang-related activities and other social relationships which make them feel strong and invulnerable whilst actually increasing their vulnerability. Mental health difficulties can be high in this group, with increased anxiety, depression and trauma-related symptoms such as hearing voices, experiencing flashbacks and troubling dreams and nightmares.

Daniel displays a disorganized-controlling attachment pattern

Daniel is an angry, hyperactive six-year-old who is exhausting to his mother. He is on the go all the time, playing loud, active games. He frequently puts himself in danger and needs constant supervision. He is bossy, telling his mother what she must do. When she asks him to do something he ignores her. When Daniel sees the wasp enter the room, he runs around chasing it. When Mum tries to remove the wasp, Daniel gets angry, telling her to leave it alone.

Daniel arrives at school and everyone knows it. He comes in loudly and tries to tell the other children what to do. When staff approach, he becomes angry towards them. Difficult to contain indoors, Daniel prefers to be outside, running around and chasing the other children. He does not like to come back indoors and it is difficult to help him adjust to being back in the classroom. Daniel does not settle to his work; he is too busy seeing what everyone else is doing. He can explode with anger, and often has to be taken out of the classroom.

Occasionally he will spend time drawing – he likes to draw soldiers in battle, frequently with lost limbs and lots of blood. Soon, however, he is running around again or fighting with one of the other children. When staff try to intervene, they can be physically attacked.

When he reaches ten years, Daniel will often run out of the classroom when he feels challenged by work or relationships. He has difficulty accepting teacher authority and will respond with verbal and occasionally physical aggression.

By 15 Daniel regularly absconds from school, and is often to be found in the middle of town smoking with other discontented peers. He enjoys being seen as one of the tough kids and will enjoy coercing younger children into shop-lifting. He has begun to experiment with alcohol and cannabis. When in school he is disruptive, getting into fights with peers and becoming angry with adults. He likes to boast about his out-of-school activities. Whilst he displays an attitude of not caring, staff suspect that he is very unhappy. At times he becomes sullen and withdrawn, but then bounces back into another wave of hyperactive, angry behaviour.

Elaine displays a disorganized and withdrawn attachment pattern

Elaine is a quiet, withdrawn six-year-old who spends a lot of time in her bedroom. As her mother approaches, Elaine is vigilant, keeping an eye on her. At times she will approach her mother, as if to check that she is all right. She is very compliant, doing as she is told and urgently trying to help her mother with household jobs. When Elaine sees the wasp in the room, she runs to Mum and then quickly away again. She is clearly distressed, but appears confused about whether to go to Mum for help or not.

Elaine arrives at school late. She appears unconcerned when Mum goes but remains hypervigilant, watching what is going on around her but not able to settle to her work either with or without staff. At other times Elaine appears quiet and 'switched off' as she sits at a table paying little attention to what is going on around her.

This behaviour pattern continues when she reaches ten years, and by 15 Elaine is difficult to engage in most school work. Her learning is patchy, with evidence that she doesn't have the basics in place so that she appears inconsistent in what she can do. She can become overly concerned about small details but finds it hard to see the bigger picture. Her peers tend to leave her alone and Elaine seems content to drift along in her own world.

Within the DMM, attachment researchers have shown how these controlling patterns of behaviour are organized around the self-reliant avoidant and coercive ambivalent patterns of relating. Young people may tend towards one or the other of these or show combinations of both (see Crittenden *et al.* 2001).

Controlling avoidant patterns

The child inhibits strong negative feelings of anxiety, fear or the need for comfort. The older child may also display false positive feelings to hide negative feelings.

Young people with these patterns tend to be withdrawn, unusually compliant and anxiously eager to please. As they experience increased stress, they become compulsively self-reliant and sometimes even care-giving towards their parent.

Controlling ambivalent patterns

The child alternates between displaying anger and vulnerability. The parent is caught in a trap of coercive interactions. If the parent ignores or habituates to the child's behaviour, the child will increase their demanding and 'attention-needing' behaviour, including provocative behaviour (doing the thing the parent most doesn't want them to do) and risk-taking behaviour (if I am in danger will you rescue me?). In this way the child maintains adult attention.

As they experience increased stress, they become even more obsessively preoccupied with adult attention, becoming more controlling in their use of aggressive and coy behaviours.

Disorganized-controlling patterns in school

Whether quiet and withdrawn or loud and aggressive, these young people make their presence felt by the way that they maintain control within relationships. Others tend to feel quickly manipulated. They demonstrate a diminished range of emotions, lacking the contentment and joy in activities of their peers and appearing anxious much of the time. They are frequently afraid but tend to mask this through more aggressive or powerful behaviours. They can be highly disruptive in school as they demonstrate highly compulsive or obsessive behaviours which allow them to hold on to rigid control. This may be demonstrated through a compulsive need to stay self-reliant, within which the young person appears compliant but resists attempts to be helped or comforted. Some young people try to take on a pseudomature caregiving role within the classroom, while others demonstrate more obsessive preoccupations with being noticed through a combination of aggressive and coy behaviours. These students are hypervigilant to what is going on around them, making it difficult to concentrate or attend to a task. Many of these students remain in a hyper-aroused state, but some students cope with excessive feelings of stress by dissociating – appearing 'switched off'.

Relationships can cause distress with little provocation, leading to violent anger and anxious dependence. Strong feelings are overwhelming, and they find it hard to understand, distinguish or control emotions in themselves or others.

While some students remain reluctant to engage with their peers, many do seek friendships, but their immaturity and rigid, controlling style of relating to others can lead to social isolation.

In the classroom these students tend to be anxious and inattentive. They have poor stress tolerance, which detracts from learning. Their need to maintain feelings of being in control overrides learning as they provoke, bully or challenge others. The young person feels very anxious, preventing engagement in activities. Often the anxiety is masked by angry or aggressive behaviours as they try to control the teacher or teaching assistant. These students find relating to adults and engagement with activities difficult.

Patterns of non-attachment

A small proportion of young people have been severely neglected or raised in an institution with multiple caregivers. These young people have had no experience of an early attachment relationship. Without this experience they will not be able to develop a selective attachment. Having no early attachment experience, they do not know how to draw support from the people caring for them. These young people can be disinhibited. They are indiscriminate in who they go to, being friendly to anyone but unable to engage in a mutually satisfying relationship with their parent. Alternatively they can be inhibited, being fearful of others and not approaching anyone when distressed.

Katie displays signs of non-attachment

Katie is a quiet but apparently contented child. She potters around, flitting from activity to activity. When her carer is in the room she tends to ignore her. When visitors arrive, she goes over to them and chats to them as if she has always known them. If distressed Katie fusses, but is difficult to soothe, often pushing the carer away as she attempts to respond, while simultaneously crying out to her. Katie pays no attention to the wasp in the room; she remains absorbed in pouring water from cup to cup in her tea set.

At school Katie appears contented but quite oblivious of what is going on around her. She wanders from activity to activity, taking little notice of the other children. When a visitor comes into the classroom, Katie goes over to her and takes her by the hand. The visitor crouches down and talks to her, Katie turns away and wanders up to one of the other adults, again taking hold of their hand. As the other children gather their things together in preparation for going home, Katie is still wandering around picking up materials that the adults are trying to put away. As she gets older, Katie continues to appear 'unaware' of her surroundings, both in terms of her peers and tasks set. She has great difficulty in settling to and completing activities and appears surprised when adults are frustrated with her limited work output.

Non-attachment within school

These young people are relatively few compared to other young people with attachment difficulties. For a young person to have non-attachment, an experience of severe neglect, institutional care or a large number of placement moves will be apparent in the early history. These students are notable in school by a lack of connection with adults, even appearing autistic at times. This has been termed a 'quasi-autism' to emphasize the acquired nature of the difficulties because of the early history (Rutter *et al.* 2009). The students may be very withdrawn, although more usually they appear highly sociable, approaching anyone for comfort, but appearing dissatisfied by the contact with an adult. These students generally appear very immature and respond more like younger children, tending to get on with their own thing and appearing unaware of normal rules and routines.

Summary: insecure attachment patterns

Insecure avoidant pattern

PARENT ◄──────► CHILD

- Distant and rejecting.

- Finds it difficult to cope with the child's emotional needs.

STUDENT ◄──────► ADULT

- Withdrawn or quiet.

- More self-reliant than peers of same age.

- Less likely to turn to parent or teacher for support and help.

- Can appear isolated, or friendships lack depth.

- Apparent indifference to uncertainty in new situations.

- Finds physical closeness threatening.

- Inexplicable tantrums or outbursts – appear from nowhere, which can be quickly over.

- More likely to be focused on 'doing' than relationships with people.

Insecure ambivalent pattern

PARENT ◄──────► CHILD

- Parent will sometimes meet the child's needs depending on their own mood. Therefore, unpredictably available.

STUDENT ⟷ *ADULT*

- High level of anxiety and uncertainty.

- Attention-needing.

- Hypervigilant to what adults are doing.

- May talk excessively, or act as a 'clown' in order to keep the adult's attention.

- Accept negative or positive attention from adults.

- Difficulties attempting the task if unsupported.

- Difficulty concentrating and focusing.

- Poor understanding of cause and effect.

- May present as highly articulate but this does not correlate with achievement levels.

Disorganized/disorientated and controlling attachment pattern

PARENT ⟷ *CHILD*

- Parent is frightened of or frightening to the child.

- May be because they were frightened as a child so become unresponsive when their child needs them the most.

- May be overtly frightening to the child by exposing them to family violence, odd behaviour or harsh discipline. May be abusive or neglectful.

STUDENT ⟷ *ADULT*

- Sees the parent as both the potential source of comfort and terror – 'I need you, but you frighten me.'

- May react to unseen triggers.

- Very controlling in their relationships.

- May be hyper-aroused or dissociated for much of the time.

- Their early brain development has developed over-responsive fight-or-flight reactions, leaving a diminished capacity to concentrate or think.

- May be unable to accept being taught, and/or unable to 'permit' others to know more than they do, as this triggers overwhelming feelings of humiliation.

- Struggle in relatively unsupervised settings such as the playground or moving between lessons.

Appendix 4
Supporting Traumatized Adolescents in Educational Settings

Revisiting challenges of adolescence

As we explored in Appendix 2, adolescence is a time of change and transition. This can impact on all aspects of development and can impact on the capacity of the young person to benefit from education. Educators of adolescents need to be aware that settling to learn can be especially challenging when much emotional energy is devoted to managing the changes of this developmental stage. The cultural context within which these changes are occurring also needs to be considered. For example, Western adolescents living in the twenty-first century are growing up during an age of rapid technological change. Their ability to master this technology is often vastly better than the adults who could potentially support them with it. However, their emotional capacity to deal with the consequences can be immature, leaving adolescents vulnerable and adults struggling to catch up sufficiently to provide the emotional support needed.

What happens when early relational trauma is thrown into the adolescent mix?

Some young people who have experienced early trauma do develop smoothly during adolescence and appear to have benefited fully from their intervening experience at home and at school.

Others can find this developmental stage more difficult than their peers. Adolescence is a time of revisiting identity, discovering who you are. With increased maturity young people revisit their life stories and what has happened to them in their life and they question why. Many adopters can testify how destabilizing this can be to family relationships as the young person questions whether they belong here, and wonders whether there is something wrong about themselves that such bad things happened in the past.

The increased stress can lead to a return to some earlier behaviours which families thought were long behind them, for example rejection of parents, increased controlling behaviours and non-compliance.

Case example 1

Jake had a stressful start to being part of his adoptive family as a toddler. His early experience of frightening parenting led to his resistance to being parented by his new parents. This however resolved and his middle years were settled and stable.

At 13 this young man became extremely unsettled; he became convinced that he was not a good person and that his parents did not want him, he fell out with friends and complained of bullying by his peers and he developed fantasies that perhaps he had been kidnapped from his birth family. He became angry and hostile to his parents and siblings, he engaged in some very risky behaviours and he stopped attending school.

It was only the sensitive support of his parents, supported by mental health professionals, and close working with understanding school staff, that helped this young man to work through his confusion and once again to be settled at home, re-engaged with friends and able to focus on school work again.

In trying to deal with the uncertainty and confusion of this self-exploration some young people will engage in new behaviours that are concerning to those around them. Self-harm, lying and stealing, use of alcohol or drugs and even sexual exploitation are sadly behaviours that adolescents can experiment with to try to deal with strong doubts about their own self-worth.

Case example 2

Megan had lived in a chaotic and frightening home for her first four years. Her father was violent and her mother neglectful. Megan was regularly exposed to prostitution and to drug dealers. She then moved to live with her grandparents and had a settled three years until her grandmother developed a life-limiting illness. At 7 Megan moved to a foster placement where she eventually stayed long term. Megan thrived in this family and there were no notable concerns until she was 14.

At this age Megan made friends with Julie, a troubled girl who could be dominating and bullying within her friendships. Megan found her earlier friends drifted away from her, intimidated by Julie's possessiveness. Megan became surly and more defiant at home, became disengaged with her school work and gave up rowing, an interest she had sustained since living with her grandparents. At the same time she became more preoccupied with her appearance. She would wear lots of make-up, and spend a long time styling her hair and applying false nails. Megan started going into town after school and would be unpredictable about returning home. When questioned about where she was or what she was doing she would become angry and even violent on occasions.

When Julie was expelled from the school for selling cannabis Megan began to skip school herself so that she could meet up with her. At calm times her foster parents tried to talk with Megan and encourage her to meet up with past friends or start rowing again. Megan would become tearful, confessing that she did not think anyone at the rowing club liked her and that she was not good enough for her other friends. Her biggest fear was that she was going to end up just like her mother.

This came to a head when Megan returned home with a brand new mobile phone and insisted that she had to go out again later that evening. When told she could not go she became very frightened. The foster carer and the social worker working closely with the sexual exploitation team supported Megan to get out of the situation she had got into, but it was a long time before Megan could feel confident in her friendships again.

The young person might start to search for birth family to try to get some answers. Unfortunately social media has made this easier, and it is not uncommon for young people to find and make contact with birth relatives without any awareness by the parents. Without preparation and support such contact can be very destabilizing.

Case example 3

Josh was a popular boy at school, good at music and at sports. He was adopted at a relatively young age and always seemed settled into his family. He always knew he was adopted but his parents did not encourage him to talk about this. They believed that the past was best left alone and that Josh would be more settled without being faced with details about his early experience.

At 14 Josh became more withdrawn. He spent less time with friends and more time in his bedroom on his computer. When asked, he would tell his parents that he was playing Minecraft with friends. He spent less and less time with the family and became quite cruel towards his younger sister, undoing the close relationship that they had always had. He continued to attend school regularly and always had good reports from his teachers.

At 16 Josh went missing. It was only after a frantic 48 hours for his parents that Josh rang to let them know that he had gone to live with his birth mother. Only then did they realize that he had made contact with a sibling and been communicating with him over Facebook for a couple of years. This sibling had convinced Josh that he should not be living with his adoptive family and that he was being disloyal to his birth mother who had never really done anything wrong. It was vindictive social workers that put him into care.

> Josh remained living with his birth mother for six months, but arrived back at his adoptive parents' door one day looking dishevelled and smelling of alcohol. He told them that his mother had kicked him out and he did not know what to do. Luckily for Josh his parents were happy to have him home again and to support him through a difficult time whilst he came to terms with what had happened and rediscovered that he did belong with his adoptive family.

All of these case examples illustrate the complexity of becoming an adolescent and the possibility of past history coming back to haunt the present. 'Ghosts from the nursery' was the phrase used by Robin Karr-Morse and Meredith Wiley (1997), adapted from the original expression coined by psychoanalyst Selma Fraiberg, to describe the way that past experience of being parented can impact on present behaviour in adolescence. In all three case examples the ghosts from the nursery are evident as the young people struggle with adolescent worries and confusions.

Educational staff are therefore advised to be aware of the earlier experiences of their students, and to know what the risk factors are for a more than usually troubled adolescent. Understanding the continuing emotional and social needs of students as they enter educational settings during this developmental stage of their life is as important as understanding those of children just entering nursery and infant school. School staff can just as easily become a supportive attachment figure to these young people as they can for younger children. Sensitive educational practitioners are able to help their students experience school as a secure base, providing some stability in their life as they navigate their way through their teenage years. Understanding how to do this for the most emotionally troubled of young people can be a challenging but very rewarding aspect of working within education.

Table A4.1 summarizes the key challenges that all adolescents will face to some extent, which can impact on learning and being able to benefit from education. Alongside this, consideration is given to the additional challenges this might present to young people who have experienced relational trauma early in their life.

Table A4.1 Challenges of adolescence for education

Challenge	Additional difficulties for traumatized adolescent
Major change of educational setting in early adolescence	Transition is particularly difficult as novelty and change are experienced as threats and not challenges Students may additionally have to manage transitions of educational setting at different times from their peers, e.g. • family mobility • placement changes for children living in foster or residential homes • need to change educational settings for students who are presenting challenges that a current setting can't cope with
Educational setting is bigger and more complex: • travelling to school over larger distances and using public transport • loss of secure base of consistent classroom and teacher at centre of school day • need to relate to a larger range of adults • need to navigate around large educational site • a lot of students moving around at the same time • additional noise and crowding	Find it harder to feel safe in the bigger secondary settings: • may find getting to school challenging • more reliant on the safety provided by consistent place and teacher • struggle to use multiple relationships with adults for safety • struggle more with inconsistencies between adults • can struggle to remember and find way around the site • can be overwhelmed emotionally and at sensory level experiencing large numbers of students, crowding and noise
Increased demands for organization and independence: • the pace of learning increases during the secondary school • more independent study and more project work involving self-study	Immaturity leads to insufficient independence skills: • fear of being in wrong place, late or with wrong materials can increase stress levels • may not have skills for independent study
Need to arrive at lessons organized, calm and ready to learn: • two-week timetables can add to this complexity	Increased stress can mean that students arrive at school/lessons already hyper-aroused, and without the means to quickly adjust to the demands of the lesson. Difficulties can quickly escalate Fragile executive functioning, which reduces further under stress, can make it harder for a student to manage demands for organization
Not all education staff that the student relates to during the day may have a good knowledge of that student and what is going on for them in their life	Protecting the privacy of the student may mean that adults have information on a need-to-know basis. This can mean that individual staff may not know or understand the student's particular needs. External changes may not be shared quickly enough or at all, e.g. a change of placement, problems with contact, family changes

Peer pressure increases as peer relationships become increasingly important. This can raise challenges for all adolescents, e.g. • Who do I want to impress? • What will my peers think if I answer the question, complete the homework? • I don't want to be seen to be needing help. • Do I look attractive enough? • Am I liked, accepted, wanted by my peers? • Do I have the latest gadget?	Challenges are increased for students who are more immature and less socially skilled. The need to fit in and be accepted by peers can clash with the need to rely on and be helped by adults: • having a secure base to go to in school may not be 'cool' • worries about developing friendships mean student is unable to focus on learning • may fall prey to bullying or grooming behaviours from peers • need to feel in control may lead to bullying behaviours to peers • peer pressure can lead to engagement in risk-taking behaviours such as truanting, smoking, alcohol/drug abuse, self-harm
Students have greater access to and less supervision with technology in the form of computers, phones, tablets, etc. They also have a great desire to connect with peers and thus social media is very attractive	For students who are struggling to fit in with their peer group, social media can appear attractive as a virtual way of relating to peers, but these young people are also more vulnerable to the dangers of interacting in this way, e.g. • do not realize and can't handle the fast spread of information • need to interact with ever-increasing friendship group • unaware that the virtual person may not be who he or she seems • vulnerable to pressures to use media inappropriately, e.g. sending revealing photographs • vulnerable to cyber bullying, and may be less aware that this is happening
As they progress through secondary education, students have to make choices that will have implications for their future: • options, choosing subjects to follow • planning career path • thinking about what to do next • increased academic pressure from formal examinations	Students living outside of their birth family have additional pressures connected with understanding their origins – revisiting their life story As well as planning future career paths they may also be facing future changes in family: • looked after young people have worries about leaving care and what will happen to them • adopted young people may be facing choices about seeking for birth family or dealing with birth family members making contact • students may be facing placement instability or difficulties living with birth family as increasingly challenging behaviour puts a strain on the family

Managing the transition to a secondary setting

Transition and change can be a time of excitement for young people. Healthy students will generally thrive on the new challenges that these transitions bring and will have a thirst for novelty, whether within peer relationships or in learning. Of course some students will need more support than others in managing the change, but generally the move to secondary education will be a positive one, with the student making the most of the new experiences on offer.

This is much less likely to be true for the students who have experienced early relational trauma. Trauma has a restricting impact on an individual; change and novelty are experienced as threats, and the loss of familiar adults will trigger memories of previous losses. Transition can increase the fears of abandonment that the young person has been struggling with throughout their primary education. These fears, stemming from inexplicable early loss, leave the young person fearing that they are bad in some way, that things have happened to them because of some fault of their own and that ultimately they will not be liked or wanted by others. These are difficult fears to carry into a completely new educational setting with the demands to make a new set of relationships. Louise Michelle Bombèr (2009) stresses the importance of relationship and stability to support young people with necessary change and transition during adolescence. She suggests providing preventative support rather than waiting for difficulties to arise. Her experience suggests that if students are left to 'sink or swim' they will often survive Years 7 and 8 (11–12 years) but will completely fall apart in Years 9 and 10 (13–14 years). It is important to keep these students in mind, actively intervening on a consistent basis and not waiting for a crisis before reacting.

It is important to be aware that these young people do not have helpful frames of reference to support them in adapting to change. They will need support to manage a completely new environment. This requires additional planning and preparation. It is also important to think about change which is happening at unscheduled times, for example because of exclusion from a previous school or a change in care arrangements. Bombèr (2009) suggests, in these circumstances, beginning with a part-time timetable and building up to full-time and full integration.

Education and support staff need to find out as much about a young person as possible before they arrive so that they can plan a supportive environment tailored to the student's individual needs. Whilst very personal background information will only be revealed to a few staff who will closely support the vulnerable student, there is a range of information that needs to be more widely shared. Bombèr (2009) recommends the use of a fact file which is included at the front of the student's school records. This can be updated as the student progresses through his or her education and can be moved with him or her if there is a planned or sudden move at any time. In this way those involved in the education and support of the student can have this important information available and accessible. In particular this fact file should include:

- a summary of relational traumas and losses

- a list of known triggers, for example raised voices

- strategies known to be effective.

It is also important that the student arrives at the new setting having had the opportunity for a healthy ending of the previous stage of their education. Opportunities for goodbyes are even more important for students moving unexpectedly or between scheduled transition times. These students also need honest explanations of why they are moving.

The following box provides some ideas for supporting students moving from primary to secondary education.

Supporting students with transitions

Leaving primary school

- Trusted adults from the current school can talk to the student about their feelings about moving, research the new school, visit and learn how to get around in the new environment and help him or her to get to know new key staff.

- Familiarity can be built in through visits, maps and photographs prior to the move.

- Bombèr (2009) recommends three to four visits with familiar adults. This aims for a slow and gradual transition.

Moving to the new school

- Provide a buddy to support the young person into school.

- Support the young person to become familiar with new experiences, for example moving around the school when it is busy, buying and eating lunch in the canteen, using the library and school shop, etc.

- Identify a secure base within the school and help the young person learn how to get back there from different parts of the school. Ideally this will be somewhere supported such as a learning base or inclusion department, where there will be familiar faces and supportive adults.

Managing challenging behaviour at adolescence

Heather Forbes (2012, pp.44–45), in her book *Help for Billy*, suggests that:

> Trauma impacts a child's ability to concentrate, organize, and process information. So by age sixteen, Billy may still be unable to keep his backpack organized, his note-taking skills are probably non-existent, and he likely has no ability to plan out the timing of a four-week project. His level of frustration with school has been continually building since the second grade, and by now he hates learning and has no tolerance for doing work he believes is 'busy work'. At this point in his academic career, Billy is truly viewed as nothing short of a problem student in the classroom.

The adolescent who has not yet experienced security within attachment relationships will experience the secondary school environment as highly stressful. The increased pressure on the young person to develop relationships with peers and to manage a bigger range of adult relationships will significantly increase the pressure upon him or her. In addition the emotional gap between the young person and the peer group is widening, further adding to the emotional toll of coping in the educational setting. All of this pressure adds up to significant distress, often communicated through challenging behaviours.

With large numbers of students all with a range of their own needs, these challenging behaviours can put considerable stress on the educational staff. On top of this their tried-and-tested behavioural management strategies are tested to their limits and often found wanting. New ways of managing behaviour are needed for the relationally traumatized adolescent, but these differing approaches do not always sit comfortably alongside the existing policies and procedures. Fortunately there is a range of advice based on our latest understanding of neuroscience and the impact of trauma on young people to guide the educational staff (see Bombèr 2009; Forbes 2012; Gott 1999; Howard 2013). Forbes (2012, pp.21–22) states this advice very succinctly:

> Instead of asking children to make a better 'choice' in their behaviors, it is time that we ask ourselves to make a better choice in the creation of their environments. We must develop stronger relationships that will increase their window of stress tolerance and hence increase their capacity to learn, thrive and succeed.

She recommends that education staff move away from consequences-based approaches to managing behaviour to those that are more regulatory based. This recognizes that many of the problems being displayed are an outcome of dysregulated nervous systems rather than poor choices being made by the student.

Behavioural management procedures are based on assumptions about relationships that do not hold true for relationally traumatized adolescents, in particular the assumption that the student wants to be appreciated and valued by the teacher and therefore will behave in a way which earns this appreciation. Actually their behaviours are more often a consequence of trying to defend against expectations of not being appreciated and valued. They rarely feel that they are good enough and they expect others to be uncaring and manipulative towards them. They therefore view the actions of the teacher through this lens of mistrust. They view rewards as manipulation and discipline as cruel or mean. They respond with the range of controlling behaviours that they learnt to survive earlier relationships; this in turn often earns them the label of manipulative, which of course then reinforces their beliefs of being bad and unwanted and feelings of rejection. Howard (2013) suggests that if the adults don't work on the relationship with the students then their efforts to reward, praise and provide fair and appropriate discipline will simply reinforce the beliefs and fears that are guiding the student.

Case example 4

Mark Brown is 12 years old and in his second term at high school. The transition from primary school was done carefully with additional visits and good information being shared between the schools. This has alerted the new school that Mark lives within a troubled family where he has been exposed to substantial domestic violence. His mother left this home a few years previously taking Mark's younger sister with her, but leaving Mark in the care of his father, who is deaf and has struggled to get employment. He can be quick to anger and is highly critical of the teachers who have worked with Mark. Parent evenings can be challenging when Mr Brown comes along! Within the primary setting Mark has needed considerable support. He has poor self-esteem, is very self-critical and quickly becomes hyper-aroused. When feeling stressed he demonstrates quite challenging attention-needing behaviours. He is achieving at a below-average level.

Armed with this information Mark has been provided with a teaching assistant to support him at the beginning and end of the day, and to help him manage the numerous transitions within the school. He has also been introduced to the support base where he receives some catch-up lessons and can also retreat to if he experiences difficulty. Mark's teachers have been alerted to his additional needs, and a list of activities that help him successfully join and settle into his classes is available to them all. This includes a personal greeting at the start of each lesson, and maintaining brief contact with him throughout the lesson so that he never feels forgotten about. For example, a teacher might give the occasional thumbs up when not directly attending to him. He is additionally given clear instructions and time frames to complete work. Regular support and checking in from the teacher and teaching assistant ensure that he is remaining on task. Mark has also been given some responsibilities to help increase his confidence around the school. For example, he has the task of taking the register to the office after form time at the beginning of the day.

With this structure in place Mark made an excellent start to the year. He especially responded to the literacy work, and his good progress in reading even helped the first parents' evening to go smoothly! He had a couple of wobbles when he needed the support of the teaching assistant and the support base. However, he was given time and help to calm before the teaching assistant talked through with him what had gone wrong. Her PACE approach (see Chapter 9) helped him to talk about some difficulties he was having out in the playground. He experienced the other children not wanting him to join in with the football game. A responsible older student was given the task of helping Mark with this unstructured time and soon he was a regular member of the football game.

Towards the end of term Mark began to wobble again. He started to display some rudeness to teachers, and was loud and disruptive in his classes. He was also experiencing some peer difficulties again, not helped by his buddy being less available as he was rehearsing hard for his central role in the Christmas performance. Mark was getting tired from the continuing pressure of holding it together across the term, and was unsettled by some changes to the structure he had become used to. It was decided to give Mark, some additional time with his buddy by giving him a small part in the performance. It was recognized that this was adding some stress for Mark, but his English teacher, Miss James, volunteered to give him some additional help and all went well.

The new term began well but quickly Mark began to unravel. He began turning up late to school, his disruptive behaviour increased so that he frequently had to leave lessons, he was falling out with his peers again, and his rudeness to teachers was beginning to get them all feeling very frustrated with him. Some teachers began pushing for a tougher approach with more focus on consequences for these difficult behaviours. The staff group became divided about how to support Mark, and this added to Mark's stress and his difficult behaviour continued to escalate. A clue to helping Mark came one day from Miss James. This astute teacher was at the receiving end of Mark's rudeness when he came across her during break. In front of his peers he laughed at her and shouted out that she had been sacked. Miss James quietly separated Mark from his friends and suggested they take a walk. Reluctantly and angrily Mark followed her. They walked for a while, with Miss James commenting on things she was noticing around the school: the frost in the tree, the frozen pond. Despite himself Mark found himself looking at what she was seeing and he slowly became more regulated. When Miss James judged that he was calmer she commented in the same tone of voice that Mark seemed angry with her today. Mark denied this, and Miss James wondered how he was finding school this term. Angrily Mark responded: 'I'm stuck in that lesson for English with that new teacher, and I don't like him and you just left us.'

The English groups in Year 7 had been moved around so that Miss James could cover for a teacher who was taking an extended leave of absence. She now realized that she had failed to talk with Mark about this, and that he was particularly vulnerable to people leaving him given his history with his mother. She needed to let him know that she understood and to repair the relationship because of her error: 'Mark, I am sorry that you aren't in my group this term. I guess it must feel like I don't want to teach you. I made a mistake not explaining this to you and it makes sense that you are angry with me. You need to go in for your next lesson now, but let's make a time when you and I can talk about this.'

Miss James met with Mark to explore his anger about the change of teacher. Responding with PACE she validated his anger that she was not his teacher any more. She expressed her sadness that this was the case and assured him that she was still in school and available to talk to him should he need to. She also learnt from Mark that things had been more difficult at home, thus explaining why he was struggling more this term. Miss James apprised the staff group of this and then met with Mark's new English teacher to let him know of the situation. Miss James then checked in with Mark on a monthly basis. She remained a key adult in his school life for the next couple of years until he no longer needed this. By happy chance Mark was in Miss James' (although now Mrs Burnett!) group for his GCSE years. She was delighted with his progress and proud that his best grade in the formal exams was for English!

The value of relationship

Relationship is the key to managing the challenges of distress communicated through behaviour. In primary education this is relatively easy to provide. Teachers have a closer relationship with their pupils, and the relative youth of the children means that it does not feel uncomfortable to meet dependency needs and the need for nurture. By secondary education teaching staff expect to offer a different sort of relationship: one that provides wise guidance to foster the developing independence of their students. The focus is on learning and achievement, and this is separated from providing emotional support, with the latter often being viewed as the province of school counsellors or nurses. They might look kindly on the insecurities of the younger secondary students, expecting to provide support alongside their teaching. As these young people move through the school, however, they are expected to be more independent and more in need of teaching than support. Relationally traumatized students are very much square pegs unable to fit into these round holes. They remain highly stressed, emotionally immature and in need of, although still unsure or resistant to using, an increased level of support offered through a warm and nurturing relationship. They do need discipline and boundaries; but by adolescence they have become accomplished at not responding to these. Their range of controlling behaviours has become more sophisticated to help them feel safer in what they view as unsafe relationships. These students want to influence the others around them, but they fear being influenced in turn. The world of reciprocal relationships is closed to them as they try to manage rather than respond to the relationship overtures of others. When the adults, in their turn, also seek to manage the student with a focus that is more on behaviour than the young person, then the relationship will close down completely and opportunities to help the young people experience safety in reciprocity, pride in being valued and joy in accomplishment is lost.

Of course students need rules and regulations, some boundaries and discipline to guide their development; they also need praise and rewards to mark their successes. These will only be successful, however, if these relationally troubled young people also experience connection with the adults: connection which demonstrates they are understood, valued for who they are, not their behaviour, and validation for what they experience. They need to know that their emotional experience is neither right nor wrong – it is just how they feel, and that this makes sense to others, even when the way that this experience is expressed causes some problems. The troubled adolescent is likely to fight this connection; after all they have had 11 and more years of managing without it, and they still carry the scars of earlier experiences when they were open to connection and were hurt by it. They have learnt to mask their vulnerability, to not need relationships. However, we, the wiser adults, know that to truly heal and to have the deeply rich and rewarding futures that they deserve, they need these relationships; they need the experience of being vulnerable and not being hurt, and they need to move towards their futures open to the reciprocal relationships which will help them to be successful at work and in their more intimate relationships. Any education they receive during the secondary years will fall on infertile ground if these young people do not also learn to be emotionally resilient and open to relationship.

The ideas about using DDP-informed ways of relating based on the attitude of PACE and connecting with students which we introduced in Chapter 9 are as relevant in the adolescent years as they are for younger children. However, these can be more challenging to apply when educational staff have less time to connect with their students and they are met by growing young people whose defences have become stronger and whose resistance to relationship has become more entrenched. For these young people it is even more important that the adults develop ways of:

- remaining open and engaged to their students, even when they are being pushed into defensive responses reflecting their feelings of anger, frustration or hopelessness

- noticing and wondering about the emotional inner lives of their students so that the students get an experience of being safely understood and a sense of the relationship being unconditional

- co-regulating the dysregulated feelings that are threatening to overwhelm the student

- co-constructing by making sense together of the experience of the young person so that he or she can more flexibly respond to it

- talking with the young person to strengthen the connection and, when this is too intense for this student, finding ways to talk about the young person indirectly so that they still get a sense of being understood and valued.

When students get this relationship experience consistently from the adults that they are relating to on a daily and termly basis, over time their levels of fear will reduce and their experience of school as a safe place to be will increase. They will become open to learning and achievement and their educational experience will be a success.

Building self-regulation at adolescence

Adolescent students who continue to be troubled by early relational trauma will almost certainly be struggling to regulate their emotional experience. This relates to their lack of good early nurturing, which means that their nervous system has developed to manage stress and to be alert for danger. If the middle childhood years have provided experience which can calm the nervous system down but have not offered them sufficient compensatory experience to radically rewire it, then this nervous system will certainly 'rev up' again as the young person faces the additional challenges of this developmental stage. The limbic system in the brain will be in charge and the fight/flight/freeze responses will be on full alert as the young person draws upon the strategies that helped them survive previously. Whether these responses are dissociative or hyper-aroused, the young person will be in survival mode, not relating mode.

One of the important tasks therefore for all adults who are supporting traumatized adolescents is to help develop the self-regulatory capacity of the adolescents, by creating environments which are regulating, by using the relationship to co-regulate and by gradually helping the adolescents to move away from survival and towards relationship. With their thinking brain back in charge these adolescents will have the flexibility to manage the stresses they encounter and to seek help for this when needed.

Secondary education coincides with the time when students are developmentally re-organizing their nervous systems. Education staff are well placed therefore to provide the experience needed to move the students from reactive to calm nervous systems in a way that can get built in to this reorganization. In order to do this the level of stress that students are experiencing and the low levels of stress tolerance at their disposal needs to be taken into account so that the school environment becomes a place where stress is reduced and safety increased. Heather Forbes (2012, p.21) notes that:

> The amount of pressure students are asked to handle in academic environments frequently goes far beyond what their nervous systems are equipped to

handle. Staying at this heightened level of stress diminishes their ability to self-regulate and their ability to learn.

It is essential therefore that educational staff are aware and alert to challenging behaviours being a sign of regulatory difficulties, and have ways of helping the student move out of these stressed, defensive, dysregulated states and back into the calm, alert and regulated states which will increase stress tolerance and which are conducive to learning. This requires an environment that provides external regulation as scaffolding to allow the young person to begin to develop internal regulation (see Forbes 2012). This requires proactive strategies used by the adults to build the self-regulation of their students (see Howard 2013). Judith Howard notes how levels of adrenalin and cortisol are raised in the students' systems when they are in a highly stressed and dysregulated state. When adults move to disciplinary responses they are risking escalating the outbursts from the young person, putting themselves and others at risk. It is essential that low-stimulus activities and a calm and safe environment are provided to calm the dysregulated state; only then will the student be open to discussing the incident or benefit from behavioural interventions if it is felt that these are needed, for example to allow the student to show the genuine remorse that develops when they experience being understood by the adult. Now they can begin to think about others who they may have hurt in the process and will accept help to repair these relationships. Howard recommends at least an hour is given to calming a dysregulated adolescent before trying to help them to reflect on what has happened.

Case example 5

Philip was severely neglected in his early years with some evidence of cruelty and food being withdrawn for punishment. He moved into foster care with his younger brother when he was five. They had a number of placements before finally settling into a long-term placement.

Philip engaged well with school, giving teachers few problems. He had gained 100 per cent attendance from Years 7 to 10. The difficulties with food he had displayed at primary school (taking food from other pupils' lunch boxes and eating his own lunch before school in case it was stolen or taken from him) had decreased and were no longer an issue. Philip was eager to please, but quite a socially isolated student.

At 16 years old and as the exam period approached, Philip's timetable changed, building in more independence and time for self-study. The expectation was that he would turn up to revision sessions and study at home rather than attending lessons. Suddenly with this change of responsibility and structure things started to go wrong for Philip. He stopped turning up to sessions and started to lie about where he had been. When staff talked to his foster parents they reported changes in his behaviour at home as well. They were also trying to deal with some local lads who had been bullying him and trying to get him to steal for them.

Philip's teachers responded sensitively to this. They brought him into a small meeting together with his foster carers. They initially discussed his difficulties outside of school and explored what Philip and his carers had done to help with the local peer group. They then said they had noticed that he seemed to be finding the changes at school tricky and wondered with him how they could help and support him to try to remedy the situation. A plan was drawn up that they all agreed to. It was arranged for him to have a mentor from the Virtual School for looked after children who helped him to reorganize his time, and made sure he had the correct revision equipment and books. Philip's mentor also responded with PACE when he minimized his difficulties due to embarrassment and shame. She showed him empathy and acceptance and via this built up a positive relationship with him so that he trusted her to guide him and give support in an inconspicuous way. In this way his peers did not react negatively towards him having extra support.

Staff were concerned that leaving school might be scary for Philip. They remembered that earlier changes of placement meant that he had never yet left a school at the same time as his peers. They started planning how they could help him have a good ending. They gave Philip a goal to think about and work towards by involving him in plans for the end-of-school prom. They made sure he had his ticket, took him to buy his suit, and made sure transport to the prom was organized. They also arranged to visit the local colleges with him so that he could make some choices about what he would do next. He chose a local horticultural college as he was developing an interest in gardening, and they supported him with several visits to the college before the term ended.

Philip sat and passed all of his exams. He also began tending the garden of an elderly neighbour and became friends with her grandson of a similar age. Happily he enthused his new friend with an interest in gardening and they both planned to attend the same college.

Philip attended the prom and left the school having maintained a very positive relationship with both learning and the staff who supported him.

Sticking with it

Educating young people who have relational trauma in their background is a challenging task. By adolescence, if they have not been able to benefit from corrective emotional experiences in alternative relationships, these young people can be extremely difficult to relate to. They have learnt and are well practised in defensive ways of relating to adults.

These are mainly centred around the need to stay in control at all costs. This makes them very resistant to entering a reciprocal relationship and being open to your influence. This would require that they give up their one-way, controlling influence of you. They additionally have long-held and deep-seated beliefs about their own inadequacy, that others will hurt them and that things won't change. On top of this their struggles to relate within their peer group can be further reinforcing these beliefs. For some young people they try to defend against these certainties, appearing arrogant, 'cocky' and 'hard', to mask their huge vulnerabilities. If you start to connect with these students and get under these defences they will feel highly vulnerable; they may react very angrily, sometimes aggressively, when this happens. It is a truism that these young people are often most hurtful to those they feel closest to for this reason. These young people need good relationships with adults who can support and guide them more than most young people, and yet they will resist these relationships at every turn. To make a long-lasting difference, to open up a future that their potential deserves, these young people need you to stick with them – to hang on in there and persevere. As they experience repeated connection with you, as they experience safety in your presence and as they discover that they can be vulnerable and not get hurt, they will truly begin to change, and you will be rewarded by knowing that this young person's future is there waiting for him or her. Howard (2013) stresses the importance of persevering with relationships whilst expecting these to be tested. Try not to take the behaviours personally. You will be helped to stick with these students if you do the following:

- Make sure you have time for continuing professional development, so that you can:
  » gain a good understanding of adolescent development and the impact of trauma upon this development, and in particular understand how traumatizing experience sensitizes the nervous system and how this influences behaviour
  » understand and have lots of ideas to draw upon for regulation management as an alternative to behaviour management
  » understand and have lots of ideas to draw upon in order to keep the importance of relationship central.

- Understand and practise using PACE (see Chapter 9). Try practising with less complex students so that this starts to feel like a familiar way of relating to them. These young people will enjoy the deeper connection with you, giving you confidence in your abilities before they become challenged by the more resistant students.

- Ensure you are part of a team around the particularly challenging students so that you are not doing this alone. This is a group of staff who come together on a regular basis to reflect upon a young person's needs and his or her impact upon them (see Bombèr 2009).

- Ensure that there is one key adult (who may or may not be you) who is coordinating the support for the young person (see Bombèr 2009).

- Access supervision from someone outside of the school who has a good understanding about educating traumatized adolescents. This might be an educational psychologist, a clinician from a local looked after children or adoption team or a mental health practitioner (see Bombèr 2009).

- Support each other – in particular look out for secondary trauma. It is possible to become traumatized vicariously when working closely with traumatized individuals. It is not always possible to notice this in yourself, but if you are open to support, others might be able to alert you and help you to get the help with this that you need (see Bombèr 2009). Secondary trauma is not something you can always avoid, but good support and good self-care (e.g. regular relaxation, meditation, time for you, friends, hobbies, etc.) can minimize the impact of this experience.

- Ensure you are aware of your own attachment and relationship history. Young people who are relationally traumatized are excellent 'button pushers'. They know they have control if they can predictably make you react defensively towards them. They will do this most easily if you have a vulnerable point. Understanding your strengths and vulnerabilities will allow you to remain open to and engaged with the student, however unpleasant he or she is being, instead of reacting defensively.

Taking care of yourself, good support and being well informed will help you to stick with the students, giving them the help that they need, if not want. With these things in place you can focus on the individual student, and explore and plan ways of helping him or her. With a good understanding of the young person you can tailor your support in a way that will aid regulation, increase safety and increase trust that the adults are acting from the student's best interest. Anticipate resistance and keep things in place for long enough to have an effect. Stopping and starting or chopping and changing the support provision can be deeply unsettling for both of you. Trust in the process and allow time for this to be effective. Having said that, don't be afraid to review and make changes if a particular strategy is clearly not helpful for this student. Getting the balance between sticking with something and being adaptive to the responses of the student can be tricky, but these are judgements that will get easier the better you know the student. The following box provides a range of ideas for supporting traumatized adolescents, many of them drawn from the wisdom of Louise Michelle Bombèr (see Bombèr 2009).

Practical ideas for supporting the adolescent

- Bombèr recommends that a key adult is physically and emotionally available, ideally for two to three years. This needs to be a genuine relationship, not a name on paper, with an adult who is supported to actively get to know the student and develop a relationship with him or her. When possible, allow the student to choose a key adult from a small group of possible adults. For especially challenging students two or three key adults may be needed to allow the primary adult to get a break when needed.

- Match the percentage of direct time spent with the student to the specific needs being presented. This is likely to reduce for a well-supported student as he or she progresses through the school.

- Ensure a consistent approach across staff where possible. This will require good communication between staff. It will be helpful if, as far as is possible, staffing is kept consistent with any necessary changes being explained to the student. This is particularly important for key adults and adults who support in bases where the student can go as needed.

- Allow dependency so that the student can develop successful independence over time.

- The key person supports the student with breaks from school as well as during term time. For example, transitional objects can be used by asking the student to look after something of yours, or swapping items to be looked after, write postcards ready to be posted during the holidays and help the student to know that you will continue to think about him or her during the break.

- Meet and greet the student at the beginning of the day. This provides grounding and an opportunity to be supported to get organized. Be aware of what has happened before coming to school, and help the student to focus on the day ahead.

- Within the setting provide appropriate structure. Don't wait for the student to misbehave and be put on report to get the structure needed. Use check-in cards (instead of report cards) to allow the student to meet with a key adult at certain points during the school day and week, without the experience of being in trouble.

- Track the progress and the whereabouts of the student; get to know what school life is like for the student so that you can be alert to potential difficult moments.

- Provide key messages that are repeated and reinforced, for example that school is a safe place, that the student will be supported when feelings are overwhelming, that adults want to support. Communicate this through words and actions.

- Provide and model organizational support. Include support to understand and follow the timetable.

- Keep in touch with parents/carers and be the gatekeeper for other staff to share information between home and school. Weekly communication about positives as well as negatives can help to foster a sense of working together. This can be done relatively easily via email.

- Provide stepping stones matched to the developmental age of the student. As term progresses, monitor this developmental age and level of maturity, and help all staff understand this. Be especially aware of increased stress which is likely to lead to a regression in age and ability, and the need for increased support while the stress reduces again.

- Have an action plan ready for when particular challenges arise. This will include planning who will step in. At these times school needs to feel smaller and the number of people dealing with the student needs to reduce.

- Provide 'time in' with a trusted adult during times of distress and dysregulation, however this is displayed through behaviour. 'Time out' such as seclusion or being sent away will only increase distress and thus escalate the dysregulation.

- Adults are only human, and will get things wrong or become defensive when a student is being particularly difficult. Always take responsibility for repairing the relationship. This conveys that the relationship is unconditional and, whatever has happened, you remain committed to supporting him or her.

- Ensure that the student has access to a safe place in school and permission to access this when needed. Permission cards that the student hands to the teacher can allow the student to retreat quickly to this place when needed.

- Providing food and drink can be both nurturing and regulating.

- Allow brain breaks and opportunities for physical regulation and exercise. Consider any sensory integration difficulties that the student might have and be aware of how large a chunk of task-centred activity he or she can manage.

- If a nurture or support base is provided within the school it is helpful if this is seen by all students as somewhere to go, and the expectation is that everyone will need it from time to time. If it is a 'cool' place to be, the challenged student will not feel different or bad because they need to use the base.

Supporting traumatized adolescents in secondary education is not easy. An approach that recommends supporting dependency, building connection and providing regulatory support does not sit comfortably with an ethos of encouraging independence, reducing need for support and expecting students to increasingly make good behavioural choices. Without a good understanding of the impact of trauma upon the adolescent this approach can appear time and resource heavy and to be working in the opposite direction to the explicit aims of secondary education. Building successful independence, becoming a self-directed learner and allowing students to have the opportunity to make good behavioural choices will only happen for traumatized students if their dependency and support needs are met. Far from being resource and time heavy, this approach will reduce the time and resources needed to manage highly distressed and very dysregulated students. It will reduce the need for temporary or permanent exclusions or having to provide managed moves, and ultimately it will allow the students to access the curriculum and reach their potential.

In order to achieve this, however, these different approaches will also need to be part of the ethos of the school. There needs to be a whole school consistency of approach supported from the top down. The headteacher, senior staff and governors can provide leadership which generates a sense of team work around the support provided to traumatized adolescents. They can develop champions within the school who can develop the specialist skills and knowledge needed and share this with the rest of the team. They can ensure that the key adults working with these most challenging of students get the support and the status that they need. Adults who know these students best can be the lowest paid and least powerful in the school. Recognizing the expertise that these adults bring through their knowledge, experience and skill can allow them to be central to ensuring that the school is a truly trauma-informed community.

Summary

Revisiting challenges of adolescence

- Settling to learn can be especially challenging when emotional energy is devoted to managing the changes of this developmental stage.

- The cultural context within which these changes are occurring also needs to be considered.

- Consideration needs to be given to the additional challenges this might present to young people who have experienced relational trauma early in their life.

The impact of early relational trauma

- Adolescence is a time of revisiting identity. This can be destabilizing, as the young person questions whether they belong and wonders whether there is something wrong about themselves.

- The increased stress can lead to a return to some earlier, challenging behaviours.

- Some young people will engage in new behaviours that are concerning to those around them.

- The young person might start to search for his or her birth family. Social media can make this easier. Without preparation and support, such contact can be very destabilizing.

- Educational staff need to be aware of the earlier experiences of their students, and to know what the risk factors are for a troubled adolescence.

- School staff can become a supportive attachment figure to these young people.

Managing the transition to a secondary setting

- Trauma has a restricting impact on an individual; change and novelty are experienced as threats, and the loss of familiar adults will trigger memories of previous losses.

- Transition can increase the fears of abandonment that the young person has been struggling with throughout their primary education.

- Relationship and stability are needed to support young people with necessary change and transition during adolescence. This needs to be preventative support rather than waiting for difficulties to arise.

- Traumatized young people do not have helpful frames of reference to support them in adapting to change. They will need support to manage a completely new environment.

- This also applies to change which is happening at unscheduled times, for example because of exclusion from a previous school or a change in care arrangements. Begin with a part-time timetable and build up to full-time and full integration.

- Find out as much about a young person as possible before they arrive. Plan a supportive environment tailored to the student's individual needs.

- Use a fact file at the front of the student's school records. This can be updated as the student progresses through education.

- Ensure a healthy ending of the previous stage of their education with opportunities for goodbyes.

Managing challenging behaviour at adolescence

- Traumatized adolescents can experience significant distress often communicated through challenging behaviours.

- These challenging behaviours can put considerable stress on the educational staff.

- Behavioural management strategies are less useful for these students. New ways of managing behaviour are needed.

- Behavioural management procedures are based on assumptions about relationships that do not hold true for relationally traumatized adolescents.

- There needs to be a move from consequences-based approaches to regulatory-based approaches.

The value of relationship

- Relationship is needed to manage the challenges of distress communicated through behaviour.

- Relationally traumatized students remain highly stressed, emotionally immature and in need of, although still unsure or resistant to using, an increased level of support offered through a warm and nurturing relationship.

- Students also need discipline and boundaries but will often not respond to these. They want to feel in control and therefore fear being influenced by others.

- Boundaries, discipline, praise and rewards will only be successful if these young people also experience connection with the adults.

- The troubled adolescent is likely to fight this connection.

- DDP-informed ways of relating based on the attitude of PACE and connecting with students are as relevant in the adolescent years as they are for younger children.

- However, these can be more challenging to apply when educational staff have less time to connect with their students and they are met by growing young people whose defences have become stronger and whose resistance to relationship has become more entrenched.

- When students get relationship experience consistently from the adults that they are relating to, their levels of fear will reduce and their experience of school as a safe place will increase. They will become open to learning and achievement.

Building self-regulation at adolescence

- Traumatized adolescent students will struggle to regulate their emotional experience. Their nervous system has developed to manage stress and to be alert for danger.

- The level of stress that students are experiencing and the low levels of stress tolerance at their disposal need to be taken into account so that school environments become a place where stress is reduced and safety increased.

- They need help to develop self-regulation. Create environments which are regulating. Use the relationship to co-regulate.

- Be aware and alert to challenging behaviours being a sign of regulatory difficulties, and have ways of helping the student move out of these stressed, defensive, dysregulated states and back into the calm, alert and regulated states which will increase stress tolerance and which are conducive to learning.

- This requires an environment that provides external regulation as scaffolding to allow the young person to begin to develop internal regulation.

Sticking with it

- These young people need good relationships with adults who can support and guide them, but they will resist these relationships. Therefore adults need to stick with them.

- As they experience repeated connection and safety in an adult's presence, and as they discover that they can be vulnerable and not hurt, they will begin to change.

- Persevere with the relationship whilst expecting to be tested. Try not to take the behaviours personally.

- To stick with these students adults need:

  » continuing professional development to gain understanding of adolescent development and the impact of trauma

   » to understand and practise using PACE

   » to develop teams around the challenging students

   » to ensure that there is one key adult who is coordinating the support for the young person

   » to have access to supervision

   » to support each other, and look out for secondary trauma

   » to have good support and good self-care to minimize the impact of this experience

   » to be aware of their own attachment and relationship history. Understanding their strengths and vulnerabilities allows a person to remain open and engaged to the student, however unpleasant he or she is being, instead of reacting defensively.

- Tailor support in a way that will aid regulation, build safety and build trust that the adults are acting from the student's best interest.

- Anticipate resistance and keep things in place for long enough to have an effect. But don't be afraid to review and make changes if a particular strategy is clearly not helpful for this student.

- These different approaches will need to be part of the ethos of the school. There needs to be a whole school consistency of approach supported from the top down.

- The headteacher, senior staff and governors can provide leadership which generates a sense of team work around the support provided to traumatized adolescents.

- Develop champions within the school who can develop the specialist skills and knowledge needed and share this with the rest of the team.

- Ensure that the key adults working with these most challenging of students get the support and the status that they need. Recognize the expertise that these adults bring through their knowledge, experience and skill.

Appendix 5
Glossary

ADHD

Attention deficit hyperactivity disorder (ADHD) is the diagnosis given to a range of difficulties that children and young people can display because they have difficulty attending to and staying focused on a task, controlling impulses and regulating their activity levels.

Affect matching

Affect is the outward expression of the emotion being experienced. These affects are conveyed through non-verbal patterns marked by the intensity of expression, the quality of the voice and gestures or movements being made. Affect matching involves one person matching these non-verbal expressions in the other. This is how empathy and understanding of the other's inner experience is conveyed. One person experiences the emotion, expressing this through affect; the other person expresses his or her understanding and empathy for this experience by matching this affect.

Ambivalent attachment

The young child develops ambivalent-resistant attachment when a parent is experienced as inconsistent and unpredictable. The child learns to maximize displays of emotion in order to maintain the parent's availability and thus appears very attention-needing. This early experience of an inconsistent parent leads to an expectation that other adults, such as teachers and teaching assistants, will also be inconsistent, leading to the attention-needing behaviours also appearing in the classroom.

Attachment

Attachment is an affectional bond that develops from a child to the parent or attachment figure. This leads to an attachment pattern, a style of relating to carers and other significant adults based on the early experience of attachment relationships.

Attachment difficulties

When a child experiences difficulties in experiencing security and comfort from a caregiver, the child develops an insecure attachment. This increases the risk that the child or young person will experience difficulties in feeling secure with alternative caregivers and other significant adults. Children experiencing caregivers as frightening are at most risk of attachment difficulties extending into adolescence.

Attuned relationship

An attuned relationship is an emotional connection between two people in which one person mirrors or matches the vitality and affect (externally displayed mood) of the other. When an adult gets into an attuned relationship with the young person, the adult will be able to co-regulate the emotional experience of the young person, soothing high arousal and stimulating low arousal.

Autism

Autism is a diagnosis given to children who display a pattern of difficulties in social communication, language and imaginative play. Onset is before three years of age. It is recognized that children and young people can display autistic difficulties in different ways and therefore an autism spectrum is described.

Avoidant attachment

The child develops avoidant attachment when a parent is experienced as rejecting. The child learns to minimize displays of emotion in order to maintain parent availability, and thus appears self-reliant. This early experience of a rejecting parent leads to an expectation that other adults, such as teachers and teaching assistants, will also be rejecting, leading to the self-reliant behaviours also appearing in the classroom.

Behavioural management

Behavioural management is a set of strategies based on social learning principles that are designed to influence the behaviour of the student. The student is rewarded for good behaviour and given consequences for bad behaviour in order to increase good and reduce bad behaviours. An over-reliance on behavioural management can lead to too much focus on behaviour and not enough on relationship. The student feels influenced, or coerced, by the other, with little opportunity to influence back.

Chronological age

The chronological age of a person reflects the passage of time. For example, if a child has lived for six years, his or her chronological age is also six years.

Coercive behaviour

Coercive behaviour is displayed in order to ensure a particular reaction from others. The behaviour compels others to behave in a particular way.

Cognitive

Cognitive or conscious thinking processes take place in the cortex of the brain, and are central to learning.

Compliant behaviour

Compliant behaviour is performed in order to please another person, that is, to fit in with another person's wishes.

Compulsive behaviour

Compulsive behaviour is governed by an impulse to do something in order to reduce anxiety and maintain feelings of safety. Adolescents who have to wash their hands whenever they touch a door handle would be demonstrating compulsive behaviour.

Controlling behaviour

Controlling behaviour is performed in order to feel in control within a relationship, because the behaviour causes a predictable response in the other person. Controlling behaviours interfere with the development of reciprocal relationships because the young person seeks to influence others without being influenced by them.

Developmental delay

Developmental delay is when a young person's abilities are immature for the young person's chronological age. Young people can be developmentally delayed globally, across all areas of development (generalized learning difficulty), or specifically in some areas of development but not others (specific learning difficulty).

Disinhibited

Indiscriminately friendly but superficial behaviours usually relate to an inability to engage in mutually satisfying relationships. A child is disinhibited when he or she approaches strangers and seeks a cuddle or sits on their lap. Similarly a young person who discloses personal information to a visitor to the classroom would be described as disinhibited.

Disorganized-controlling attachment

The child develops disorganized-controlling attachment when a parent is experienced as frightening or frightened. The child experiences difficulty organizing his or her behaviour at times of stress. As they grow older, these young people learn to control relationships to force predictability. This early experience of a frightening parent leads to an expectation that other adults, such as teachers or teaching assistants, will also be frightening. This leads to the controlling behaviours also appearing in the classroom.

Dissociation

Dissociation is a term to describe the process by which a person defends against overwhelming stress by cutting off from conscious awareness what is being sensed or felt. At its extreme the person cuts off from contact with others or the world, becoming numb, unfeeling or unaware. Dissociation reduces the ability to make sense of self or others.

Emotional age

Emotional age is the age level at which the young person's emotional needs are expressed. This can be discrepant from the chronological age, represented as emotional immaturity or emotional maturity.

Emotional co-regulation

The capacity to regulate emotion is influenced by the experience of co-regulation. This occurs when adults interact with young people to help them to manage their emotion and emotional arousal.

Emotional dysregulation

Dysregulation represents a lack of regulatory capacity. It occurs when individuals fail to control and modulate emotions and emotional arousal. The emotion overwhelms them, controlling them rather than them being in control of the emotion. A young person who feels angry and physically attacks another young person in this rage is demonstrating emotional dysregulation.

Emotional regulation

Emotional regulation is the capacity to control and modulate emotions and emotional arousal. A young person who feels angry but is able to soothe him or herself and take appropriate action is demonstrating good emotional regulation.

Empathy

Empathy is an ability to imagine and share what another is experiencing. By identifying what another is thinking or feeling, we can respond to that person with an appropriate emotion of our own. A young person recognizing that a peer is hurt may feel upset for the peer and therefore seek to comfort him or her. Empathy is at the heart of relationship, as without empathy we cannot influence and be influenced by another.

Executive functioning

Psychologists use the term executive functioning to define a group of brain processes which are responsible for a range of cognitive processes including attention, planning, flexibility and impulse inhibition.

Generalized learning difficulty

See *developmental delay*.

Hyper-arousal

Hyper-arousal describes arousal which is extreme for the situation. A person is hyper-aroused when he or she responds to stress with a high state of arousal. This is an automatic response to perceived threat or danger, marked by increase in heart rate and a fight-or-flight response.

Hypersensitivity

A person is hypersensitive when he or she has a low threshold for sensory input. The individual is easily overwhelmed by sensory input and reacts defensively to it with strong negative emotion.

Hypervigilant

A person is hypervigilant when he or she constantly scans the environment for threats. When such individuals are in a state of hypervigilance, they will show enhanced attention to what is happening on the periphery while having difficulties focusing on what is happening in front of them.

Hypo-arousal

Hypo-arousal describes arousal which is less than would be expected for a situation. A person is hypo-aroused when he or she responds to stress with a low state of arousal. It is therefore an under-responsiveness with minimal reactions to stimuli.

Hyposensitivity

A person is hyposensitive when he or she has a high threshold for sensory input. The individual ignores or is relatively unaffected by sensory stimuli which most people would respond to. This individual may seek intense sensory stimulation.

Impulsive behaviour

Impulsive behaviour occurs without thinking. An impulsive individual does not 'look before leaping'. Impulse control requires that a person thinks about the consequences that might occur following the behaviour, and inhibits the action if the consequence is unacceptable.

Inhibited behaviour

An inhibited individual shows restraint in his or her behaviour. A shy individual can be described as socially inhibited.

Innate drive

An innate drive describes an instinct leading to behaviour that does not need to be learnt. The drive to attach is an innate drive, a child needs no learning to attach to parents, and the child will attach even if the parent is abusive or frightening in some way. The instinct is not easily overridden.

Interactive repair

Interactive repair is a psychological term used to describe the behaviour when one individual wants to become close to another following an episode when closeness between them was lost. It is important for healthy adolescent development that adults re-establish a positive emotional connection between themselves and a young person (attunement) following a time when the relationship was ruptured, either because of the behaviour of the young person or of the adult. This is also called relationship repair.

Internal working model (IWM)

IWM is a term used in attachment theory to describe cognitive models or templates of the attachment relationships that a child has experienced. This model influences how the young person will respond to future relationships.

Mentalization

Mentalization, or the ability to be mind-minded, is when we treat others as individuals with their own minds. We use our own theory of mind – the understanding that the other has thoughts, feelings, beliefs and desires which might be different to our own.

With this understanding, the other's behaviour is more understandable and our response to it more compassionate.

Mind-mindedness

See *mentalization*.

Neurodevelopmental difficulty

Neurodevelopmental difficulty arises when neural development has been impaired in some way. The brain and nervous system have not developed optimally, leading to difficulties in functioning.

Non-compliant behaviour

A person is non-compliant when he or she behaves in a way that is counter to the wishes of another person. The individual behaves in a particular way in order to thwart another person. A young person who continues to walk around the classroom when asked to sit down is demonstrating non-compliant behaviour.

Obsessive behaviour

Obsessive behaviour is governed by anxiety linked to a preoccupation with certain ideas or needs. A young person is demonstrating obsessional behaviour when he or she continually approaches the teacher and asks if there is a rehearsal after school today, despite already being reassured of this fact.

Passive-aggressive

Passive-aggressive describes the expression of anger towards others through indirect acts of aggression, which happen behind the other's back. For example, a young person might experience anger towards a peer but does not express this anger directly. Instead, when no one is looking, he or she steals the peer's folder of work and damages it.

Pattern of attachment

The stable pattern of relating to an attachment figure and other significant adults develops in response to the way that the attachment needs of the child have been met by the caregiver early in life.

Protective behaviours

Protective behaviours is a practical approach to help people to experience personal safety, which is easily adapted to use in schools. It is an approach that can be used with individual students or as part of a class-based activity. It helps students to understand when they are not feeling safe and to seek help from a network of support at these times.

Proximity-seeking

Proximity-seeking is a term used in attachment theory to describe behaviour that is displayed in order to achieve closeness to an attachment figure. This increases feelings of safety and security for the young person.

Pseudomaturity

Pseudomaturity is a term used to describe a person who behaves in a way that is more mature than he or she is emotionally ready for. A six-year-old child trying to cook a meal for his three-year-old sibling would be described as demonstrating pseudomature behaviour.

Reflectivity

Reflectivity is a cognitive ability that requires the individual to notice, think about and understand experience. A young person who can talk about visiting the zoo at the weekend, explaining both what happened and how he or she felt about this, is demonstrating reflectivity. For example, a girl might say that she visited the lion enclosure and that she felt scared of the lions.

Relationship-based play

Relationship-based play is modelled on healthy parent–infant relationships. The focus of the play is the relationship and enjoying being together. This allows the young person to:

- feel safe, calm and comforted

- re-establish trust

- learn that it is good to be a young person and safe to play

- learn the pleasure of joyful engagement

- enhance self-esteem

- feel more confident and competent

- develop skills in all areas of development.

This type of play has been recommended for children with attachment difficulties. It also forms the basis of Theraplay® (Booth and Jernberg 2010). This is a therapy designed to enhance the relationship between the child and parent. Many of the relationship-based games can be adapted for use with adolescents.

Relationship repair

See *interactive repair.*

Secondary trauma

Working with someone who has been traumatized can result in secondary trauma. This is when the parent or teacher develops symptoms, as if they have been traumatized themselves.

Secure attachment

The child develops secure attachment when a parent is experienced as sensitive and responsive to his or her emotional needs. The child learns trust in others and appropriate self-reliance. This early experience of a sensitive parent leads to an expectation that other adults, such as teachers and teaching assistants, will also be sensitive. The young person is able to demonstrate age-appropriate self-reliance, seeking help from the adult when needed.

Secure base

Secure base is a term used in attachment theory to describe an adult being used as a source of security for the child. A secure base occurs when a child is able to feel secure with a parent or significant adult and is therefore able to engage in confident exploration. Adolescents also need a secure base, whether at school, home or within their peer group.

Self-esteem

Self-esteem describes how people perceive themselves, their sense of their own worth. The opinion we hold about ourselves leads to our self-esteem. High self-esteem suggests that we perceive ourselves positively, while low self-esteem represents a low opinion of ourselves and our worth to others.

Self-reliance

Self-reliance describes the ability to depend upon the self. Ideally self-reliance is balanced with the ability to use support from others when available. A young child who is able to sit and eat an apple is demonstrating appropriate self-reliance. If the child attempts to cut up the apple without seeking help, and the task is beyond him or her, this child would be described as being inappropriately self-reliant.

Sensory integration

Sensory integration describes the ability of the brain to take in information from the senses and to use this information in a joined-up way.

Sensory systems

The senses provide us with the information we need to function in the world. We have seven sensory systems:

- the tactile system (touch)
- proprioception (body sense)
- vestibular system (balance)
- auditory system (sound)
- visual system (sight)
- olfactory system (smell)
- gustation (taste).

Separation protest

Separation protest is a term used in attachment theory. It describes the behaviour that a child displays when accessibility to an attachment figure is threatened. A very young child might cry or crawl after the adult. An older child might call out or try to call him or her back. An adolescent might persistently text a parent whilst they are out.

Shame

Shame is a complex emotional state within which a person experiences negative feelings about him or herself – a feeling of being not good enough. Shame develops as part of the normal socialization process for young children. A child displays an unacceptable behaviour, and the adult disciplines the child. The break in attunement between the child and adult is experienced as shame because the relationship has been disrupted. Shame is uncomfortable for children, and therefore children will learn to limit shame-inducing behaviours. In this sense it is protective, because it helps children to behave in a way that is safe, socially acceptable and helps them to develop relationships. However, the child also needs experience of the adult repairing the relationship following the break in attunement. This communication that the child is still loved is an important part of healthy child development, allowing the child to develop the capacity for emotional and behavioural regulation and learning to express appropriate and inhibit inappropriate behaviours.

Theory of mind

See *mentalization*.

Transitional object

Transitional object is a psychological term to describe the use of a toy or object by a child or young person to 'stand in' for a parent or significant adult, while being separated from him or her. The object has a special significance which helps the child or young person to know that he or she is still being kept in mind by the parent despite them not being together.

Unconditional positive regard

Unconditional positive regard describes acceptance and positive feelings for another without reservation or judgement. These feelings towards the other are not conditional upon any particular behaviour from the other. A parent demonstrates unconditional love to a young person when he or she continues to love the young person despite any challenging behaviour being displayed. The parent loves the young person no matter what.

Wondering aloud

A supportive adult can 'wonder aloud' to help young people make sense of their experience, especially their inner emotional life. This is modelled on the way parents talk to their infants, wondering about how they are feeling linked to the behaviour being displayed. For example, a teaching assistant might wonder: 'I wonder if Michael is feeling angry because he had to leave the computer. He was really enjoying this session and he didn't want it to end.' In order to do this the adult has to mentalize – taking the perspective of the young person in order to understand how he or she is feeling underneath the behaviour which is an expression of these feelings.

Appendix 6
Glossary for the UK Education System

Educational health care plan (EHC)

A single pathway plan available for young people between the ages of 0 and 25, replacing the Special Educational Needs (SEN) Code of Practice. The pathway includes five stages – referral; considering if an assessment is required; coordinated assessment; planning; and sign-off – drawing together the previous SEN Statement and Learning Difficulty Assessments into a single process and set of paperwork and including a new focus on preparing for adulthood. The EHC planning process enables wider aspects of the student and family's life to be built into the assessment and plan, while SEN Statements had been generally confined to the student's time within the school premises and school day.

Educational psychologist (EP)

An educational psychologist is a chartered psychologist often trained as both a teacher and a psychologist. EPs are employed by the local authority to carry out specialist assessment with children and young people and to give advice and support to teachers and parents on how a student's needs in school can be met.

First/middle/high school

In some parts of the UK local education authorities have a three-tiered system of education whereby children attend first school (nursery [in some cases] and Years 1–4/1–5), middle school (Years 5–8 or 6–8) and high school (Year 9 upwards).

Inclusion

Inclusion represents the educating of students with special educational needs, together with students who do not have special educational needs, in mainstream schools, wherever possible.

Individualized education plan (IEP)

The IEP is a written document that describes the educational plan for a student with special educational needs or disability. Among other things, an IEP talks about the young person's difficulties, what skills they need to learn, what the school will do to support this learning and what services the school might involve in delivering the appropriate learning opportunities.

Key person/adult

A member of staff is given the role of forming a special relationship with a student so that he or she can help the student to feel safe in school, and can support the student emotionally, socially and educationally. The key person is often a teaching assistant (learning support assistant), designated by the school to provide support to an individual student.

Key stages

The National Curriculum in England, Wales and Northern Ireland defines five key stages. These are:

- Foundation Stage (age 3 to end of reception year, which is pre-Year 1)
- Key Stage 1: Years 1 and 2 (up to age 7)
- Key Stage 2: Years 3, 4, 5 and 6 (age 7 to 11)
- Key Stage 3: Years 7, 8 and 9 (age 11 to 14)
- Key Stage 4: Years 10 and 11 (age 14 to 16).

Key Stages 1 and 2 are taught in primary schools, and Key Stages 3 and 4 are usually taught in secondary schools. Most pupils transfer from primary to secondary school at age 11 years. However, a system of middle schools also exists in some areas: here pupils are transferred from primary school to middle school at either 8 or 9 years of age, then on to secondary education at age 12 or 13 years.

Scotland has a different, flexible qualification framework that is separate from the National Curriculum-based framework used in England, Wales and Northern Ireland. The Curriculum for Excellence provides education from the ages of 3–18.

PACE

PACE is an attitude to help teachers connect with the children they are teaching. Through a playful, highly accepting, curious and empathic approach, teachers can more deeply connect with the child's internal experience. This is modelled on the way that parents connect with their infants in healthy parent–child relationships, and can be used by teachers as the foundation for healthy relationships and the development of attachment security within education

Personal education plan (PEP)

A personal education plan (PEP) is required for every looked after child or young person and this should clearly demonstrate how a school is going to ensure the student receives a personalized programme to aid progress through focused, targeted work. This document should also identify advice and support to education staff about behaviour issues and learning needs so that bad behaviour 'triggers' can be avoided and all the student's teachers across the curriculum can put in place effective learning strategies.

Provision map

A provision map documents the range of supports available for students with special education needs, to assist with the planning process for individual students. Some schools use provision mapping, while other schools use individual education plans. These serve the same function.

Pupil Referral Unit (PRU)

A PRU (or Pupil Reintegration Unit in some local education authorities) is an establishment maintained by a local authority which is specifically organized to provide education for children who are excluded, sick or otherwise unable to attend a mainstream or special maintained school.

Special educational needs (SEN)

Students have special educational needs if they have a learning difficulty which requires special educational provision to be made for them.

Special educational needs coordinator (SENCO)

The SENCO is the education practitioner in the school who has been designated as responsible for coordinating the help given to students in the school who have special educational needs.

Teaching assistant (TA)

Sometimes called a learning support assistant, the teaching assistant is a non-teacher employed by the school to provide support for students with special education needs or disabilities. The TA will work closely with an individual student or with a group of students to support individual needs. The TA may be employed as a key person for a student with attachment difficulties.

Virtual School

Every local authority, through the role of the Virtual School Head (VSH), identifies and supports looked after children and young people by defining attainment targets and ensuring education. Teachers and mentors within the Virtual School are responsible for engaging with individual schools through liaison with the designated teacher to discuss particular issues (funding, placement, education, analysis of data) for individual students. The Virtual School ensures all looked after children and young people have regular and consistent access to a broad, balanced and relevant curriculum in the most appropriate educational setting (i.e. mainstream, specialist, outreach, one-to-one tutoring), including having one-to-one counselling, if deemed necessary, to ensure progress in education is made. The Virtual School mentioned in the text is the Virtual School for Looked After and Adopted Children, Worcestershire.

References

Ainsworth, M.D.S., Blehar, M.C., Waters, E. and Wall, S. (1978) *Patterns of Attachment: A Psychological Study of the Strange Situation.* Hillsdale, NJ: Erlbaum.

Ayres, J.A. (1972) *Sensory Integration and Learning Disorder.* Los Angeles, CA: Western Psychological Services.

Bhreathnach, E. (2006) *The Just Right State Programme.* Unpublished document.

Bombèr, L.M. (2007) *Inside I'm Hurting: Practical Strategies for Supporting Children with Attachment Difficulties in School.* London: Worth Publishing.

Bombèr, L.M. (2009) 'Survival of the Fittest! – Teenagers Finding Their Way Through the Labyrinth of Transitions in Schools.' In A. Perry (ed.) *Teenagers and Attachment: Helping Adolescents Engage with Life and Learning.* London: Worth Publishing.

Bombèr, L.M. (2011) *What about Me? Inclusive Strategies to Support Pupils with Attachment Difficulties Make It Through the School Day.* London: Worth Publishing.

Booth, P.B. and Jernberg, A.M. (2010) *Theraplay: Helping Parents and Children Build Better Relationships Through Attachment-Based Play.* San Francisco, CA: Jossey-Bass.

Bowlby, J. (1973) *Attachment and Loss. Volume II: Separation, Anxiety and Anger.* New York: Basic Books (1975; Harmondsworth: Penguin).

Bowlby, J. (1980) *Attachment and Loss. Volume III: Loss, Sadness and Depression.* New York: Basic Books (1981; Harmondsworth: Penguin).

Bowlby, J. (1982) *Attachment and Loss. Volume I: Attachment.* London: Hogarth Press; New York: Basic Books (original work published 1969).

Bowlby, J. (1998) *A Secure Base: Clinical Applications of Attachment Theory.* London: Routledge (original work published 1988).

Brisch, K.H. (2009) 'Attachment and Adolescence: The Influence of Attachment Patterns on Teenage Behavior.' In A. Perry (ed.) *Teenagers and Attachment: Helping Adolescents Engage with Life and Learning.* London: Worth Publishing.

Cairns, K. and Stanway, C. (2004) *Learn the Child: Helping Looked After Children to Learn.* London: BAAF (British Association for Adopting and Fostering).

Comfort, R.L. (2008) *Searching to be Found: Understanding and Helping Adopted and Looked After Children with Attention Difficulties.* London: Karnac.

Crittenden, P.M. (2008) *Raising Parents: Attachment, Parenting and Child Safety.* Cullompton: Willan.

Crittenden, P.M., Landini, A. and Claussen, A.H. (2001) 'A Dynamic-Maturational Approach to Treatment of Maltreated Children.' In J.N. Hughes, A.M. La Greca and J.C. Conoley (eds) *Handbook of Psychological Services for Children and Adolescents.* Oxford: Oxford University Press.

Cunningham, H. and Morpurgo, M. (2006) *The Invention of Childhood.* Bath: BBC Audio Books.

Davis, D. (1994) *Reaching Out to Children with FAS/FAE: A Handbook for Teachers, Counselors, and Parents Who Live and Work with Children Affected by Fetal Alcohol Syndrome.* New Jersey: Prentice Hall Direct.

Delaney, M. (2009) 'How Teachers Can Use a Knowledge of Attachment Theory to Work with Difficult to Reach Teenagers.' In A. Perry (ed.) *Teenagers and Attachment: Helping Adolescents Engage with Life and Learning.* London: Worth Publishing.

Forbes, H.T. (2012) *Help for Billy: A Beyond Consequences Approach to Helping Challenging Children in the Classroom.* Boulder, CO: BCI.

Geddes, H. (2006) *Attachment in the Classroom: The Links Between Children's Early Experience, Emotional Well-Being and Performance in School.* London: Worth Publishing.

Gerhardt, S. (2014) *Why Love Matters: How Affection Shapes a Baby's Brain*, 2nd edn. Hove: Brunner-Routledge.

Golding, K.S. and Hughes, D.A. (2012) *Creating Loving Attachments: Parenting with PACE to Nurture Confidence and Security in the Troubled Child.* London: Jessica Kingsley Publishers.

Golding, K.S., Fuggle, P., Harrop, C. and Raynes, M. (2006) 'Bridge over troubled water: Working with young people during the transition from adolescence to adulthood.' *British Psychological Society, Faculty for Children and Young People, Service & Practice Update,* 5, 2, 23–27.

Gott, S. (1999) *Teach to Inspire Better Behaviour: Coping with Aggressive, Disruptive and Unpredictable Behaviours.* London: Optimus Education.

Greene, R.W. (2010) *The Explosive Child: A New Approach for Understanding and Parenting Easily Frustrated, Chronically Inflexible Children*, 2nd edn. New York: Harper Paperbacks.

Hetherington, E.M. and Parke, R.D. (1993) *Child Psychology: A Contemporary Viewpoint*, 3rd edn. New York: McGraw-Hill.

Hobson, P. (2002) *The Cradle of Thought: Exploring the Origins of Thinking.* London: Macmillan.

Howard, J.A. (2013) *Distressed or Deliberately Defiant? Managing Challenging Student Behavior Due to Trauma and Disorganized Attachment.* Toowong, Queensland: Australian Academic Press.

Howe, D. (2011) *Attachment across the Lifecourse: A Brief Introduction.* Basingstoke: Palgrave Macmillan.

Hughes, D.A. (2011) *Attachment Focused Family Therapy: The Workbook.* New York: W.W. Norton.

Karr-Morse, R. and Wiley, M.S. (1997) *Ghosts from the Nursery: Tracing the Roots of Violence.* New York: Atlantic Monthly Press.

Koomar, J., Kranowitz, C., Szklut, S., Balzer-Martin, L., Haber, E. and Sava, D.I. (2001) *Answers to Questions Teachers Ask about Sensory Integration: Forms, Checklists, and Practical Tools for Teachers and Parents.* Arlington, TX: Future Horizons.

Koren-Karie, N., Oppenheim, D., Dolev, S. and Yirmiya, N. (2009) 'Mothers of securely attached children with autism spectrum disorders are more sensitive than mothers of insecurely attached children.' *Journal of Child Psychology and Psychiatry 50*, 5, 643–650.

Kranowitz, C.S. (2005) *The Out-of-Sync Child: Recognizing and Coping with Sensory Processing Disorder.* New York: Perigee, revised edn (original work published 1998).

Main, M. and Solomon, J. (1986) 'Discovery of a New, Insecure Disorganized/Disorientated Attachment Pattern.' In T.B. Brazelton and M. Yogman (eds) *Affective Development in Infancy.* Norwood, NJ: Ablex.

Music, G. (2011) *Nurturing Natures: Attachment and Children's Emotional, Sociocultural and Brain Development.* Hove and New York: Psychology Press.

Nash, J.M. (1997) 'How a child's brain develops.' *Time Magazine*, 3 February.

O'Driscoll, D. (2009) 'Psychotherapy and Intellectual Disability: A Historical View.' In T. Cottis (ed.) *Intellectual Disability, Trauma and Psychotherapy.* London: Routledge.

Panksepp, J. (2007) 'Can PLAY diminish ADHD and facilitate the construction of the social brain?' *Journal of Canadian Academic Child and Adolescent Psychiatry 16*, 2, 57–66.

Pianta, R.C. (2006) 'Teacher–Child Relationships and Early Literacy.' In D.K. Dickinson and S.B. Neuman (eds) *Handbook of Early Literacy Research, Volume 2.* New York: Guilford.

Rutter, M., Beckett, C., Castle, J., Kreppner, J., Stevens, S. and Sonuga-Barke, E. (2009) *Policy and Practice Implications from the English and Romanian Adoptees (ERA) Study: Forty-Five Key Questions.* London: BAAF.

Van IJzendoorn, M.H. and Sagi, A. (1999) 'Cross-Cultural Patterns of Attachment: Universal and Contextual Dimensions.' In J. Cassidy and P.R. Shaver (eds) *Handbook of Attachment: Theory, Research and Clinical Applications.* New York: Guilford.

Vostanis, P. (2014) *Helping Children and Young People who Experience Trauma: Children of Despair, Children of Hope.* London and New York: Radcliffe Publishing.

Further Reading and Useful Websites

Further reading
Attachment theory

Bowlby, J. (1988/1998) *A Secure Base: Clinical Applications of Attachment Theory.* London: Routledge.

Cairns, K. (2002) *Attachment, Trauma and Resilience.* London: BAAF (British Association for Adopting and Fostering).

Howe, D. (2005) *Child Abuse and Neglect: Attachment, Development and Intervention.* Basingstoke: Palgrave Macmillan.

Howe, D. (2011) *Attachment across the Lifecourse: A Brief Introduction.* Basingstoke: Palgrave Macmillan.

Silver, M. (2013) *Attachment in Common Sense and Doodles: A Practical Guide.* London: Jessica Kingsley Publishers.

Supporting children in secondary schools

Bebbington, E. (2012) *Stop Wasting My Time! Case Studies of Pupils with Attachment Issues in Schools with Special Reference to Looked After and Adopted Children.* Available at www.postadoptioncentralsupport.org (accessed 6 May 2015).

Bombèr, L.M. (2007) *Inside I'm Hurting: Practical Strategies for Supporting Children with Attachment Difficulties in School.* London: Worth Publishing.

Bombèr, L.M. (2011) *What about Me? Inclusive Strategies to Support Pupils with Attachment Difficulties Make It Through the School Day.* London: Worth Publishing.

Bombèr, L.M. and Hughes, D.A. (2013) *Settling to Learn. Settling Troubled Pupils to Learn: Why Relationships Matter in School.* London: Worth Publishing.

Cairns, K. and Stanway, C. (2004) *Learn the Child: Helping Looked After Children to Learn.* London: BAAF.

Forbes, H.T. (2012) *Help for Billy: A Beyond Consequences Approach to Helping Challenging Children in the Classroom.* Boulder, CO: BCI.

Geddes, H. (2006) *Attachment in the Classroom: The Links Between Children's Early Experience, Emotional Well-Being and Performance in School.* London: Worth Publishing.

Gott, S. (1999) *Teach to Inspire Better Behaviour: Coping with Aggressive, Disruptive and Unpredictable Behaviours.* London: Optimus Education.

Howard, J.A. (2013) *Distressed or Deliberately Defiant? Managing Challenging Student Behavior Due to Trauma and Disorganized Attachment.* Toowong, Queensland: Australian Academic Press.

Perry, A. (2009) *Teenagers and Attachment: Helping Adolescents Engage with Life and Learning.* London: Worth Publishing.

Children in care and those adopted

Barton, S., Gonzalez, R. and Tomlinson, P. (2012) *Therapeutic Residential Care for Children and Young People: An Attachment and Trauma-Informed Model for Practice.* London: Jessica Kingsley Publishers.

Downes, C. (1992) *Separation Revisited: Adolescents in Foster Family Care.* Surrey: Ashgate Publishing.

Gilligan, R. (2001) *Promoting Resilience: A Resource Guide on Working with Children in the Care System.* London: BAAF.

Golding, K.S. (2006) *Thinking Psychologically about Children Who are Looked After and Adopted: Space for Reflection.* Chichester: Wiley.

Golding, K.S. (2008) *Nurturing Attachments: Supporting Children Who are Fostered or Adopted.* London: Jessica Kingsley Publishers.

Hughes, D.A. (2006) *Building the Bonds of Attachment: Awakening Love in Deeply Troubled Children,* 2nd edn. Lanham, MD: Aronson.

Taylor, C. (2010) *A Practical Guide to Caring for Children and Teenagers with Attachment Difficulties.* London: Jessica Kingsley Publishers.

Parenting

Elliott, A. (2013) *Why Can't My Child Behave? Empathic Parenting Strategies that Work for Adoptive and Foster Families.* London: Jessica Kingsley Publishers.

Golding, K.S. and Hughes, D.A. (2012) *Creating Loving Attachments: Parenting with PACE to Nurture Confidence and Security in the Troubled Child.* London: Jessica Kingsley Publishers.

Hughes, D.A. (2009) *Attachment Focused Parenting: Effective Strategies to Care for Children.* New York: Norton.

Hughes, D.A. and Baylin, J. (2012) *Brain-Based Parenting: The Neuroscience of Caregiving for Healthy Attachment.* New York: Norton.

Useful websites

All websites were accessed on 21 February 2015.

General

Adoption UK

Charity providing support, awareness and understanding for those parenting or supporting children who cannot live with their birth parents.

www.adoptionuk.org

CoramBAAF Adoption and Fostering Academy
Association supporting, advising and campaigning for better outcomes for children in care.
www.baaf.org.uk

Dyadic Developmental Psychotherapy and Practice (DDP) Network
Information about Dyadic Developmental Psychotherapy and Practice, including how to become certified in DDP, the parenting approach, resources, training courses and conferences. Includes sites for the UK, the USA and Canada.
http://ddpnetwork.org

Help in educational settings

Nurture Group Network
The Nurture Group Network provides advice, support and information to support its aims of raising the profile of nurture and enabling access to nurture provision.
www.nurturegroups.org

Post Adoption Central Support (PACS)
Post Adoption Central Support has developed a leaflet about adoption attachment issues and school.
www.postadoptioncentralsupport.org

Yellow Kite
Attachment support service for schools. Yellow Kite offers a range of services supporting children in care and adopted children.
www.theyellowkite.co.uk

Young Minds
Young Minds is a UK charity committed to improving the emotional well-being and mental health of children and young people. This includes the Young Minds in Schools Programme which supports the emotional well-being of children and young people in school. It aims to support educational professionals' understanding of the link between emotional well-being and learning. This includes a section covering the links between attachment, behaviour and learning.
www.youngminds.org.uk

Helping children with neurodevelopmental difficulties

ADHD
This site provides an introduction to the ADHD pages available on the Hi2u 4 people with hidden impairments website. A site centred around ADHD, Asperger syndrome, dyslexia and similar neurological differences along with any other type of hidden impairment.
www.adhd.org.uk

Brain Gym®

The Brain Gym® model of learning promotes play and the joy of learning while building awareness of the value of movement in daily life. It encourages creativity and self-expression and inspires an appreciation of music, physical education and the fine arts.
www.braingym.org

Global Autism Collaboration

The Global Autism Collaboration is an organization created in response to a global need for networking and communication among autism groups.
www.globalautismcollaboration.com

Gray Center

The Gray Center is the official home of Carol Gray and Social Stories™. This site provides samples and instructions for creating and using this educational tool to promote social understanding and social effectiveness.
www.thegraycenter.org

Sensory Integration Network

The Sensory Integration Network promotes education, good practice and research into the theory and practice of sensory integration.
www.sensoryintegration.org.uk

Theraplay® Institute

The Theraplay® Institute is an international organization with headquarters in Chicago, USA. The website provides information, resources and details of training in Theraplay®.
http://theraplay.org

Author Biographies

Kim S. Golding Kim is a consultant clinical psychologist with a special interest in supporting foster carers and adoptive parents. After 30 years with the NHS Kim is now in independent practice. Following a career break, when her son and daughter were young, Kim was involved in the setting up and evaluation of an inter-agency project in Worcestershire. This team is now part of the Integrated Service for Looked After and Adopted Children (ISL). The team provides support for foster, adoptive and residential parents, schools and the range of professionals around the child growing up in or moved from care. Within this service Kim has developed a range of direct and indirect interventions based on attachment theory and an understanding of the impact of trauma and loss. She has carried out research exploring the use of a consultation service for foster carers and other professionals and the efficacy of the Nurturing Attachments Group, a groupwork programme for foster carers and adopters. Kim has a passionate interest in getting the emotional needs of children better understood within schools and early years settings. She is concerned that too much focus on behavioural management and a focus on learning without strengthening emotional and social development means that some children are not able to get the best out of their time in school, with continuing difficulties in forming healthy relationships. Kim has authored a range of books and offers consultation and training, with the aim of supporting carers, parents, teachers and other practitioners involved with this vulnerable population of children and young people.

Mary T. Turner Mary is a qualified business and economics secondary school teacher who specializes in working with SEN and inclusion students. She worked for eight years in a local secondary school and progressed to be a headteacher for a school attached to a children's home in Solihull, West Midlands. She is at present working as a teacher for Key Stage 3, 4 and 5 students at the Virtual School, Worcestershire. She has high aspirations for her students and believes in supporting them with strategies to enhance confidence and self-esteem, improve social relationships, impact on success, promote academic achievement and improve social competence and encourage happiness. She has a Masters Degree in health care policy and law, and before having her two beautiful daughters she worked as a hospital manager for eight years at the Queen Elizabeth Hospital.

Helen Worrall Prior to working in her current role as a Key Stage 1 and 2 support teacher for ISL and now the Virtual School for Looked After and Adopted Children in Worcestershire, Helen was a primary school teacher working in schools in Wolverhampton and Walsall from

1995 to 2004. She soon found that she had a particular passion and high level of skill in working with children with special needs – particularly those with a variety of emotional needs that impacted upon their learning. In 2004 she took up her post in Worcestershire and began working to support looked after and adopted children to be able to settle to learn and enjoy and achieve within education. Helen's role has led her to gain a significant level of expertise in working with children who have a range of emotional and attachment difficulties in schools and offering training and guidance to parents, carers and educational staff to help them to understand and effectively support those children in their education setting. Helen was a co-author of *Observing Children with Attachment Difficulties in School: A Tool for Identifying and Supporting Emotional and Social Difficulties in Children Aged 5–11* (2012).

Jennifer Roberts Jennifer graduated in 2000 with a degree in sociology and law and politics. After going to university she was employed in residential settings for looked after children. She quickly learnt how important it is for looked after children to have an adult who believes in them and that they are one caring adult away from success. This was brought into sharp focus when a young person who she looked after when they were 13–15 came up to her at 19, gave her a massive hug and said, 'Thank you for being the one who believed in me, Jen.' This has shaped her work with each young person she has worked with and it made her even more passionate about making a difference in their lives. In 2003 Jennifer joined Worcestershire County Council as a social work assistant. She worked with families and young people who were going through times of crisis and where relationships had broken down. Again attachment and the role of key adults became her focus and she became acutely aware of how our early year experiences shape how we develop and succeed in life. In 2006 Jennifer began work as a child support worker for ISL, which has since become the Virtual School. She now supports young people, schools, foster carers, parents and grandparents to meet the needs of the young people. She has furthered her knowledge by gaining training in Theraplay® principles, drawing and talking therapy, DDP principles and cognitive behavioural therapies to continue to meet the needs of looked after children.

Ann E. Cadman Ann qualified as a teacher in 1974 and started her career teaching physical education in a high school in North Worcestershire. She became very interested in children with special needs and worked for six years in an observation and assessment centre with a school on the premises. She loved this work, helping children with a wide variety of social and emotional difficulties and disrupted attachments and behaviours which impacted on their learning. In 1982, Ann started teaching in the school attached to a children's home for 22 children. She found the most rewarding parts of the work were communicating with the children through art, music, sport and gardening and tapping into their talents and interests, where they would relax and feel safe, developing at their own pace. For 15 years Ann worked in an education team attached to ISL, thoroughly enjoying supporting pupils, carers, teachers and schools in raising the attainment of looked after children. She supported and advised on an alternative curriculum to prevent exclusion of these children and to support colleagues in education, social services and health in the understanding of these education processes and holistic practice. After qualifying as an Arts Award assessor, she also worked on a sessional basis with the Greenfingers Project, which offers theraputic art, music and gardening sessions to looked after children and their carers within Worcestershire. Ann retired in 2014 after 40 wonderful years working with these children and the adults and professionals who helped them. Ann has two grown-up daughters and is an avid animal lover, supporting animal rights and welfare. She is President of the National Union of Teachers for Worcestershire.